Spielberg's Holocaust

Spielberg's Holocaust

Critical Perspectives on
Schindler's List

Edited by
Yosefa Loshitzky

Indiana University Press

Bloomington and Indianapolis

The paper used in this publication meets the mimimum require-
ments of American National Standard for Information Sciences—
Permanence of Paper for Printed Library Materials,
ANSI Z39.48-1984.

Manufactured in the United States of America

Library of Congress Cataloging-in-Publication Data

Spielberg's Holocaust : critical perspectives on Schindler's List /
   edited by Yosefa Loshitzky.
        p.   cm.
   Includes index.
   ISBN 0-253-33232-X (cl : alk. paper). — ISBN 0-253-21098-4 (pa :
alk. paper)
   1. Schindler's list (Motion picture).   2. Holocaust, Jewish
(1939–1945), in motion pictures.   I. Loshitzky, Yosefa.
PN1997.S3133S65   1997
791.43'72—dc20   96-35930

1 2 3 4 5   02 01 00 99 98 97

Dedicated to the memory of my family
who were murdered in Treblinka

Contents

Acknowledgments

THE SYMPOSIUM ON Steven Spielberg's *Schindler's List* which led to this volume was held at the University of Pennsylvania, Philadelphia, on March 24, 1994; it was organized under the auspices and with the help of the Annenberg School of Communication at the University of Pennsylvania. The originator of the idea for this symposium—which was held three days after Steven Spielberg received the Academy Award for best director—was Elihu Katz; I am very grateful for his support. I would also like to thank Barbara Darhun Grabias who helped to organize this event. It was the initiative of the panelists who participated in this symposium (Omer Bartov, Sara Horowitz, Jeffrey Shandler, Liliane Weissberg, and Barbie Zelizer) to use it as a basis for an anthology. I wish to thank them for supporting me all the way through and for keeping to the sometimes strict deadlines. All the other contributors, whom I approached later, were also very supportive and helpful in different ways, and I extend my gratitude to them. I also wish to thank Jerry Siegelman for his kindness and good professional advice. Thanks to the Authority for Research and Development at the Hebrew University of Jerusalem for its financial support and to Shmuel Zamir and Shoshana Blum-Kulka, who were very helpful in obtaining and securing this support.

A very special thank you to Joan Catapano, Assistant Director and Senior Sponsoring Editor at Indiana University Press, and to two anonymous readers who recommended the book for publication. Another special thanks to Paul Frosh, my assistant, and to Robin O'Neil, who gave me access to his materials on the "real" Oskar Schindler.

Some of the material used in this book has already appeared in print in somewhat different form. A slightly different version of Geoffrey Hartman's article appeared in *Salmagundi*, nos. 106–107 (Spring/Summer 1995), pp. 127–46; and a more or less identical version appeared in his book *The Longest Shadow: In the Aftermath of the Holocaust* (Indiana University Press, 1996). Miriam Hansen's article appeared in *Critical Inquiry*, vol. 22, no. 2 (Winter 1995), pp. 292–312. A shorter version of Omer Bartov's article appeared in his book *Murder in Our Midst: The Holocaust, Industrial Killing, and Representation* (New York: Oxford University Press, 1996), pp. 166–75.

Spielberg's Holocaust

Fig. 1: A drawing by Josef Bau, a "Schindler Jew" living in Israel.

Introduction

Yosefa Loshitzky

I promised that Schindler's name will be a household name
—Leopold Page (Poldek Pfefferberg)

. . . and for the six million who cannot watch it tonight with the one billion who are watching us now
—Steven Spielberg at the Academy Awards (the Oscars) on receiving the award for Best Director.

In the last decades there has been new importance to the question of "whether or not" as Marc Ferro puts it, "cinema and television modify our vision of History."[1] It has generated extensive debates among historians and media scholars regarding the right of cinema and television to constitute a new form of expression for history, as well as controversies concerning the contribution of this new form of historical "writing" to the transformation of our understanding of history.

Sergei Eisenstein's *Battleship Potemkin* (1925) provides a classic example of this problem. Images from this film have dominated our "memory" of the Revolution of 1905 (they even appear in some history books and historical documentaries on the period), although they belong to Eisenstein's space of imagination more than to any real space of historical events. In much the same way, as Anton Kaes observes, millions of Europeans have "experienced" the Vietnam War through the lens of Francis Ford Coppola's 1979 film *Apocalypse Now* or Michael Cimino's *The Deer Hunter* (1978).[2] This applies even more radically to a film such as *Schindler's List*, whose popular success on a global scale has surpassed all expectations. Will this film not only preserve the Holocaust in the world's historical memory but also define the shape and dominant imagery of this memory? Although most historians still hold the view that history books are "our designated preservers of memory,"[3] many of the official custodians of memory, notably Pierre Sorlin, will admit that it is no longer necessary to justify an interest in films as "important pieces of evidence for any study of the twentieth century."[4] Myths and symbols constructed and perpetuated by Hollywood have become permanent features of America and the world's historical consciousness.

As the first studio film to deal directly with the enormity of the Holocaust, one made by the most commercially successful director in movie history, *Schindler's List* attempts to provide the popular imagination with a master narrative about the Holocaust. Challenging "the limits of representation,"[5] Spielberg's 1993 film has become a media event, generating extensive discourse on the Holocaust and its mediation by popular culture in a way not seen in the United States since the 1978 NBC television series *Holocaust*. By now no one can deny the impact of Spielberg's film on an ever-growing viewing audience. Publicly celebrated with multiple Academy Awards and screened as an antidote to racism in New Jersey, the film has been widely acclaimed as a moving, powerful, and truthful depiction of historical atrocity, affirming the veracity of survivor testimony and historical documentation for a public in need of initiation or convincing.

Schindler's List provides fertile ground for general reflections about the limits and problems associated with the representation of the Holocaust precisely because it challenges those limits by making the unimaginable imaginable, the unrepresentable representable. The film, as Miriam Hansen suggests, throws into crisis the ideational foundations of post-Holocaust aesthetics with its rigorous, Bible-inspired purist demand: Do not make the Holocaust into an image. *Schindler's List* (along with the Holocaust Museum in Washington) can be viewed as part of a symbolic rite of passage introducing the Holocaust into mainstream American culture. The irony is that of all the films made on the Holocaust, *Schindler's List*, which is a mainstream Hollywood film (unlike the highly experimental *Shoah* [1985] or *The Memory of Justice* [1976]), crystallizes a moment of rupture with past representational forms. Even the films (mostly German and Italian) which constitute part of what Saul Friedlander calls "the new discourse"[6] have not achieved this degree of rupture. Distributed mostly in art cinemas and consumed by an intellectual elite, films such as Luchino Visconti's grand, operatic *The Damned* (1969), Liliana Cavani's semipornographic *The Night Porter* (1974), Lina Wertmuller's anarchic black comedy *Seven Beauties* (1975), and Hans Jürgen Syberberg's Wagnerian *Hitler, a Film from Germany* (1978) have failed to reach the masses. Their effect on global historical consciousness has therefore been limited. In contrast, *Schindler's List* has penetrated historical consciousness on a global scale and has transformed the image of the Holocaust as perceived by millions of people all over the world.[7]

Contemporary fascination with the Holocaust mediated through film, television and museums may be seen as part of a larger cultural phenomenon: a postmodern obsession with the past characterized by a cultivation of "memorial, or *museal*, sensibility."[8] Yet the emerging interest in the Holocaust, particularly in the United States,[9] transcends postmodern fads and fashions. What might seem an obsession is anything but trivial. Rather, it is grounded in real needs, fears, and concerns. Today, the desire to represent (as well as to "consume") the Holocaust is motivated by a deep anxiety nurtured by the gradual disappearance of Holocaust survivors—the last eyewitnesses to a catastrophe—from the land of the living. Steven Spielberg's *Schindler's List* may thus be seen as the great locus of this angst. The film, which was released almost two years before the fifty-year anniversary memorializings of the end of World War II, appeared precisely at the moment in which the generation for whom the Holocaust remains a personal memory is disappearing. Hence the film reifies the fragile moment of transition in historical consciousness from lived, personal memories to collective, manufactured memory. Furthermore, this moment signifies the victory of collective memory as transmitted by popular culture over a memory contested and debated by professional historians. We all well know that most people derive their historical knowledge from popular culture and not from scholarly sources. "A hit movie," as Frank Rich claims, "will eternally preserve the Holocaust in the world's memory."[10] Time, history, and memory become qualitatively different concepts in a media-saturated world where "instead of relating to the past through a shared sense of place or ancestry," film and television consumers "can experience a common heritage with people they have never seen; they can acquire memories of a past to which they have no geographic or biological connection."[11]

As an anxiety-induced film motivated by fears of disappearance and consequent oblivion and denial, *Schindler's List* also marks a shift in Holocaust narrative tropes and in generational sensibilities. *Schindler's List* can be viewed as an "epistemological break" in Holocaust cinematography through its introduction of the Holocaust into mainstream cinema. This process is, perhaps, not different from what Michael Marrus calls the current "entry of the Holocaust into the mainstream of historical writing." For Marrus this is a positive turn, a result of "a natural process as the event marks its anniversary of a half-century and a generation of writers appears for whom the Holocaust is discovered, instead of being contemplated as a lived experience."[12]

Like Agnieszka Holland's *Europa, Europa* (1991), *Schindler's List* is a film about survival rather than death, redemption instead of annihilation.[13] After all, as Omer Bartov suggests, *Schindler's List* presents a palatable version of the Holocaust in which individual talent allegedly could have helped victims survive. Spielberg, Bartov argues, creates a disturbing illusion which suggests that everything which Auschwitz destroyed actually lives on, at least on the screen. *Schindler's List* is a film generated by an American post–Cold War generational sensibility distanced from the Holocaust both temporally and spatially. The taboo on explicitly imagining the Holocaust, and the preference for the dignity of metaphorical and literal silence over explosive memorabilia, was both advocated and practiced by artists of the generation of survivors such as Elie Wiesel. This taboo begins to lose its moral grip as second generation artists appear on the Holocaust scene. For a director like Spielberg (as for the American Jewish community at large), what matters is survival. The mourning over the six million Jews who perished in Europe is symbolically transformed into a celebration of the approximately five million Jews living in America today. It is as though American Jews are the imaginary survivors of the Holocaust, the reincarnation of the six million dead European Jews. Thus *Schindler's List* can be seen as a turning point in the politics of Holocaust representation.

Desacralizing the taboo on imagining the Holocaust—especially through its famous shower scene—*Schindler's List* symbolically passes the torch from one generation to the next, reaffirming the role of generational identity in the symbolic memory culture of the Holocaust. Furthermore, *Schindler's List* epitomizes the process of the "colonization" of the Holocaust by American culture. Prior to Spielberg's film, the most important films on the Holocaust (*Night and Fog* (1955), *Shoah, Kitty: A Return to Auschwitz* (1980), *The Memory of Justice*) were made in Europe by European filmmakers and artists who had firsthand experience of World War II. Though some of these films won artistic, critical, and popular acclaim, none of them ever enjoyed the visibility and exposure granted to *Schindler's List*. Hence, Spielberg's film displaces not only a generational but also a continental sensibility. It shifts, symbolically, Holocaust consciousness from the "old world" (Europe), the "stage" on which the drama of the Holocaust was enacted, to the "new world" (America), the distant participant in or spectator of this drama. After all, firsthand American experience of the Holocaust (not of World War II at large) was limited to those U.S. soldiers who took part in the liberation of the camps.[14]

In the 70s, the cinematic imagination of the Holocaust (as produced and consumed by an intellectual elite) was monopolized by a European sensibility typical of the films of the "new discourse." It was an imagination constituted from decadent, morbid, and erotic visions inspired by the great western European artistic traditions: German Romanticism, French Decadence and Symbolism, and Italian Grand Opera. In the 80s these baroque spectacles were displaced by more realistic and sober representations conveyed through the great documentary masterpieces of the French filmmakers Claude Lanzmann and Marcel Ophuls. It was for Spielberg, the American colonizer of the popular imagination of the 90s, to merge and Americanize these European cinematic traditions into a single film conceived and designed as the *summa* of the Holocaust film genre. Thus, as my article explains, the film combines film noir iconography and stylized mise-en-scène borrowed from the high-camp tradition of the films of the "new discourse,"[15] with a simulation of the documentary coda of the great French documentaries of the 80s.

The irony is that Spielberg deliberately worked without a studio and without American stars. His crew was a mixture of Britons, Poles, Israelis, Germans, and Croats. The lack of Americans was intentional: "Spielberg—the most Californian of all the Hollywood virtuosos" was "making a 'European' film."[16] The most commercial director, associated with the "classics" of American popular culture, "Europeanized" his film on the Holocaust as though a "European look" guaranteed critical respectability and an authoritative claim to historical authenticity and artistic accomplishment. *Schindler's List* is an American pastiche of European cinematic traditions. Thus the "Americanization of the Holocaust" was paradoxically achieved through the "Europeanization" of the film. Similar to the films of the "new discourse," which reveal a not so latent fascination with the Nazis, the hero of Spielberg's film is German, a member of the Nazi party. The focus of fascination is still a perpetrator and collaborator. Even for an American Jewish director, evil is still more interesting than suffering, and the oppressor is more titillating than the victim. The tragic grandeur attributed to the character of Amon Goeth, and the redemptive version of the Faust-Mephistopheles contractual dilemma between mystic "good" and "evil," reveals once again a heightened fascination with the Nazis. While earlier cinematic studies such as *Anne Frank* (1959) and *The Pawnbroker* (1965) focused on the plight of the victims and survivors, films of the "new discourse" such as *Mephisto* (1981), *Lacombe Lucien* (1974), and *The Conformist* (1970), have concentrated on the Nazis and their collaborators.

Spielberg's film, as many critics have noted, culminates the process of the Americanization of the Holocaust. The "Holocaust boom," to use Frank Rich's suggestive phrase,[17] reached its zenith in 1993–94, especially on the American front. This was "the year of the Holocaust." Among the more salient Holocaust-related events of this year in the United States were: the opening of the United States Holocaust Memorial Museum in April 1993,[18] the signing of a bill on April 7, 1994 (the official Holocaust Memorial Day in Israel and in the Jewish Diaspora) by New Jersey Governor Christie Whitman requiring New Jersey school children to be taught about the Holocaust and other genocides,[19] and the decision to rebroadcast the 1978 NBC television miniseries *Holocaust*. On the international scene Pope John Paul II welcomed the Chief Rabbi of Rome to the Vatican on April 7, 1994, as guest of honor at a concert to commemorate the victims of the Holocaust. It was the first time that Pope John Paul, who has sought to heal the strife between Catholics and Jews, officially honored the memory of the millions of European Jews killed by the Nazis on the day Jews set aside for this commemoration. And it was the first time Rome's Chief Rabbi, Elio Toaff, had been received as an honored guest at a Vatican ceremony.

Schindler's List was the "jewel in the crown" in "the year of the Holocaust," confirming once again the power of popular cinema to shape collective memory and to generate topics for public conversation. All these Holocaust-related events, and especially the phenomenal success of *Schindler's List*, have had a cross-fertilizing effect on one another. The success of the Holocaust Museum attracted audiences to Spielberg's film and vice versa, while both in turn helped provoke a flood of television programs on the Holocaust.

Perhaps what is most fascinating about the current "Schindlermania" is the film's engagement with public controversies about group hate. Despite some historians' objections, history on film and television is as much about the present as about the past; often it intervenes in ongoing debates. "Holocaust history, as perhaps any history, goes through fashions that may reveal as much about the contemporary era as the past it is peering into."[20] The Holocaust as memorialized by Spielberg's film has been mobilized as an educational tool in the fight against contemporary racism, reinforcing the thesis of French historian Pierre Sorlin that the historical film always interprets the past from the perspective of the present.[21] This is most evident in the way the film has been used as a "weapon" in the multicultural wars dividing the contemporary ethnic landscape of American society. Spielberg's testimony in the summer of 1994 before a congressional committee examining the issue of "hate crimes" itself testifies to the fact that the most successful commercial filmmaker in Hollywood's history has suddenly achieved "expert" status on a controversial and complex social phenomenon—purely by virtue of having directed a film whose subject is the rescue of a handful of Jews from the Nazis.

Schindler's List has been invoked in different contexts concerning the delicate and problematic relationship between African Americans and American Jews.[22] In response to the controversy that followed an inflammatory statement made at Kean College, New Jersey, by Khalil Abdul Muhammad—assistant to Nation of Islam leader Minister Louis Farrakhan—that the Jews are the bloodsuckers of the Black people, and that "everybody always talk about Hitler exterminating six million Jews. But don't nobody ever ask what did they do to Hitler," New Jersey Governor Christie Whitman proposed showing *Schindler's List* at a discussion on racism at Trenton State College, New Jersey, to which Khalil Muhammad was invited as a keynote speaker. It is reported that after seeing the film on February 28, 1994, Khalil Muhammad admitted that he was moved. Nevertheless, he also said: "That was a Holocaust but African Americans pay a hell of a cost."[23] After a visit to the Holocaust Museum in Washington in September 1994, Khalil Muhammad stated: "We were given swindler's list." These "witticisms" give voice to African Americans' frustration with attempts to frame their victimhood through the experience of other groups. For African Americans such efforts are ways of silencing their own victimhood and making it invisible.

The fact that *Schindler's List* has been abused in the current American "victim contest" demonstrates the dangers inherent in such reactions, where discussion of racism is displaced by a competition about victimization. "The hunger for memory," as Charles Maier observes, "has brought about a change in the status of victimhood."[24] In contemporary American society there is a desperate quest for repressed history as a vehicle for constructing ethnic or postethnic identity, and everyone—with the exception of white bourgeois males—has a claim to being victimized. For American Jews this search is expressed by the transformation of the Holocaust into a new locus of identity. This fact, as Philip Gourevitch and others note, "points to the centrality of victimology in contemporary American identity politics."[25]

An interesting historical parallel for the new status of victimhood in American society developed in consequence of the television series *Holocaust* (1978), which itself was made as a reaction to the commercial success of the television series *Roots* (1977). *Holocaust*, as the television counterpart to *Roots*, cultivated the idea (which since then has become pervasive in American Jewish discourse) that being Jewish is primarily an ethnic rather than a religious category and that Jewish identity can be affirmed through the Holocaust.[26] It is perhaps not altogether an accident that Spielberg also directed the film *The Color Purple* (1985), whose subject is racism against American blacks. There is also another interesting intertextual reference to African Americans in *Schindler's List*. The final scene of the film is documentary footage shot in color of *Schindlerjuden* survivors, including Schindler's widow, Emilie, joined by the actors who have impersonated them. They are gathered around Schindler's grave in Jerusalem, where he was buried (at his own request) in 1974, at the age of 66. Indeed, Thomas Keneally was worried that the result of this scene "might be a bit trite" and he drew a parallel with Nelson Mandela's lecture at the end of the movie *Malcolm X* (1992).[27] The memorial sequence of Schindler Jews and their offspring laying stones on Schindler's grave carries, according to Armond White, "the moral conviction Lee hoped to get from Nelson Mandela's appearance at the end of *Malcolm X*."[28] Governor Whitman's response to the film, as well as Spielberg's testifying before the American Congress, attest to the status that *Schindler's List* has already achieved in American historical consciousness. It has attained the status of historical document, the final and undeniable proof of the ultimate catastrophe endured by the Jewish people.

The historian Peter Burke, reflecting on the idea of "thick narrative"—

based on anthropologist Clifford Geertz's notion of "thick description"—suggests that the "so-called 'non-fiction novel' might have had something to offer historians, from Truman Capote's *In Cold Blood* (1965) to Thomas Keneally's *Schindler's Ark* (1982), which claims 'to use the texture and devices of a novel to tell a true story.' "[29] However, these literary models, Burke acknowledges, do not grapple with the problem of structures because they condense the problem of an epoch into a story about a family. We may argue that this incapacity to explore macrostructures is all the more problematic in a film such as *Schindler's List* which, following the model of classical Hollywood narrative, represents the individual as the protagonist of history.

Memorial narratives, Geoffrey Hartman claims, "asserting the identity of nation or group, are usually *modern* constructs, a form of antimemory limiting the subversive or heterogeneous facts. Invented to nationalize consensus by suggesting a uniform and heroic past."[30] *Schindler's List* has created this kind of narrative and its almost universally celebratory reception especially in the USA offers, as Jeffrey Shandler suggests, an opportunity to reflect on the dynamics of Holocaust culture in America over the past fifteen years and the emergence of the Holocaust as a master moral paradigm in American consciousness. This dynamic, however, does not apply to other countries, as the discussion of comparative receptions in different national contexts suggests. The critical and popular reception of *Schindler's List* in Germany and Israel represent, perhaps, the most problematic cases. Whereas Germany is the land of the perpetrators, Israel is perceived—according to the Zionist view of the Holocaust—as the representative of the victims. It is no accident that the film opened in Germany and Israel almost simultaneously: in Germany on March 1, 1993, and in Israel on March 3. Both openings were treated as national media events with Spielberg present at both premieres. In both countries the reactions (unlike those in the United States) were mixed. The film and the American director were subject to early attacks by a surprising number of both Israeli and German critics. In both countries, obviously for different reasons, both Spielberg's Americanness and Jewishness were the source of a feeling of discomfort, if not blatant hostility. For the Germans, Spielberg's Americanness was, in some cases, viewed negatively as yet more evidence of American cultural imperialism threatening to turn Europe and Germany—as its emerging power—into "little America." Latent xenophobia and Judeophobia were disguised through criticism leveled at Hollywood's vulgarization of the Holocaust. In Israel some of the more vicious attacks on the film (for example, the one made by the historian and journalist Tom Segev) expressed latent hostility toward the American Jew who "stole our Shoah." A persistent, negative and patronizing attitude toward the Diaspora Jew, as Haim Bresheeth observes, was behind some critical Israeli reviews. This negativism was supported by the emerging competition between Israel and America regarding the status of the two countries as official custodians of the memory of the Holocaust. Israel's privileged position as "speaker" for the dead European Jews has recently been challenged by America, especially through the foundation of the Holocaust Museum in Washington, which has threatened the status of the Israeli Yad Vashem as *the* Holocaust museum. In both countries, however, it was recommended that the film be screened for school children and integrated into the educational curriculum.

The film's opening in Germany generated an overwhelming response: During the first week alone the film drew more than 100,000 viewers. An emotional explosion emerged, paralleled only by the broadcast of the 1978 NBC television miniseries *Holocaust*. Released in a period of violent assaults against foreigners, the burning of a synagogue in the northern German town of Lübeck, neo-Nazis marching in the streets, and continuing discussion about the role of the Holocaust in German history, the media debates about *Schindler's List* have become a seismograph for the current emotional and intellectual climate in the newly unified Germany. An overwhelming majority of German reviewers and film audiences followed the American line and praised *Schindler's List* as the best representation to date of the Holocaust. But the importance of this movie and its reception in a reunified Germany goes far deeper than a collective and educational recalling to consciousness. For through its positive reception, Spielberg's Hollywood film was effectively Germanized during its initial run in Germany: that is, it became "volkseigen."

The success of *Schindler's List* duplicates the success of the 1978 television series *Holocaust*, which was viewed by approximately 120 million Americans. This television series had a totally unanticipated and unintended impact in America, but its effect was even more intense in West Germany. In Germany it was the first encounter of many people, especially the young, with the Holocaust, and it triggered heated debates. In this instance, the television series definitely played a role in what we might call consciousness-raising. It placed the Holocaust on the agenda and opened the long-repressed subject for public discussion. Years after the television screening of *Holocaust*, the *Historikerstreit* (the historians' debate)—the debate of German scholars about whether the Holocaust should assume a unique status in history—and the coming down of the Berlin Wall, Spielberg's film has reopened yet another discussion of the German past. The paradox, of course, is that with *Schindler's List*, an American film is reaching out across the ocean once more to negotiate a "new" German past and to explain events in the country where it all began.

The reception of *Schindler's List* within the framework of Israel's struggle with the memory of the Shoah and its conflicted integration in Israeli consciousness and national rituals is another major example of how national identity is negotiated through popular culture. In fact, the Zionist view of the Holocaust is predicated on the perception of the State of Israel as the most suitable monument—the secular redemption—to the memory of European Jewry. Indeed, the United Nations' decision in 1947 to divide Palestine into two states, one Arab and one Jewish, was directly connected to Western guilt regarding the extermination of European Jewry. It was also an attempt to solve the problem of Jewish refugees. Ben-Gurion's statist ideology regarded the Holocaust as the logical culmination of Jewish life in exile. Consequently, during the 50s the Holocaust occupied a marginal place in Israeli public discourse and survivors were subject to alienation, latent repression, and self-suppression. A turning point in Israel's attitude toward the Holocaust occurred as a result of Adolf Eichmann's trial in 1960: "Holocaust survivors were finally given the chance to speak" and overnight "they became the focus of national attention."[31] The Eichmann trial, " 'historic' in the fullest sense of the term, compelled," as Haim Gouri observes, "an entire nation to undergo a process of self-reckoning and overwhelmed it with a painful search for its identity."[32] The June 1967 war opened a new phase in the perception of the Shoah, followed by an ideological polarization which reached its peak with the rise to power of the right-wing Likud party in 1977. Since the early 80s the memory of the Shoah has been institutionalized and ritualized in Israeli official discourse on the Holocaust, with a growing awareness toward what came to be known as the "second generation." Organized visits of Israeli and Diaspora Jewish youth (known as the March of the Living) to the death camps in Poland, and the appropriation of the symbols of the Holocaust (such as the yellow Star of David) by racist ultraright-wing movements (*Kach* and *Kahana Hay*) have become a part of Israeli civil religion.

Recently, Israeli public discourse on the Holocaust shows more openness toward its more contradictory and disturbing aspects. The emergence of the Israeli "new historians"[33] and their revisionist reading of the history of the Israeli-Palestinian conflict, the corrosive effect of the Intifada (the Palestinian popular uprising) on the Israeli public, and the start of the peace process with the Palestinians and other Arab neighbors have synthesized the concerns of Israel's artistic, intellectual, and academic communities, encouraging the Israeli public at large to reexamine the space occupied by the Shoah in the grand narrative of Zionism. In an age which has been called "post-Zionist" by some Israeli scholars and intellectuals, it is only natural that the contradictory "lessons" of the Shoah (if one can talk at all about the "lessons" of this catastrophe), such as Israeli attitudes toward the Palestinian "Other," the disturbing charges of collaboration between Zionism and Nazism,[34] as well as the traditionally arrogant and patronizing attitude of Israelis toward the Jewish Diaspora, had to be publicly discussed and debated.

As in Germany—where most of the discussions of Nazi crimes against the Jews took place in the cultural and aesthetic spheres—so in Israel art preceded purely political debate. Films such as Orna Ben-Dor Niv's *Because of That War* (1988), as well as the music of Yehuda Poliker, have opened a new space in Israeli public discourse to the formerly suppressed plight of the Diaspora (*galuti* in Hebrew) survivors and to the effect of their lived experience on their sons and daughters, the so-called "second generation." In a play such as *Arbeit Macht Frei*,[35] the Israeli and the survivor's self are disturbingly mirrored in/by their Palestinian "other." Moti Lerner's controversial play *Kasztner* was recently adapted into a television drama, *The Kasztner Trial*, by the filmmaker Uri Barbash—director of *Behind the Walls* (1984)—and scandalized the Israeli public even prior to its actual broadcasting due to its revisionist post-Zionist reading of the affair and particularly its demythification of the heroic figure of the Hungarian/Palestinian parachutist, Hannah Senesh.[36] A transition from representation to "life" has already occurred: Polish President Lech Walesa invited Yasser Arafat (as a Peace Nobel Laureate) to attend the commemoration of the fiftieth anniversary of the liberation of Auschwitz. As expected, this invitation—which further strengthens the symbolic link between the Israeli self and its Palestinian mirror/other—elicited a great deal of controversy among Holocaust survivors, especially in Israel. In the light of these vociferous objections, Boris Goldstein, the head of the committee organizing the commemoration, announced on November 17, 1994, that the invitation to Arafat had been withdrawn.

A passionate response to *Schindler's List* also characterized the reception of the film in France, where the Holocaust, as Natasha Lehrer observes, remains an insistent presence in the volatile memory-politics that dominate French public life today. The polemics in the French press surrounding Spielberg's film were evidence that the traumatic memory of the Occupation remains imprinted on French consciousness to this day; the juxtaposition of the opening of the film with the beginning of the trial of Paul Touvier exactly two weeks later underscored the ambiguities and discontinuities inherent in integrating the role of the Vichy regime in the Final Solution into contemporary French memory of the period.

Paradoxically, the worldwide success of the film and the consequent infiltration of the Holocaust into the historical consciousness of a global audience creates a new situation. The limits of representation seem somehow no longer to be appreciated in the fullest sense of the word. As Spielberg has forcefully gone beyond these limits—has in fact transgressed, violated, and desacralized them (according to critical intellectuals such as Claude Lanzmann)—he has somehow made the whole debate concerning them obsolete. *Schindler's List* not only violates the taboo on graven images (*Bilderverbot*) which has been at the core of the debate on post-Holocaust aesthetics, but it goes one step further: It opens a (post?) "new discourse" on the Holocaust.

The question, then, is what space does Spielberg's film occupy in relation to the Holocaust? Is *Schindler's List* the beginning of a post–"new discourse" that signifies a rupture with mass-produced fantasies about the Nazi past and a call for a more stable "truth" of the Holocaust? *Schindler's List*, despite its acknowledged debt to the traditions of European art cinema, is different. For one thing it is a film made by an American Jew who is perceived by many as *the* formative representative of American popular culture. Furthermore, Schindler's transformation from a war profiteer into an altruistic "Jew lover" allegorizes Spielberg's own journey from a "nondidactic" popular entertainer to his much publicized "rebirth" as a Jewish artist. With *Schindler's List*, one may argue, the Holocaust has entered mainstream culture. It remains to be seen whether Spielberg's film will heighten fascination with Nazism or will open popular avenues in the quest for new, disenchanting images of the Holocaust. It also remains to be seen whether the filmmaker turned "historian" can give back to society a history of which it has been deprived by institutionalized history, which despite its "impressively productive and crucially important work seldom finds its way back to the mainstream of scholarly discipline and cultural life in general—much like most other specialized interests in our world of specialists and specializations."[37] The global scope of the reactions to Spielberg's *Schindler's List*, and the controversies it has engendered in scholarly circles (of which this book is a part), the media, and the public at large are perhaps evidence that through this film the Holocaust has found its way back to the world's historical consciousness and conscience.

Released a few months after the inauguration of the United States Holocaust Memorial Museum—a museum which has enjoyed sweeping popular success—Spielberg's film both "capitalized" on and contributed to the Holocaust Museum's popularity. Quenching public thirst for "historical voyeurism," *Schindler's List* not only invites a renewed scholarly and intellectual discussion about the "limits of representation" but also proves the necessity of such a discussion for a larger public. The critical and popular reception of *Schindler's List* and the public conversations it has triggered in different national and ethnic contexts touch upon a variety of issues: the representation of history by cinema and popular culture; the right to dramatize the "unrepresentable" (the Holocaust has, traditionally, been conceived of as defying representation); the relationship between public/popular memory and personal memory, such as survivors' memory; the role of national identity in the shaping and selective reception of popular memory; the place and role of the Holocaust in ongoing debates about racism and group hate; and the authority of popular culture, and Hollywood in particular, to retell and ultimately shape public perceptions of the Holocaust. Such questions are not easily answered. It is to provoke reflection on them that this critical anthology has been designed. However, it should be stated from the start that this book does not attempt to present a monolithic view of the film, or to offer an intellectual consensus on how to represent the Holocaust correctly on film. It is more interesting and illuminating, I believe, to problematize the film and its critical and popular reception rather than to come out with any unified vision of the Holocaust in popular consciousness. As readers of this book will realize, some of the perspectives offered here are more celebratory than others; some, indeed, are critical, even hostile. Others acknowledge ambivalence. Together the articles give voice to the ongoing debate about the representation of the Holocaust and its current initiation into mainstream culture. This book, which benefits from the privilege of reflection, offers diverse and controversial readings of the film in the hope of engaging its readers in an ongoing, provocative debate.

Notes

1. Marc Ferro, *Cinema and History*, trans. Naomi Green (Detroit: Wayne State University Press, 1988), p. 158.

2. Anton Kaes, *From Hitler to Heimat: The Return of History as Film* (Cambridge: Harvard University Press, 1989), p. 195.

3. Lucy S. Dawidowicz, *What Is the Use of Jewish History?* (New York: Schocken Books, 1992), p. xiv.

4. Pierre Sorlin, *European Cinemas, European Societies 1939–1990* (London: Routledge, 1991), p. 5.

5. The notion of "the limits of representation," which has become so prominent in contemporary scholarly discourse on the Holocaust, was coined by Saul Friedlander. See Saul Friedlander, ed., *Probing the Limits of Representation: Nazism and the "Final Solution"* (Cambridge: Harvard University Press, 1992). For a further and more recent discussion of the topic, see *History and Theory* 33, no. 2 (1994). This is a special issue devoted to a "Forum on Representing the Holocaust."

6. As Saul Friedlander and others have observed, most of the discussions on Nazi crimes against the Jews have taken place in the cultural and aesthetic spheres. Miriam Hansen and Michael Geyer claim that in Germany, "The transition from lived experience to representation has already occurred. . . . The individual labor of remembering was overlaid by the mass-production of memory. The film *Hitler: A Career* (1977), television broadcasts of *Holocaust* (1979), and then *Heimat* (1984) were stages in this development, each production moving Germans very deeply—and each leading them in very different directions." See Michael Geyer and Miriam Hansen, "German-Jewish Memory and National Consciousness," in Geoffrey H. Hartman, ed. *Holocaust Remembrance: The Shapes of Memory* (Oxford: Blackwell, 1994), p. 177. For an excellent discussion of German struggles with memory in the "aesthetic dimension," see Saul Friedlander, "Some German Struggles with Memory," in *Bitburg in Moral and Political Perspective*, ed. Geoffrey H. Hartman (Bloomington: Indiana University Press, 1986), pp. 27–42. During

the last two decades, as Friedlander has shown, "an ongoing shaping and reshaping of the image of the Nazi epoch" has been in effect, particularly in Germany (Friedlander, introduction to *Probing the Limits of Representation*, p. 2). During the 70s and 80s, film (in particular films made by Hans Jürgen Syberberg, Rainer Werner Fassbinder, and Edgar Reitz) opened the way to some sort of "new discourse" (see Saul Friedlander, *Reflections of Nazism: An Essay on Kitsch and Death* [New York: Harper and Row, 1984]), which was followed in the mid-80s by a new historiography in what came to be known as the *Historikerstreit* (the historians' debate).

7. The film had done exceptionally well in Germany where it was No. 1 at the box office for a long time and was shown in 500 theaters. It also dominated the box office in Austria and Italy as well as in Japan and in Latin America. The film also succeeded in Poland despite a number of negative reviews.

8. Andreas Huyssen, "Monument and Memory in a Postmodern Age," in *The Art of Memory: Holocaust Memorials in History*, ed. James Young (New York: Prestel, 1994), p. 11. According to Huyssen this postmodern *museal* sensibility, which celebrates the material quality of the object, is a response to our media-saturated reality in which the fleeting image of the television screen denies the permanence of the object: "Far from suffering from amnesia, it seems, we suffer from an overload of memories and have too many museums," p. 11. Huyssen's thesis seems to go against the grain of Jean Baudrillard's postmodern theory. According to Baudrillard, ours is a culture of amnesia due to the dominance of simulacra in contemporary Western societies. See Jean Baudrillard, *Selected Writings* (Cambridge: Polity Press, 1988).

9. For a further discussion of the place of the Holocaust in American culture, see James Young, *The Texture of Memory: Holocaust Memorials and Meaning* (New Haven: Yale University Press, 1993). See in particular the chapters on the United States. See also Peter Novick, "Holocaust Memory in America," in *The Art of Memory*, ed. Young, pp. 159–65. See also Jeffrey Shandler in this book. A recent example of the dissemination of *Schindler's List* in American political culture is the use of the name "Lautenberg's List" by Democratic U.S. Senator Frank P. Lautenberg of New Jersey as "a cheap hook to raise money for his reelection campaign against his Republican challenger, State Assembly Speaker Garabed 'Chuck' Haytaian" (Editorial, "Lautenberg's List: Using the Holocaust as a Campaign Gimmick," *Philadelphia Inquirer* [May 13, 1994], p. A22). Another example of the penetration of the title and the concept of the film into American journalistic discourse is an article about French war criminal Paul Touvier, which appeared in the *New York Times*. The heading of the article read: "Caught after decades of hiding, Paul Touvier presented a 'Schindler defense'—that actually he was saving Jews." See Ted Morgan, "The Hidden Henchman," *New York Times Magazine* (May 22, 1994), pp. 31–39, 56–57, 78.

10. Frank Rich, "Extras in the Shadows," *New York Times* (Sunday, January 2, 1994), section 4, p. 9.

11. George Lipsitz, *Time Passages: Collective Memory and American Popular Culture* (Minneapolis: University of Minnesota Press, 1990), p. 5.

12. Michael Marrus, "Reflections on the Historiography of the Holocaust," *Journal of Modern History* 66 (March 1994), p. 115.

13. Raul Hilberg said he finds the emphasis on rescue misleading: "There is nothing to be taken from the Holocaust that imbues anyone with hope or any thought of redemption. But the need for heroes is so strong that we'll manufacture them." Quoted in Diana Jean Schemo, "Good Germans: Honoring the Heroes and Hiding the Holocaust," *New York Times* (Sunday, June 12, 1994), section 4, p. 6E. There is not only a need for heroes but also for happy endings. As Urs Jenny has pointed out, "good old Spiel-

berg has succeeded in acquiring from amongst all the Holocaust stories the one which has a happy end." See Urs Jenny, "Holocaust with a Happy End?" *Der Spiegel* (May 24, 1993), p. 8 (translation from the Israel office of UPI).

14. It is not surprising, therefore, that the exhibition at the United States Holocaust Memorial Museum begins with the American liberation of the camps. The initial sounds the visitors to the museum hear inside are the shocked voices of American troops who liberated some of the camps in 1945. As Philip Gourevitch observes, "discovering that hell through American eyes" comforts Americans "by identifying them immediately as heroes." See Philip Gourevitch, "Behold Now Behemoth: The Holocaust Memorial Museum: One More American Theme Park," *Harper's Magazine* (July 1993), p. 58.

15. The scene which epitomizes the aesthetics of the "new discourse" is the erotic one between Amon Goeth and his Jewish slave, Helen Hirsch. The beautiful Jewish woman is wearing a revealing dress which, because it is wet, brings out the shape of her body and breasts in particular. The scene courts the spectator's voyeurism, seduces and excites him through titillation. The scene's blend of violence and sex recalls the sadomasochistic relationship between the oppressor and the victim portrayed in Liliana Cavani's *The Night Porter* (1974). The fantasy of erotic links between the tormentors and the victims is typical of other films of the "new discourse" such as *Seven Beauties* and *Lacomb Lucien*.

16. Jenny, "Holocaust with a Happy End?" p. 3 (translation from the Israel office of UPI). It is also interesting to point out in this context the many similarities and allusions to Orson Welles's *Citizen Kane*. Many critics have noticed this intertextual layer. Spielberg himself referred to the "rosebud question": What drove Schindler along this incredible path?

17. Frank Rich, "The Holocaust Boom: Memory as an Art Form," *New York Times* (Thursday, April 7, 1994), p. A27.

18. For further critical assessments of the Holocaust Museum, see Young, *The Texture of Memory*. It should be mentioned, however, that the discussion of the museum was written before it opened. See also Liliane Weissberg, "Memory Confined," *Documents* 4 (Spring 1994), pp. 81–98.

19. The states of California and Indiana already require genocide education, but according to the new bill New Jersey will be the first state where teaching the Holocaust is required.

20. Schemo, "Good Germans," p. 3E.

21. Pierre Sorlin, *The Film in History: Restaging the Past* (New York: Oxford University Press, 1980).

22. The Jewish Museum, in collaboration with the National Association for the Advancement of Colored People (NAACP), has organized an exhibition entitled "Bridges and Boundaries: African Americans and American Jews" in response to recent tensions between the two ethnic groups. See the book catalogue which was published in conjunction with the exhibition: Jack Salzman, Adina Back, and Gretchen Sullivan Sorin, eds., *Bridges and Boundaries: African Americans and American Jews* (New York: The Jewish Museum, 1992). The *Oprah Winfrey Show* on March 18, 1994, which was broadcast three days before the Oscar ceremony, was entitled "Angels of the Holocaust." It was devoted to stories of gentiles who saved Jews during the Holocaust. In this show Oprah (who a few months before interviewed Elie Wiesel in a very reverential fashion, untypical of her usual televisual style) "begged" the audience to go and see *Schindler's List*. "I think that I'm a better person as a result of seeing *Schindler's List*" she confessed to the audience. It is perhaps no accident either that the African American actress

Whoopi Goldberg was master of ceremonies for the 1994 Oscar award. She herself was involved during 1994 in public controversies regarding racial issues. One incident, which included a comic remark about the correct way to prepare traditional Jewish chicken soup, was interpreted as anti-Semitic. In fact the year 1994 was one of the most explosive years in terms of the rising tensions between African Americans and American Jews.

23. Minister Farrakhan, under intense pressure from mainstream black leaders, appeared on the Black Entertainment Network and condemned Muhammad's tone but not his words. Farrakhan added: "Why is it that we have so many stories about a Jewish Holocaust? . . . Why is it that we can see a *Schindler's List* but there is nothing that is said of the Holocaust to black people, which was 100 times worse than the Holocaust of the Jews." Arsenio Hall, an African American late night talk show host, gave Minister Farrakhan a forum to explain his remarks in which he continued his accusations of a Jewish-saturated media that is after him. On March 11, 1994, Khalil Muhammad said in a gathering in west Philadelphia (a predominantly black neighborhood), in reference to the Holocaust and the exhibition "Bridges and Boundaries: African Americans and American Jews": "We have to go beyond boundaries."

24. Charles R. Maier, *The Unmasterable Past: History, Holocaust, and German National Identity* (Cambridge: Harvard University Press, 1988), p. 164.

25. Gourevitch, "Behold Now Behemoth," p. 62.

26. For a further discussion of the relationship between *Holocaust* and *Roots*, see Judith E. Doneson, *The Holocaust in American Film* (Philadelphia: Jewish Publication Society, 1987), pp. 145–46.

27. Reported in Juliet Herd, "Spielberg Takes on the Holocaust," *The Australian Magazine* (July 17–18, 1993), p. 12.

28. Armond White, "Toward a Theory of Spielberg's History," *Film Comment* 30, no. 2 (March–April 1994), p. 56.

29. Peter Burke, "History of Events," in Peter Burke, ed., *New Perspectives on Historical Writing* (University Park: Pennsylvania State University Press, 1992), p. 241.

30. Geoffrey H. Hartman, "Public Memory and Its Discontents," *Raritan*, vol. 13, no. 4, (Spring 1994), p. 31.

31. Haim Gouri, "Facing the Glass Booth," in *Holocaust Remembrance*, ed. Hartman, p. 154.

32. Ibid., p. 155.

33. For a further discussion of this issue, see *History and Memory* 7, no. 1 (Spring/ Summer 1995). This is a special issue devoted to "Israeli Historiography Revisited." The introduction by Anita Shapira (pp. 9–40) includes a section on "Zionism and the Holocaust" (pp. 17–23).

34. For a new publication on this issue that has generated heated debate in Israel, see Daniel Frenkel, *Al Pi Tehom: Hamediniyut Hatziyonit Veshelat Yehuday Germanya, 1933–1938* (On the abyss: Zionist policy and the question of the German Jews, 1933–1938) (Jerusalem: Magnes, 1994).

35. The play was first performed at the Akko (Acre) Theater Festival in 1991 by the Center for Akko Theater. It is still playing in Acre and from time to time in Germany as well. Two documentaries (Israeli and German) have been made about this play, which is an example of total theater.

36. Giyora Senesh appealed to the Israeli Supreme Court because of one sentence uttered in the drama by Kasztner, in which he claims that Hannah Senesh broke under torture and informed the Nazis about the two other parachutists. His appeal was dismissed by the judges. However, the creators of the television drama eventually decided

to remove the controversial line from the broadcast version. It is interesting to note at this point that Spielberg replaced "Jerusalem of Gold" with Senesh's "To Caesarea" (known in Israel as "Eli, Eli") in the Israeli version of the film. For a discussion of this replacement and its ideological implications, see the essays by Bartov and Bresheeth in this book.

37. Zygmunt Bauman, *Modernity and the Holocaust* (Cambridge: Polity Press, 1989), p. ix.

1 | Every Once in a While
Schindler's List and the
Shaping of History

Barbie Zelizer

Every once in a while, a movie arrives that appears to triangulate the link between culture, history, and collective memory in peculiar ways. *Schindler's List* is such a film. Its release in December 1993 captured much of the international cinema-going audience with a captivating version of one of the horrific events of contemporary history. In the weeks following the movie's release, director Steven Spielberg was hailed for having accomplished the "best directing of his career," while the film was applauded as "the movie of the year."[1] Both the film and its director appeared to have taken Hollywood by its overly commercial bootstraps, raising the filmmaking industry to new levels of concern about humanity. Or so, at least, went the popular gloss surrounding the film.

This chapter contests that gloss. It argues that the seemingly unidimensional applause surrounding *Schindler's List* and Steven Spielberg in fact hides a far more basic ambivalence about film and history, filmmakers and historians, and ultimately about popular culture. Like other popular cultural representations of real-life events of the past, *Schindler's List* has generated a slew of unresolved questions about who has the right to tell the story of past events, and in which ways. Ultimately, discourse about the film has reinstated the preferred position of traditional modes of historical documentation, bypassing the strengths derived from using popular culture to address events of the past.

History and Representing the Past through Popular Culture

By definition, the shaping of history has long been seen as the terrain of the historian. Historians have traditionally taken on the role of the premier spokespeople when representing events of the past, and their use of historical records to craft versions of the past has come to be seen as the preferred way of addressing such events. Their record has tended to depend on the recovery of certain types of documents that are typically transmitted through a preferred mode of transmission—the book. In most cases, the constitutive narratives of such a record receive the status of "history."

The fundamental practice with which historical recording has long been associated is one of truth-telling. According to one typical overview, history is a "discipline which [seeks] to establish true statements about events which have occurred and objects which have existed in the past."[2] Historians have produced a record that is thereby predicated on truth. It is also predicated on distance, and many historians have attempted to uphold their distance through the perspectives, narrative standards, and analytical methods they employ.

We know, however, that history is far less uniform than the traditional view implies. For one, it has been differently shaped by its various makers. Scholars such as Fernand Braudel, Pierre Nora, and Philippe Aries have demonstrated the complexity of the link between history and truth by showing that historical recording not only accounts for a so-called truth but actively attends to the needs of those doing the accounting.[3] Work by Hayden White, Michel de Certeau, Lionel Gossman, and Hans Kellner has demonstrated that history-making evolves in conjunction with another activity—that of history-writing.[4] Narratives about the past have been shown to be carefully constructed in accordance with certain world views about how the world should, and should not, look. This means that many practices are brought to bear upon the stories about the past that we group together as authoritative narratives and consequently label "history."

Moreover, the marking of one group of narratives as "history" has been out of step with a general thrust in the academy to diversify history-making with the presence of voices other than that of the historian. As public discourse has grown more complex, multidimensional, and dependent on a variety of media technologies, other spokespeople—such as politicians, journalists, and the creators of popular culture, including filmmakers, novelists, and television screenwriters—have increasingly attempted to address events of the past. In some quarters, we have seen the privileged authority of one type of historical document give way to a more negotiated status across many types of documents, records, and images. Similarly, we have begun to admit that even the "safest" venue for weaving historical record—the history textbook—has been subject to the adjustments of the past.[5] This has necessarily begun to expose the domain of history-making to an array of records, all of which rely strongly on "the materiality of the trace, the immediacy of the recording, the visibility of the image."[6] It has also enhanced the relevance of an array of archival possibilities for recording events of the past. Historical memories and historical evidence "can no longer be found solely in archives and libraries; they pervade popular culture and public discourse as well."[7] Pieces of history can be found equally in artifacts, images, and other kinds of records, and they are broadly institutionalized in museums, theme parks, the cinema, and mail-order catalogues as well as libraries.

How has the growing diversification of history-making affected our understanding of the past? On the one hand, the involvement of other venues for shaping history has begun to generate a voice for popular culture in addressing the past. Popular culture has demanded from audiences at least a partial suspension of disbelief about the particulars in the stories it tells. Because the past is retold in ways that render it potentially more entertaining, compelling or even controversial, audiences have tended to give license to popular cultural representations that might not be forthcoming for so-called serious modes of historical recording. The outlines of a fact-based historical event have tended to be retained while many of its particulars have been fictionalized.[8] In representations as diverse as *Civil War* or *Homefront*, the original linkage to an event has thereby been underscored through only partial adherence to its particulars. Via blurred demarcations between fact and fiction, an event has been readily adapted to the spread of presentational formats made available by popular culture.[9] Usually, this has been accomplished without the fictionalized presentation losing its grip on the original event. And in certain modes of representation, the visual image—and the media of television and cinema that most directly employ it—has lent an aura of verisimilitude to historical recording that can be difficult to contest. This suggests that popular culture has created new spaces from within which it has become possible to associate oneself with the past.

Yet these new spaces have not been universally recognized, particularly not by those favoring traditional modes of historical recounting. In fact, the preference for traditional historians, proven modes of history-writing, and traditional means of gathering and presenting historical facts has worked against the entry of other voices into discourses about how history is made.[10] The privileging of the historian's voice has generated an unspoken ranking concerning who is allowed to speak for the past. Professional historians have traditionally come first, followed by journalists, politicians, and perhaps members of the clergy. Only then has a space been made for those who use popular culture as their raw terrain when crafting stories about the past. It is here that filmmakers have woven their narratives about historical events. Together with playwrights, novelists, poets, and television screenwriters, they have skillfully blended fact and fiction to create certain types of representations of events that occurred long ago. Through it all, however, their role has been continually contrasted with the role played by historians themselves, a contrast that has further estranged them from being able to claim a primary voice when addressing events of the past.

The legitimation of popular culture for addressing the past has thereby evolved in ways that have prejudiced the full recognition of popular culture. In fact, there have been only scattered attempts to recognize the virtues of popular culture's own voice in representing the past. This chapter examines public discourse about *Schindler's List* and Steven Spielberg, as it appeared in the American popular press, in an attempt to demonstrate this very tension between history and popular culture when addressing the past. It considers the ways in which the recognition of popular culture has been partial and contested, even when it appears to be wholehearted. It argues that the popular celebration surrounding this particular piece of popular culture has been shaped in accordance with the basic privileged position accorded history, rendering praise for Spielberg's Holocaust at best a muffled applause. Such applause recognizes only in contained ways the authoritative voice of popular culture in representing the past.

The Shape of Containment: Discussing Spielberg's Holocaust

Ground zero of historical representation is, and must be, the event itself. On such a point, *Schindler's List* earned its most vocal accolades. Even before the film swept off with its seven Academy Awards—two of them for "Best Picture" and "Best Director"—it had earned awards from the National Society of Film Critics, the Los Angeles Film Critics' Association, the New York Film Critics' Circle, and the National Board of Review.[11] Many observers contended that the movie's garnering of awards was "predictable."[12] At first glance, observers appeared to laud Spielberg for his masterful attempt to transcend the disjunctions created by using popular culture to make a movie like *Schindler's List*. The film was given nearly every celebratory label in the lexicon, from "soul-inspiring" on the part of the *Philadelphia Inquirer* to "monumental" by *The Christian Century*.[13] The *New York Times*, calling it "a masterpiece," commented somewhat ironically that perhaps the film deserved new labels—such as "Most Wrenching," "Most Cathartic," or "Most Accessible Treatment of an Impossible Subject."[14]

Praise for Spielberg and his movie generally focused on three dimensions of its representation—technique, genre, and issue.[15] Many discussions about the film and filmmaker focused on the techniques Spielberg used in representing the Holocaust; others discussed the generic constraints which the director faced in representing the events through film; yet others concentrated on the degree to which Spielberg was able to depict the events of the Holocaust in an accurate yet reverent fashion. Only in rare cases did observers claim that Spielberg successfully met the demands of all three dimensions of his representation. Rather, in most discourse, he was found lacking in one dimension by virtue of the fact that he attended to another.

For instance, an emphasis on the generic constraints of fictional cinema was constructed as working against the ability to do justice to the Holocaust story. Spielberg, said one review, "packaged the Holocaust as tightly as a TV dinner."[16] Similarly, the ability to use certain techniques of filmmaking was codified as a necessary precondition for making a Hollywood film but one that collided with the magnitude and tenor of the issue being represented. One typical overview, which dealt with broader attempts to represent history through film, voiced the claim that "when smart directors tackle a 'controversial' issue like Vietnam or the Irish question or AIDS, they forget some of their art":

> Instead of building scenes deftly, allusively, they accumulate horrific detail to make sure you get the point. The films get longer, more ponderous; they sit on your chest until you finally surrender to their good intentions.[17]

The review went on to claim that *Schindler's List* had provided the "elevated downer of the decade."

The Event-as-It-Happened versus the Event-as-It-Is-Retold

Public discourse about *Schindler's List* was motivated by an attentiveness to the appropriateness of the roles played by popular culture and history in representing the Holocaust. Such discourse implicitly valorized the voice of the historian over that of the makers of popular culture. This was accomplished primarily through an elision of the distinction between the event-as-it-happened and the event-as-it-is retold.

Observers evaluated the film in conjunction with its fidelity to the real-life events as they had occurred. Thus, discussions about the film were filled with references to "the real" and "the accurate." The film was lavishly praised for portraying the Holocaust in what was widely agreed to be an accurate fashion; it had, said one observer, "the emotional truth of experience."[18] One critic even proclaimed it to be "more real than reality."[19]

This insistence on historical accuracy was foregrounded by both the film's makers and critics. Its promotional ad told readers that "the man was real, the story is true."[20] The *Wall Street Journal* called it a "valuable historical document . . . a film almost entirely free of artifice."[21] The *Washington Post* said that the film's "faithful" quality suggested that "Spielberg, so famous for manipulation, has let the material speak for itself."[22] And in one biting comment, an observer noted that "to question *Schindler's List* [is] to trifle with the memory of the Holocaust."[23] Such comments about the film fit in well with larger discourses about Holocaust representation, particularly those that evaluated attempts at representing the event by considering the degree to which they mirrored it.[24]

Yet Spielberg was not a reputed scholar of the Holocaust. Rather, he came from the widely contested terrain of popular culture, a known culture-monger best recognized for turning errant sharks, dinosaurs, and extraterrestrials into box-office hits. His few attempts at dealing with serious issues—best illustrated by *The Color Purple* or *Empire of the Sun*—had not done as well as had been hoped, prompting critics at the time to advise Spielberg to remain in fantasyland.[25]

How was the public to deal with the dissonance between who Spielberg was and what Spielberg did? Much of its response was reflected in the frequent references to the film's "real" and "accurate" dimensions. These remarks had much to do with larger issues about history-making and history-makers, in that they addressed a broader need to establish the historical status of both the film and its maker. To do so, however, peculiar biases needed to be created in evaluations of the representation that emerged. Thus, Spielberg was hailed for creating a movie "without glamor, without big stars, and without excessive sentiment."[26] The director referred to himself as "bearing witness" while making the film.[27] He was quoted as saying that he had experienced the events of the film "as any witness or victim would have. It wasn't like a movie."[28] The implication that Spielberg was being hailed for doing something typically *un-*Hollywoodlike was instrumental to establishing the film as a document worthy of serious attention.

Yet this has created unfortunate consequences for the full recognition of popular culture. Perhaps due to the deniers who demand such a degree of historical reconstruction that they offer the absurd claim that the Holocaust did not happen, we have let the possibility that there could—and should—be more than one mode of historical retelling fade into the background. While the event-as-it-happened remains, no doubt, the reigning force when speaking about the Holocaust, there seems to have evolved an expectation concerning *all* spokespeople trying to establish authority for the past that they neutralize the difference between the event-as-it-happened and the event-as-it-is-retold. The event-as-retold is now expected to mirror, reflect, and confirm the event-as-it-happened. And when it does not, it somehow loses its status as a historical record.

This insistence—that representations mirror the event rather than its retelling—has thereby blunted the role of popular culture as a legitimate voice in addressing the Holocaust. The details of *Schindler's List*'s three hours and sixteen minutes have come to be judged not against standards of *representation* but against some absolute standard of historical truth. Failing to recognize the strengths of popular culture has undermined the capacity of popular culture to *represent*—not mirror—the event in history. It has also placed popular culture in unsuccessful competition with the traditional role of history-making. For in the final tabulation, popular culture has come up lacking because it does not have what is required to produce a "good" historical record.

Importantly, this one-dimensional view of historical accounting has generated certain evaluations of Spielberg that recognize his achievements in contained ways. Spielberg succeeded not because he made a good movie but because he made a movie that was less movielike. He was praised not because he was a better filmmaker but because he was a filmmaker who showed audiences less of his craft. When *The Christian Century* called the movie a "film that transcends Hollywood,"[29] it struck at the core of the ambivalence about popular culture and history. This comment and others like it not only moved the film out of Hollywood—which ultimately produced the film—but it took the film out of popular culture as well.

Discursive Dissonance: Disjunctions of Identity

Not surprisingly, removing "the popular" from a film that is inherently part of popular culture has exacerbated an already-present dissonance in discussions of the film. This has been reflected in a number of disjunctions, or unnatural separations, that observers have constructed surrounding the identities central to discourse about the film. This included both the identity of Spielberg himself and the identity of the community of Hollywood filmmakers from which he emerged. Disjunctions have been twofold, in that they have separated the "old" Spielberg from the "new" Spielberg, and they have separated the traditional historians from the so-called image-makers. *Schindler's List* has thus become a benchmark for discussions about the proper mode of both a popular cultural retelling of the past and, specifically, a Spielberg retelling. This suggests that discourse has been structured in such a way as to admit Spielberg a certain voice in addressing this story, but it has stopped short of qualifying him for full recognition in shaping history. At heart, then, discourse about the film has addressed the proper and appropriate retelling of historical events, upholding the preferred position of traditional history over the contestable presence of other voices.

The Old Spielberg versus the New Spielberg

Disagreement about the appropriate way to retell history was settled first by portraying Spielberg as a transformed human being. Audiences were told about two Spielbergs—"the old" and "the new."[30] The old Spielberg was expected to tamper with the story so as to produce better drama and more intensity. "The prospect," said one review, "of Steven Spielberg directing an epic about the Holocaust is, at first glance, alarming. Reality has never been his strong suit."[31] *Schindler's List* is "not the sort of material that cries out for Steven Spielberg."[32] One person revealed that she sat at her seat's edge, not only because of the film's content but because she was anticipating the director's heavy hand, "that moment when you roll your eyes and say he gave in."[33]

But by most accounts, that moment never came. In one journal's view, "fears that the Holocaust would be trivialized by the Spielberg treatment have proved utterly unfounded."[34] *Schindler's List* "is different from anything Spielberg has done before, as far from the 'movie' movie universe of *Jaws* as it could possibly be."[35] And so discussions began to account for the new Spielberg, the "transformed" one, the "unlikely candidate" to be making such a film.[36] The film, in one critic's eyes, constituted a "positively transformative work of film art."[37] It was a work that "transformed Hollywood's greatest showman into its finest artist."[38] *Schindler's List*, said another, was "not a movie anyone could have predicted" from him.[39] Yet another observer claimed that it constituted "a defining moment for Spielberg, a turning point in which he ascends to a higher plateau of filmmaking."[40] Ultimately, "film makers like Alain Resnais, Marcel Ophuls and Claude Lanzmann will shape public perceptions of the Holocaust far less than a man best known previously for chronicling dinosaurs and extraterrestrials."[41]

Some observers codified this transformation in Spielberg as an act of maturation. Spielberg had long been seen as the "Peter Pan of the business, the filmmaker who never grows up."[42] One headline that read "Fantasy Merchant Steven Spielberg Grows Up and Tackles the Holocaust" was more explicit than other accounts only in language choice.[43] Choosing their words more carefully, others conceded that he had gone from "eternal adolescence" to "mid-life trauma."[44] Arguing that Spielberg had "waited ten years before he felt himself mature enough to make the film," accounts presumed that he had successfully let go of his "childlike instinct" and his "child's perspective."[45] Some codified the act of maturation as one that coincided with his emerging role as father to five children: "As the script matured, so did Spielberg. Becoming a father helped prepare him."[46] *Newsweek* was more generous: It told its readers that Spielberg "reached within himself for a new language . . . he's found a style and a depth of feeling that will astonish" all.[47]

Spielberg's transformation was seen as coinciding with the director's personal interest in the topic of the film. In many cases, his decision to proceed with production was portrayed as derived from his self-realization as a Jew. Spielberg, said one review, "felt a special responsibility for taking up the subject as a Jew."[48] Spielberg agreed, saying, "I think I'm prouder now of being a Jew than I ever was in my history. . . . The movie is a result of what I went through as a person."[49] Such personalization even found its way into the titles of articles discussing the film, where the linguistic possessive form under-scored some degree of ownership of the topic: Readers were told of "Spiel-berg's List," "Spielberg's Risk," or "Spielberg's Obsession."[50] At times, more colloquial forms of address informed readers about "Steven's Choice."[51]

Into what did Spielberg transform? Here arose a fundamental irony in dis-course about the film, and it rested within the many accolades that Spielberg received. The very industry that had actually somewhat snubbed Spielberg in earlier years now appeared ready to recognize him. While journals had ear-lier labeled Spielberg "Hollywood's perennial also-ran [of] Academy Award night," his garnering of awards tossed tradition aside.[52] As the *Philadelphia In-quirer* proclaimed, "Drought Ends for Spielberg."[53] Yet this occurred at the pre-cise moment that discourse about Spielberg was dissociating him from the practices of Hollywood. Accounts took care to claim that this movie, unlike his earlier ones, was fact-driven and underplayed. Spielberg himself empha-sized his different style of moviemaking, commenting that this film would not reflect, as did other Hollywood productions, a product of his always-active imagination. "I can't rely on what I've always relied," he was quoted as saying. "History is so much more extreme than anything I could possibly dream up."[54]

Most accounts thereby claimed that Spielberg was transformed into a *non*-Hollywood moviemaker. Critics observed not only that Spielberg changed his style but that he had *"deflated"* it: "Gone [were] the majestic boom shots, the pearly-slick sheen, the push-button sense of wonder."[55] Gone was the "techni-cal wizardry."[56] The assumption here—that it was possible to reach a styleless state of storytelling—was at the core of these discussions. It assumed that when all the so-called "fluff" was gone, the storytelling that remained would be more accurate, objective, and truthful. It would, in effect, be less like a movie and more like a historical record.

Historians versus Image-Makers

But that was not to say that Spielberg became a historian. While certain critics admitted that Spielberg was "doing a service to history" or that he "had brought history and film into rough but proper alignment,"[57] the role of his-torian was largely denied him. One critic, for instance, asked rhetorically whether Spielberg was restricted by the limitations of popular culture: "Will audiences ask themselves the awful questions about betrayal, brutality, and ethnic hatred that attend the Holocaust?" he wondered. "Or will they emerge speechless from the theatre, dab their tears and be glad they escaped so easily?"[58]

So who did Spielberg become? Much discourse hinged on some discus-sion of the moving image and the visual media, as observers sought to elaborate the ways in which the visual image offered a different form of historical accounting. German critic Andreas Kilb was quoted as having claimed in *Die Zeit* that with *Schindler's List*, the "question of whether the mass murder of the Jews can be represented by the moving image has been impressively and finally answered."[59] Reviewers paused to celebrate the attributes of the medium of film, raising potentially important questions about the opening of history to an array of visual records. Spielberg demonstrated "the power of the filmmaker to distil complex events into fiercely indelible images."[60] Yet while *Schindler's List* was said to "enlarge the potential of the medium itself—to teach as well as entertain, to evoke history as much as fantasy,"[61] reviewers did not fully welcome its wider list of attributes. Rather, they tended to take the narrow view, emphasizing pedagogy over entertainment, historical fact over fictional construction. *Schindler's List* was evaluated in conjunction with only a certain type of image—a fact-based one that differed from earlier Spielberg productions. In shooting footage for *Schindler's List*, then, "authenticity was the goal."[62] Again, Spielberg himself was quoted widely for his quest to use the film "to tell the truth."[63]

Why did discourse move rapidly away from discussions of the potentially variegated use of visual images by the makers of popular culture—a use that could be both entertaining and serious, both dramatic and informative—and substitute for it flattering discussions that assumed, or at least tried to find evidence for, an absolute "fact-based" use of images? This chapter suggests that by evaluating popular culture *as* history, and *on history's terms*, observers in effect underplayed the ability of popular culture to provide *both* entertainment and historical understanding, *both* fiction and fact. By presuming that it separated rather than melded fact and fiction, observers evaluated popular culture on what were essentially alien terms. The very effort to make it appear less "popular" thus deflated its authority in addressing this event.

This was accomplished by providing two alternative frames through which the public was expected to interpret the actions of Steven Spielberg. Both frames made reasonable the assumption that Spielberg had caught the horror of the Holocaust "with no preaching, no interpreting, no kitsch, just images."[64] Moreover, both frames were significant because they dissociated Spielberg from the fictionalizing practices of Hollywood moviemaking: By linking the director with communities known best for the factual tenor of their images, these frames helped position *Schindler's List* in a light in which it could be more effectively appropriated as an apparent "historical fact."

One such community of image-makers was that of documentary filmmakers. Accounts addressed at some length Spielberg's so-called obsession with documentary style. He was compared with filmmaker Sergei Eisenstein or with the Italian Neorealist filmmakers.[65] Observers lauded the fact that he had shot the "first half of the movie almost as a documentary, focusing on the Holocaust and leaving Schindler on the sidelines."[66] In one view, the film eschewed storyboards and zoom lenses, displaying "no fancy camera work."[67] Accounts dwelled on the fact that Spielberg had used little-known actors and actresses or that he had relinquished half his "tool box" to use wobbly "hand-held" cameras.[68] Similarly, observers praised his decision to shoot his scenes in black-and-white, with *Premiere* magazine calling the movie a "tribute to the heritage of the black-and-white film."[69] It "unfolds like a simulated documentary."[70] One journal lauded the film's "highly realistic tone" and "touches of cinéma verité";[71] another applauded its "crisp, stark look."[72]

Spielberg himself upheld his image as a documentary filmmaker. He admitted, "I didn't really plan a style. I didn't say I'm going to use a lot of hand-held cameras. I simply tried to pull the events closer to the audience by reducing the artifice."[73] During the film's shooting, he went on record as saying that he expected the final product to be 30 percent hand-held, which would "take a coat of wax off the finish";[74] after the film was finished, he said he had made "a document, not an entertainment."[75] Elsewhere, he admitted that he had "just limited the utensils so the story would be the strength of the piece."[76]

The second community of image-makers with which Spielberg's actions were aligned was that of television or photographic journalists. Here, Spielberg was called an "unblinking reporter."[77] He was a director who attempted to "report the facts" instead of "the drama."[78] The movie was shot, said the *Wall Street Journal*, with the "hurried urgency of news."[79] Certain observers spoke of newsreels—the newsreel-like "angles" and "cutting."[80] *Schindler's List*, said one critic, resembled "a newsreel unearthed after more than a half-century."[81] Others spoke of live television reporting.

Here too Spielberg supported the analogy between his actions and those of visual reporters. He was quoted as saying that he hoped his use of the camera would generate the aura of a CNN news report.[82] He claimed that he saw himself "as a journalist" when making the film.[83] He even went on record telling his actors not to rehearse their scenes because "you can't plan for real."[84]

What does all of this suggest about our recognition of image-makers as alternative voices for the past? Two dimensions of that recognition have been suggested here, and neither of them compliment popular culture. First, while both documentary filmmakers and journalists have come to be seen as slightly elevated above Hollywood directors, neither group has been valued as highly as historians. This means that despite the extensive praise for *Schindler's List* as having offered a popular look at the Holocaust, history—with a capital "H"—has continued to lie elsewhere. It has continued to belong to the historians, who remain the premier "other" against which all alternative voices for the past must compete.

But a second point has been made as well, and it has to do with the ille-gitimacy of popular culture itself. Discourse about the type of image-making practices employed in *Schindler's List* has dissociated the image-making from Hollywood, suggesting a need to go outside the domain of Hollywood film-making to allow Hollywood a legitimate place in crafting its version of this story. Rather than recognize Hollywood's ability to meld fact and fiction, en-tertainment and history, observers have tried to reconstruct Spielberg's ac-tions within frames of image-making associated with fact-based discourses. This renders a double-sided insult to popular culture, and particularly to Holly-wood, by proclaiming its practices deficient in not one standard but two.

Every Once in a While: Giving Pause to Historical Record

All of this raises serious questions about how we entrust our past to oth-ers. Whom do we trust more readily? How do we negotiate trust? And where are the limits of trust in representation?

Much of this may have to do with the shape of Holocaust representation itself. It may be, as Hayden White has argued, that in discussing the Holocaust we have embraced a limiting paradigm that prefers one type of representation of the past over others, recognizing that "the kind of anomalies, enigmas, and dead-ends met with in discussions of the representation of the Holocaust are the result of a conception of discourse that owes too much to a realism that is inadequate to the representation of events."[85] In Anton Kaes's view, stan-dards of appropriateness in representing these events have developed in ac-cordance with "images that have by now become so conventionalized that they determine what is a 'correct' representation of the period and what is not."[86]

Yet much of that discourse about "correct" and "appropriate" representa-tion has had to do with broader issues about history and film, historians and filmmakers—about the willingness to allow alternative voices to address the past. Not long ago Kaes argued for films on the Holocaust that "challenge the narrowly circumscribed Hollywood conventions of storytelling and not only reflect self-critically on the limits and impasses of film but also utilize its specific potential in the representation of the past."[87] This article has demon-strated that the lack of such films is embedded in a more general ambivalence about the ability of popular culture to legitimately address the past. It suggests a certain rigidity in our acceptance of alternative voices. Even in circum-stances which appear to have unidimensionally celebrated the raising of a popular voice in retelling a story of the Holocaust, we have in fact framed our acceptance in ways that make such retellings more like history and less like popular culture.

Shortly after *Schindler's List* was released, *Time* magazine used the opportunity to reflect generally upon the role of Hollywood in addressing the story of the Holocaust. For Hollywood filmmakers, it said, history was "essentially set decoration, something shimmering and elegant to place behind the well-spoken characters" of movies that come out every once in a while.[88]

Admittedly, popular culture cannot provide an ongoing, continuous, or complete record of the past. Nor can it, by virtue of its own practices of representation, offer a record that boasts fidelity to the facts as they took place. But the function of popular culture's representations—representations that appear "every once in a while"—has been to give pause to the ongoing record of historical events provided elsewhere. The explicit function of popular culture, therefore, should be not only to shake up the public and rattle its sensibilities about the content of the past but also to generate questions about the form of the past. "Every once in a while," then, might help a public think about *how* they speak for the past—to whom they allow access and from whom they deny it.

Admitting such an authority for popular culture would allow it a voice that the ongoing comparison between popular culture and traditional history has muted. To allow it, however, we need first to rearrange the disjunctions of identity through which discourse about popular culture and the past has been traditionally constructed. We need to relinquish the distinction between traditional historians and image-makers so as to allow the latter more of a place in discourse in accordance with their own merits. Similarly, we need to mute discussions of one's "old" and "new" styles of popular cultural production, facilitating a better and more effective understanding of the ebb and flow of diverse relations to the past via representation, even when such fluidity occurs within one director, one novelist, one playwright.

Yet finally, and most importantly, if we are to allow popular culture its own voice in representing the past, there is one distinction that we need to re-instate. We must build again that distinction between the event-as-it-happened and the event-as-it-is-retold. And once we have done so, we need to recognize that we can never do better than the latter. In all modes of historical recounting, including traditional history, the event-as-it-is-retold is as close as we can come.

Notes

Thanks to Larry Gross for sharing his Nexus expertise for this article.

1. Stanley Kauffman, "*Schindler's List*," *New Republic*, December 13, 1993, p. 30; Brian D. Johnson, "Hollywood Gets Serious," *Maclean's*, January 10, 1994, p. 50; see also

"Movie of the Year," *Newsweek*, December 20, 1993, front cover. Perhaps the most pointed headline in this regard was *Life* magazine's proclamation that "Spielberg Gets Real" (Lisa Grunwald, "Steven Spielberg Gets Real," *Life*, December 1993).

2. Murray G. Murphey, *Our Knowledge of the Historical Past* (Indianapolis: Bobbs-Merrill, 1973), p. 1.

3. Fernand Braudel, *On History* (Chicago: University of Chicago Press, 1980); Pierre Nora, "Between Memory and History: Les lieux de mémoire," *Representations* (Spring 1989), pp. 7–25. For a discussion of Aries, see Patrick H. Hutton, "Collective Memory and Collective Mentalities: the Halbwachs-Aries Connection," *Historical Reflections* 2 (1988), pp. 311–12.

4. See Hayden White, "The Value of Narrativity in the Representation of Reality," in W. J. T. Mitchell, *On Narrative* (Chicago: University of Chicago Press, 1980), pp. 1–23; and Michel de Certeau, *The Writing of History* (New York: Columbia University Press, 1988; trans. Edition Gallimard, 1975). Also, see Lionel Gossman, "History and Literature: Reproduction or Signification," in Robert H. Canary and Henry Kozicki, eds., *The Writing of History: Literary Form and Historical Understanding* (Madison: University of Wisconsin Press, 1978), pp. 3–40; and Hans Kellner, *Language and Historical Representation: Getting the Story Crooked* (Madison: University of Wisconsin Press, 1989).

5. See, for instance, Pierre Nora, *Les lieux de mémoire* (Paris: Gallimard, 1984). See also Frances Fitzgerald, *America Revised: History Textbooks in the Twentieth Century* (New York: Random House, 1980).

6. See Nora, "Between Memory and History: Les lieux de mémoire," p. 13.

7. George Lipsitz, *Time Passages* (Minneapolis: University of Minnesota Press, 1990), p. 36. See also Barbie Zelizer, "Reading the Past Against the Grain: The Shape of Memory Studies," *Critical Studies in Mass Communication* (June 1995), pp. 214–239. Perhaps one of the most illustrative rearrangements of conventional Holocaust retellings is Art Spiegelman's *Maus I and II: A Survivor's Tale* (New York: Pantheon, 1986), in which the author addressed the Holocaust via the ostensibly "low" genre of comic book representation.

8. See, for instance, J. Hoberman, "Vietnam: The Remake," in Barbara Kruger and Phil Mariani, eds., *Remaking History* (Seattle: Bay Press, 1989), pp. 175–96.

9. Lipsitz, *Time Passages*, offers a particularly compelling discussion of this point.

10. One typical remark pertaining to the role played by popular culture was offered in a recent review of books about Holocaust deniers. The review decried the role of television and cinema, "media that are taking increasing liberties with the truth, routinely blurring fact and fiction, and distorting real events to make dramatic or ideological points" (Michiko Kakutani, "When History is a Casualty," *New York Times*, April 30, 1993, p. C31). Such comments assume not only that film and television are incapable of doing otherwise but that other modes of representation—such as traditional history—do not engage in the practices being critiqued.

11. Janet Maslin, "New York Critics Honor *Schindler's List*," *New York Times*, December 16, 1993, p. C18; Glen Collins, "Critics Name Spielberg Best Director," *New York Times*, January 4, 1994, p. C18. See also Christopher John Farley et al., "The Week: Dec. 12–18," *Time*, December 27, 1993, p. 15.

12. "*Schindler's List* makes a predictable showing," declared the *Philadelphia Inquirer* (Carrie Rickey, "Drought Ends for Spielberg," *Philadelphia Inquirer*, March 22, 1994, p. D1).

13. Rickey, "Drought Ends for Spielberg," p. D1; John Ottenhoff, "*Schindler's List*," *The Christian Century*, February 16, 1994, p. 172.

14. Frank Rich, "Extras in the Shadows," *New York Times*, January 2, 1994, sect. 4,

p. 9; David Margolick, "Schindler's Jews Find Deliverance Again," *New York Times*, February 13, 1994, p. E4. This is not to say that there were no criticisms of the film, but they were rare. As one observer said, "the least politically correct opinion in America these days is that *Schindler's List* is a movie with problems" (Fred Bruning, "The Problem with *Schindler's List*," *Maclean's*, April 25, 1994, p. 9). Similarly, the *New York Times* contended that "negative words about *Schindler's List* are *verboten* in polite company" (Rich, "Extras in the Shadows," sec. 4, p. 9).

15. For a discussion of how these dimensions of representation figure in popular cultural retellings of the Kennedy assassination, see Barbie Zelizer, "The Kennedy Assassination through a Popular Eye: Toward a Politics of Remembering," *Journal of Communication Inquiry*, 16 (2) (Summer 1992), pp. 21–36. Also, see Barbie Zelizer, *Covering the Body: The Kennedy Assassination, the Media, and the Shaping of Collective Memory* (Chicago: University of Chicago Press, 1992) for a discussion of the Oliver Stone film *JFK* and the Kennedy assassination.

16. Bruning, "The Problem with *Schindler's List*," p. 9. Admittedly, much criticism about fictional representation has had to do with a tradition of cinematically and televisually overdramatizing the Holocaust story. One typical comment appeared in the *Wall Street Journal*, which claimed that "most of the Holocaust drama on film has simply demonstrated that this subject is beyond the grasp of most filmmakers. With rare exceptions, most dramatic films have cheapened the enormity of the event with false melodrama" (Julie Salamon, "Film: Spielberg's Portrait of a Holocaust Hero," *Wall Street Journal*, December 16, 1993, p. A14).

17. Richard Corliss, "Tidings of Job," *Time*, December 27, 1993, p. 70.

18. See, for instance, Salamon, "Film: Spielberg's Portrait of a Holocaust Hero," p. A14.

19. Margolick, "Schindler's Jews Find Deliverance Again," p. E1.

20. Advertisement for *Schindler's List*, *Newsweek*, December 20, 1993, p. 7.

21. Salamon, "Film: Spielberg's Portrait of a Holocaust Hero," p. A14. Most critical comments about visualizing the Holocaust in popular culture have centered on the 1979 TV miniseries, *Holocaust* (i.e., John Marks, "Oskar Schindler Comes Home at Last," *U.S. News and World Report*, February 28, 1994, p. 14).

22. Rita Kempley, "A Holocaust Story in Stark Black and White," *Washington Post*, December 15, 1993, p. B1.

23. Bruning, "The Problem with *Schindler's List*," p. 9.

24. By extension, these comments also underscored the limits of all representational genres in representing the event, in that no representation has been able to fully capture what happened. See, for instance, Saul Friedlander, ed., *Probing the Limits of Representation: Nazism and the Final Solution* (Cambridge: Harvard University Press, 1992). Also see Beryl Lang's discussion of the "anti-representational" status of Holocaust representation, which argues that its events can be represented only in a factual manner (Berel Lang, *Act and Idea in the Nazi Genocide* [Chicago: University of Chicago Press, 1990, p. 147]).

25. As one observer said in retrospect, "when Spielberg tried his hand at more serious subjects . . . his dependence on technological wizardry became a distraction" (Salamon, "Film: Spielberg's Portrait of a Holocaust Hero," p. A14).

26. "Movies and Videos," *Washingtonian*, March 1994.

27. Quoted in David Ansen, "Spielberg's Obsession," *Newsweek*, December 20, 1993, p. 114. This invocation raised its own problems. As Shoshana Felman has argued, the notion of "bearing witness" changes the relationship between the maker of testimony and the testimony itself: "To bear witness is to take responsibility for truth: to

speak, implicitly, from within the legal pledge and the juridical imperative of the witness' oath" (Shoshana Felman, "Film as Witness: Claude Lanzmann's *Shoah*," in Geoffrey H. Hartman, ed., *Holocaust Remembrance: The Shapes of Memory* [Oxford: Basil Blackwell, 1994], p. 90). Nonetheless, the rearranged alignment suggested here enhanced the truth-telling status of both Spielberg and the film.

28. Ansen, "Spielberg's Obsession," p. 115.

29. Ottenhoff, "Schindler's List," p. 172.

30. Tom Shales, "The Man at the Top of Schindler's List," *Washington Post*, December 15, 1993, p. B4.

31. Brian D. Johnson, "Saints and Sinners: *Schindler's List*," *Maclean's*, December 20, 1993, p. 51.

32. Stuart Klawans, "*Schindler's List*," *The Nation*, January 3, 1994, p. 30.

33. Personal Communication, March 1994. This was certainly the motivation for certain remarks in the media, too, such as the following statement which appeared in the *Philadelphia Inquirer*: "How will the *Wunderkind*, so far removed from his usual world of wonder and fantasy, confront the awful truth? How will the super showman, the wizard of high-tech emotional manipulation, make us look once more at the unwatchable?" (Desmond Ryan, "Holocaust Calls Out Best in Spielberg," *Philadelphia Inquirer*, December 15, 1993, p. E2).

34. "Spielberg's List," *The Economist*, December 25, 1993, p. 60.

35. John H. Richardson, "Steven's Choice," *Premiere*, January 1994, p. 66.

36. Ansen, "Spielberg's Obsession," p. 113.

37. Bruning, "The Problem with *Schindler's List*," p. 9.

38. Wayne Maser, "The Long Voyage Home: Steven Spielberg's Film, *Schindler's List*," *Harper's Bazaar*, February 1994, p. 134.

39. Ansen, "Spielberg's Obsession," p. 113.

40. Shales, "The Man at the Top of *Schindler's List*," p. B4.

41. Margolick, "Schindler's Jews Find Deliverance Again," p. E1.

42. "Spielberg's List," p. 30.

43. "All the Rage in 93," *Maclean's*, January 3, 1994, p. 58.

44. "Spielberg's List," p. 30.

45. Ibid., p. 30.

46. Richardson, "Steven's Choice," p. 66. Spielberg himself was quoted as saying that he had held onto the script for a decade: "I wasn't mature enough. I wasn't emotionally resolved with my life. I hadn't had children. I really hadn't seen God until my first child was born" (quoted in Ansen, "Spielberg's Obsession," p. 112).

47. Ansen, "Spielberg's Obsession," p. 113.

48. Ruth R. Wisse, "Jews in America Assess Impact of *Schindler's List*," *Philadelphia Inquirer*, May 13, 1994, p. A23.

49. Shales, "The Man at the Top of *Schindler's List*," p. B4.

50. "Spielberg's List," p. 30; Nagorski, "Spielberg's Risk," p. 60; Ansen, "Spielberg's Obsession," p. 113; Admittedly, the title of this collection of essays has also employed the possessive form, allowing Spielberg what appear to be titular claims over the Holocaust itself.

51. See Richardson, "Steven's Choice," p. 66. As one critic said, "*Schindler's List* seems very much Steven Spielberg's personal film" (Ottenhoff, "*Schindler's List*," p. 172). Interestingly, certain observers have taken the implication of ownership in other directions, as in the *Philadelphia Inquirer*'s decision to call one editorial "Lautenberg's List." The article addressed a New Jersey senator's decision to use the Holocaust as a campaign gimmick ("Lautenberg's List," *Philadelphia Inquirer*, May 13, 1994, p. A22).

52. Christopher John Farley et al., "The Week: February 6–12," *Time*, February 21, 1994, p. 15.

53. Rickey, "Drought Ends for Spielberg," p. D1. Elsewhere, Universal Pictures executive Bruce R. Feldman espoused a long line of superlatives concerning the movie's marketing capability. "It's sensational," he was quoted as having said. "We're ecstatic. For this picture to do this level of business is extraordinary" (quoted in Bernard Weinraub, "A Strong Start for *Schindler's List*," *New York Times*, December 20, 1993, p. C16). Interestingly, these were the same executives with whom Spielberg had fought for his right to film in black-and-white, a request they initially discouraged because they felt the film would lose money (see Nagorski, "Spielberg's Risk," *Newsweek*, May 24, 1993, p. 60).

54. Grunwald, "Steven Spielberg Gets Real," p. 58.

55. Ansen, "Spielberg's Obsession," p. 113.

56. "Best of Screen," *People*, December 27, 1993, p. 32.

57. Marc Silver, "Dogs and Flashlights," *U.S. News and World Report*, December 27, 1993–January 3, 1994, p. 13; Jonathan Alter, "After the Survivors," *Newsweek*, December 20, 1993, p. 117.

58. Bruning, "The Problem with *Schindler's List*," p. 9.

59. Cited in Marks, "Oskar Schindler Comes Home at Last," p. 14.

60. Janet Maslin, "Imagining the Holocaust to Remember It," *New York Times*, December 15, 1993, p. C19.

61. Alter, "After the Survivors," p. 116.

62. Grunwald, "Steven Spielberg Gets Real," p. 48.

63. Ansen, "Spielberg's Obsession," p. 112.

64. Silver, "Dogs and Flashlights," p. 13.

65. "Spielberg's List," p. 30; Maser, "The Long Voyage Home: Steven Spielberg's Film, *Schindler's List*," p. 188; Salamon, "Film: Spielberg's Portrait of a Hero," p. A14.

66. Johnson, "Saints and Sinners," p. 51.

67. Nagorski, "Spielberg's Risk," p. 60.

68. Grunwald, "Steven Spielberg Gets Real," p. 48.

69. Richardson, "Steven's Choice," p. 66. This was a particularly prominent discourse in the news magazines. See Ansen, "Spielberg's Obsession"; see also Richard Schickel, "Heart of Darkness," *Time*, December 13, 1993, pp. 75–77.

70. Johnson, "Hollywood Gets Serious," p. 50.

71. Ottenhoff, "*Schindler's List*," p. 172.

72. Joanne Kaufman, "Picks and Pans," *People*, December 13, 1993, p. 17.

73. Ansen, "Spielberg's Obsession," p. 112. In fact, following the film's release, reports claimed that Spielberg was "continuing his work as a chronicler of the Holocaust." In April of 1994, he hired a documentary film crew to interview Holocaust survivors "for educational purposes" (Mitchell Fink, "Remembrance of Evil Things Past," *People*, April 11, 1994, p. 37).

74. Richardson, "Steven's Choice," p. 66.

75. He made the comment at the film's premiere in Kraków. See Nagorski, "*Schindler's List* Hits Home," *Newsweek*, March 14, 1994, p. 77.

76. Quoted in Richardson, "Steven's Choice," p. 66.

77. Ansen, "Spielberg's Obsession," p. 114.

78. Shales, "The Man at the Top of *Schindler's List*," p. B4.

79. Salamon, "Film: Spielberg's Portrait of a Holocaust Hero," p. A14.

80. Stanley Kauffman, "*Schindler's List*," *The New Republic*, December 13, 1993, p. 30.

81. Bruning, "The Problem with *Schindler's List*," p. 9.

82. Quoted in Schickel, "Heart of Darkness," p. 75.

83. Nagorski, "*Schindler's List* Hits Home," p. 77.

84. Quoted in Richardson, "Steven's Choice," p. 66.

85. Hayden White, "Historical Emplotment and the Problem of Truth," in Friedlander, ed., *Probing the Limits of Representation*, p. 50. For a discussion of this point in conjunction with photography and the Holocaust, see Barbie Zelizer, *Snapshots of Memory: The Image, the Word, and the Holocaust* (Chicago: University of Chicago Press, forthcoming).

86. Anton Kaes, *From Hitler to Heimat: The Return of History as Film* (Cambridge: Harvard University Press, 1989), p. 196.

87. Anton Kaes, "*Holocaust* and the End of History," in Friedlander, ed., *Probing the Limits of Representation*, p. 208.

88. Schickel, "Heart of Darkness," p. 75.

Behind the Scenes: The Real Places and People

Fig. 1.1: Oskar Schindler in 1940.
Courtesy of Robin O'Neil.

Fig. 1.2: Oskar Schindler and
his workers in front of the
Emailwaren factory in Kraków.
Courtesy of Robin O'Neil.

Fig. 1.3: Amon Goeth's villa in Plaszów. Courtesy of Robin O'Neil.

Fig. 1.4: Fat and pot-bellied—far from Spielberg's glorified and romanticized version—Amon Goeth, the commandant of the Plaszów concentration camp. Courtesy of Robin O'Neil.

Fig. 1.5: Goeth's mistress, Ruth Kalder, and his dog, on the balcony of his villa. Courtesy of Robin O'Neil.

Fig. 1.6: Inmates at the Plaszów concentration camp. Courtesy of Robin O'Neil.

Fig. 1.7: A drawing of the Plaszów concentration camp by Josef Bau.

2 | Spielberg's Oskar
Hollywood Tries Evil

Omer Bartov

I<small>N THE SPRING</small> semester of 1994, during one of the first sessions of my class on the Holocaust, several students asked me whether we would discuss the film *Schindler's List*. Having not yet seen the film myself, I promised to go as soon as possible and then decide whether it was appropriate. My curiosity meanwhile aroused, I inquired how many of my students had seen the movie and quickly established that no less than three-quarters of the hundred or so undergraduates present in the lecture hall had already been to *Schindler's List*, and this just a few weeks after it was first released.

To be sure, students taking a class on the Holocaust are not wholly representative of the general student population, let alone the American public as a whole. And yet, even in this group, only a very small number of students would have watched, or even known about, such films as Alain Resnais's *Night and Fog* or Claude Lanzmann's *Shoah* had they not been screened as part of the course. Nor was there a consensus among the students which film they preferred when asked to compare Resnais's 1955 masterpiece with Spielberg's recent addition to this small and mostly quite remarkable corpus of cinematic representations of the Holocaust.[1] Indeed, one would be hard put to decide which of these films had made more effective use of the techniques of visual representation as far as these specific young American men and women were concerned, whatever historians, film critics, or intellectuals in general may think.

That *Schindler's List* has been the occasion of a renewed debate over the limits and utility of representing the Holocaust goes without saying. It is of some interest, however, that opinions expressed by American, European, and Israeli scholars and intellectuals about Spielberg's film seem to have been informed not merely by the experience of watching it (which in fact some have adamantly refused to do), but at least as much by a variety of commonly held biases and prejudices about the nature of Hollywood productions in general and the qualifications of Steven Spielberg in particular. Moreover, it is quite apparent that there often exists a gap between pure aesthetic appreciation and a willingness (or unwillingness) to evaluate the film's potential public effect and utility. Indeed, it seems that the popular success of *Schindler's List* makes it especially suspect in some intellectual circles. Conversely, the argument that the film's ability to attract large audiences is one of its merits is rejected as rooted in a snobbish attitude which assumes that only "we" can understand the higher forms of representation while the multitude has to be fed with the usual humble and simplistic Hollywood fare.

What I would like to discuss here is therefore *both* the merits and the limitations, or even pitfalls and perils, of Spielberg's film. I would like to view it critically but without bias, and to examine it within the social, political, and cultural context in which it was made, viewed, and reviewed. Moreover, I will attempt to examine the alternatives to this admittedly flawed, though nevertheless important cinematic representation of the Holocaust, and to ask whether those options, often mentioned by Spielberg's critics, are themselves free of serious defects. Finally, I will argue that *Schindler's List* has already had, and is likely to continue to have a generally positive impact on both the public perception of and the intellectual and artistic debate about the Holocaust, as well as on future attempts to represent mass murder and genocide.

Several commentators have noted that having gone to see *Schindler's List* with very low expectations, they were "positively surprised" by its cinematic qualities, relative lack of sentimentality, insistence on accuracy of fact and filming on location, the intensity of its narrative, and the power of some specific scenes.[2] Indeed, one may say that within the constraints of a Hollywood production (which were responsible for such a priori low expectations in the first place), Spielberg has managed to strike a fine balance between relatively popular appeal and relatively high artistic quality. This achievement, which to some extent qualifies previous views on the limits of representing the Holocaust, has caused a degree of consternation, even anger and frustration, among at least some scholars, artists, and intellectuals.[3]

One of the most important (and problematic) aspects of *Schindler's List* is that by choosing Oskar Schindler's story as the focus of his representation of the Holocaust, Spielberg implies that even in the heart of darkness, even within sight of the death camps, the option of hampering the Nazi murder machine never wholly disappeared. This is not to say that the victims could or should have done more to save themselves, an argument rooted mainly in the guilt feelings of survivors or potential victims who were lucky enough to be spared the genocide thanks to geographical or chronological distance from the event. Rather, the film rightly stresses that at any given point during the Holocaust, both bystanders and perpetrators were always faced with the choice to collaborate in, passively observe, or actively resist mass murder, and that resistance could come in a variety of ways and could be meaningful, even if it meant saving only a handful of victims. Hence the film qualifies the impression created by numerous historical, literary, and cinematic accounts of the Holocaust as an inherently inevitable, fateful, unstoppable event, one over which human agency had no control, except for its dubious capacity for bringing it to an apocalyptic end.

By choosing Schindler, Spielberg can therefore show that a single individual, even under the most adverse circumstances, could and did save lives. Consequently, we are left with the painful question, why were there so few Schindlers, why was his case so extraordinary? At the same time, however, the very fact that this *was* such a unique case is also one of the main problems of the film, as I shall argue below.

What makes the choice of Schindler so crucial is not only that he saved Jews but just as much the fact that he had none of the qualities normally associated with those "righteous Gentiles" celebrated by the State of Israel after the event. Schindler, after all, was a rather common and generally unsuccessful crook before he found (or installed) himself in the heart of the Final Solution. Hence he is, in a very real sense, a true Brechtian character, a crook who sets himself against a state of much worse (but officially quite "legal") criminals, a man who wishes to profit from evil but also enjoys undermining it, a potentially mediocre character who, thanks precisely to his far from respectable qualities, can become a saint in this world turned upside down. To be sure, as Schindler admits in the film, the best thing that ever happened to him was the war and, by extension, the Holocaust. But as the plot develops, Schindler's financial profits are put to moral use as he applies his newly won riches to save the people who enabled him to win them. Finally impoverished, Schindler's real profit is the innocent lives he has saved.

The crucial consequence of this juxtaposition between the crook and the criminal context in which he operates is our realization that its mirror image is the "decent" man who becomes a criminal under the same circumstances. By leading the viewers to this conclusion, without stating it outright, *Schindler's List* subtly (indeed, perhaps quite unintentionally) undermines the Hollywood convention of a cinematic world neatly divided between good and evil. Nevertheless, the film succeeds in remaining within the fold of the genre by simultaneously drawing much of its pathos from the traditional image of the tough, rough, undisciplined, and yet ultimately moral and supremely courageous hero of the classic American Western. Hence Schindler, through Spielberg, manages somehow to straddle these two modes, that of the cynical, pessimistic, corrupt, wholly un-American hero whose moral qualities can only shine in the midst of evil, and the simple, straightforward, completely incorruptible, truly American hero, who is, however, similarly motivated to action only when faced with truly bad guys (as for instance in the film *High Noon*). Schindler can exist on the Hollywood screen only because of his Gary Cooper/John Wayne facade; but he unmasks himself often enough to maintain his Brechtian characteristics and to persuade us that his is not a world of cowboys and Indians. Only at the end of the movie does Spielberg commit the error of painting a totally new face on Schindler, thus leaving him, and the movie, devoid of any credible identity and consequently on the verge of complete disintegration.

Spielberg therefore manages to complicate the popularly accepted tale of the Holocaust as consisting of victims, perpetrators, and (now especially thanks to Lanzmann, somewhat complicit) bystanders. Schindler belongs to none of these categories, yet potentially he could belong to any one of them. Initially he is a mere bystander hoping to profit from other people's misfortune; later he can choose to join the perpetrators; and, since he elects to help the victims, he stands a good chance of becoming one himself, if caught. Because Schindler chooses to act, and because by making this choice he assumes a new identity, he belies the assertion that his (bystander) world denied one the freedom of choice and the choice of identity.

Spielberg retains admirable control over his film for much (but not all) of the time, no mean achievement considering the character of the material and the conventions of the genre, successfully avoiding the kitsch and sentimentality which have plagued so many previous films on the Holocaust. His decision to make it in black-and-white is also highly effective. If it was motivated by his desire to provide the film with a documentary character, this combination of pseudo-newsreel qualities with on-location shots and historical characters played by gifted actors manages to populate a (fictive) segment of the Holocaust with living human beings and thereby to create greater empathy with the protagonists than any "real" documentary. Conversely, by refusing to shirk confrontation with the popularized and generally misunderstood cliché of the banality of evil, that is, by stressing the sheer brutality and sadism of the Holocaust as it was experienced by the victims, Spielberg has filmed some of the most haunting moments in any cinematic representation of the Holocaust. Yet when all is said and done, *Schindler's List* shares many of the failings of numerous other representations of the genocide of the Jews, be they works of fiction, scholarship, or film. The conventional difficulties of representing any historical event, the inevitable process of selection and elimination, generalization and simplification, become all the more pressing when dealing with such a traumatic and unprecedented event as the Holocaust. It is the danger of hasty generalizations, pernicious simplifications, and distortions open to abuse that must be examined here as part of our evaluation of *Schindler's List*.

Since it is a Hollywood production, *Schindler's List* inevitably has a plot and a "happy" end. Unfortunately, the positively repulsive kitsch of the last two scenes seriously undermines much of the film's previous merits. Up to this point, Spielberg's intuition led him in the right direction, even if it went against the apparent (Hollywood) rules of his trade; and since the ultimate rule of Hollywood is box-office success, Spielberg managed to show that the rules should be changed, not the film. But his desire to end the film with an emotional catharsis and a final humanization of his hero, coupled with his wish to bring the tale to a proper Zionist/ideological closure, once more raises doubts about the compatibility between the director and his chosen subject, as well as between the conventions and constraints of a Hollywood production and the profound rupture of Western civilization which was at the core of the Holocaust.

The point is of course not that Schindler did not break down upon leaving "his" Jews (he did not). The point is that by this banal humanization of Schindler, Spielberg banalizes both the man and the context of his actions. For only the kind of Schindler who precedes this scene, that do-gooder crook who gets a kick from helping Jews and fooling Nazis, that anarchist underworld character with a swastika badge who never ceases to enjoy his cognac and cigars even under the shadow of Auschwitz, that trickster who befriends one of the most sadistic of all concentration camp commanders, that incompetent failure of prewar and postwar normality who thoroughly relishes the mad universe of the SS where he is king, only that man could have saved the Jews in quite that manner. And this kind of man could not, and did not, break down. Nor was the world in which he operated an appropriate stage for sentimental scenes. Schindler's Jews did forge him a ring, and they remained grateful to him for the rest of their lives. But they did not need or expect him to weep. Tears have no place in this tale, whether "authentic" or not.

Nor does the Zionist closure, ironically accompanied by the tune of "Jerusalem of Gold," which came to symbolize first the euphoria of the Israeli victory of 1967 and then the bitter fruits of conquest, occupation, and repression of others by the young Jewish state. Looking at the joyous survivors striding down the green hill to the Promised Land, one cannot help thinking of Primo Levi's melancholy account of his own liberation in *The Reawakening*.[4] No less ironic is the fact that the only country in which the screened version of the film contained a different tune was Israel, obviously out of regard for the sensibilities of an audience which might not have approved of such a crass and yet disconcertingly ambiguous connection between the destruction of the Diaspora and the triumph of the Israeli Defense Forces. Thus the land of (by now somewhat disillusioned) Zionists was spared the Zionist punchline of the film which the rest of the world (excepting some Jewish viewers) could not appreciate in any case.[5] And meanwhile Hollywood proved once more that it could practice the technique of collage just as well as any modernist or postmodernist studio, cutting and pasting its films to suit public taste, box-office returns, political requirements, moral dictates, and the biases of its directors and producers.

Even more seriously, and similarly related to the film's box-office success, is the fact that precisely because *Schindler's List* has been watched by large numbers of people who had very little previous knowledge of the Holocaust, and cannot be expected to gain much more knowledge in the future, this specific version of the event may remain the only source of information about it for many of its viewers. Moreover, since the film is based on an "authentic" story, its authority as a true reconstruction of the past "as it really happened" is especially great. Thus, a relatively minor, and quite extraordinary case, has been transformed into a representative segment of the "story" as a whole, obliterating, or at least neglecting the fact that in the "real" Holocaust, most of the Jews died, most of the Germans collaborated with the perpetrators or remained passive bystanders, most of the victims sent to the showers were gassed, and most of the survivors did not walk across green meadows to Palestine, but either came to the Promised Land because they had nowhere else to go, remained in Europe, or settled down in other parts of the world.

Consequently, by concentrating on a particular, unique tale, whose power lies in its label of "authenticity," and considering the ignorance of many viewers regarding the historical context in which this tale took place, the film actually distorts the "reality" of the Holocaust, or at least leaves out too many other "realities," and especially that most common and typical reality of all, namely mass, industrial killing. Instead, the film caters to a certain kind of general post-Holocaust sensibility, as well as to a series of specific national and ideological biases.

In our post-Holocaust world two major requirements can be detected in public taste for representations of the past. First is the demand for a "human" story of will and determination, decency and courage, and final triumph over the forces of evil. Second is the quest for authenticity, for a story which "actually" happened, though retold according to accepted conventions of representation. Now, there is obviously a contradiction between these two demands, since authentic stories rarely happen according to conventional representations and even less frequently culminate in the triumph of good over evil. In any case, this can certainly not be said about the Holocaust where, as far as the vast majority of the victims were concerned, evil did indeed triumph. It is precisely due to this "unconventional" character of the Holocaust that Spielberg's movie is both such a success and such a distortion of the event it pretends to represent. Schindler's story manages to be both authentic and conventional precisely because, within the context of the Holocaust, it was so unique as to be untrue in the sense of not reflecting (or even negating) the fate of the vast majority of victims who were in turn swallowed up in a unique and unprecedented, and therefore (at least as far as Hollywood conventions are concerned) unrepresentable murder machine. Spielberg therefore tells an "authentic" story that (almost) never happened. But the contemporary yearning for authenticity, rooted, no doubt, in a profound sense of distrust in and incomprehension of the present reality, along with the desire for heroic plots and comforting closures, similarly related to the scarcity of such plots in the "real" world, brings crowds to the theaters and bags of money to the film industry.

Spielberg's is an evil we can live with, made in Hollywood, one that can be defeated by skill and perseverance, willpower and determination. This is troubling because so many of the millions who perished had no less will, no fewer skills, were in no way inferior to the survivors, and yet they drowned. The idea of salvation through personal gifts has no place in the Holocaust; it is just as pernicious as its opposite, namely, that the worst survived while the best perished. It was these thoughts which haunted Primo Levi as he wrote his last, heartbreaking collection of essays.[6] But such troubling ruminations are given no expression in the film since they might confuse its moral agenda and undermine its symmetry, casting doubt on the authenticity of Schindler's case as representative of anything but itself and opening the way for the horrifying distortion of humanity which was perhaps the most authentic element of the Holocaust. Indeed, placing the drowned at the center of this tale would not only have made the genocide itself unbearable to contemplate, but would also have profoundly shaken our own belief in the viability of civilized human existence after Auschwitz, since just as mass industrial murder was not created ex nihilo by the Nazis, this distortion of humanity has doubtlessly been carried over well beyond 1945. It is this that Primo Levi understood with ever greater urgency in the years between writing *Survival in Auschwitz* and *The Drowned and the Saved*, just as Paul Celan understood it between writing "Death Fugue" and "The Straitening" (*Engführung*), and Jean Améry already knew when he wrote *At the Mind's Limits*: the very stories told by the saved distort the past, not because they are not authentic (leaving aside the question of personal memory), but because, by definition, they exclude the stories of the drowned, who were the majority, and drowned not because they did not want to be saved but due to a combination of circumstances in which individual will and skills rarely played an important role and chance was paramount.[7]

Schindler's List also manages to comfort several particular sensibilities without, miraculously, causing too much offense to anyone else. For Germans (as the cover of the popular *Der Spiegel* magazine had it, reflecting much wider public sentiments), Schindler (the cinematic character, not the man) was the "good German," presumably both because of his actions and because he thereby demonstrated that not all Germans were complicit in the killing (at least not in the movies). For Zionists (but not necessarily for Israeli film critics), the film's final Zionist twist brings the whole disturbing notion of the Jews "being led like sheep to the slaughter" to a worthy conclusion, giving (retrospective) sense and meaning to an event which for its victims had neither. (Many Israelis, it seems, while saying that they did not need another film on the Holocaust, were nevertheless flattered by the fact that Hollywood had found the genocide of the Jews important enough to make it the subject of a film directed by none other than Steven Spielberg of *E.T.* fame.) For the general, well-meaning Christian/humanitarian audience, the story had all the heart-warming aspect of the Good Samaritan, the promise of human decency arising even from the darkest souls and the greatest depths of evil (thereby qualifying, even humanizing evil itself, cutting it down to a manageable size). Hence, in a sense, everything the Holocaust actually destroyed, both material and spiritual, is reestablished (on the screen) by Spielberg, with the same wave of a magic wand we have learned to expect from his earlier films. By claiming to provide us with an authentic picture, therefore, the screen does in fact what it has always done best (and recently especially at the hands of Spielberg): it creates a dream world of glimmering images that hovers momentarily over the debris of reality and then remains in our minds as a comforting tranquilizer. We do not feel the pain, ergo, the pain is no longer there.

Mass-oriented films invariably suffer from an inability to remain consistent with the more important themes they may raise. As we have seen, *Schindler's List* cannot sustain the Mephistophelean character of the main protagonist to the end. Hollywood has certainly been known to conjure up cinematic worlds of intense evil, where the few remaining old-world crooks are transformed by contrast into angels. This is, after all, a central trope of the horror film and of one variant of science fiction. But such worlds must by definition remain temporary cinematic fantasies lest they cease to entertain and consequently repel rather than attract audiences. Their success relies precisely on the assumption that they are totally different from the reality beyond the theater walls. Hence the relief felt by audiences when they return to the street, the expectation of which is at the very root of enjoying the fantasy indoors. But, of course, Nazism was no fantasy; there was no "outdoors." Nor did the inverted world it had created simply go up in smoke in 1945, either for the survivors, or for the perpetrators, or for human civilization as a whole, which has never healed since this horrific surge of modern barbarism. But all this, of course, has no room in a Hollywood production.

Another important trope of Hollywood films is the enhancement of the hero's image by a diminution of all other characters, apart, of course, from the villain he confronts. Hence, in this film we find ourselves in the curious position of watching Schindler (crook turned saint) and Goeth (the embodiment of evil) towering both physically (as tall, handsome Aryans) and personally (as clearly etched, strong characters) over a mass of physically small, emotionally confused, frantic, almost featureless Jews. The potential victims thereby serve largely as a mere background to the heroic, epic struggle between the good guy and the bad guy, cast in true Hollywood fashion and disturbingly, though unintentionally, evoking the kind of stereotypes Nazism had thrived on.

Stereotypical representations of characters, and especially of Jews, in *Schindler's List*, go beyond their portrayal as small, helpless, passive victims, waiting to be either murdered by one Aryan giant or saved by another. For reasons which I cannot quite fathom, in several scenes Jews appear terrifyingly similar to their images in Nazi propaganda, haggling over loss and profit while their brethren are being tormented and starved, selling their wares during mass in a Catholic church, vacating huge apartments, hiding diamonds and gold in their bread. How badly they come off when compared with Schindler's initially detached, cynical posture, transformed in front of our eyes into a courageous, noble stance.

Similarly disturbing is the film's portrayal and exploitation of women, where it seems that Spielberg, possibly unconsciously, catered to Hollywood's tradition of providing sexual distraction to the viewers. Most troubling of all, of course, is the shower scene, since that mass of attractive, frightened, naked women, finally relieved from their anxiety by jets of water rather than gas, would be more appropriate to a soft-porn sadomasochistic film than to its context (and here Spielberg comes dangerously close to such films as Cavani's *The Night Porter* and Wertmuller's *Seven Beauties*). The fact that this "actually" happened is, of course, wholly beside the point, since in most cases it did not, and even when it did, the only eyes which might have derived any sexual pleasure from watching such scenes belonged to the SS. Hence, by including this scene, Spielberg makes the viewers complicit with the SS, both in sharing their voyeurism and in blocking out the reality of the gas chambers.

The "graphic" violence in Spielberg's film also raises some problematic issues. As reported in several newspapers in January 1994, the field trip of sixty-nine Castlemont High School students from Oakland to a showing of *Schindler's List* ended with those teenagers being asked to leave the theater after they had disrupted the screening by reacting to some of the most violent scenes in a manner reminiscent of audience participation in Rambo-style films. This small scandal in northern California, which involved relations between inner-city African American and Latino youths and the Jewish community, and had teachers, Jewish leaders, and Holocaust survivors scrambling to the school in an effort to transform an embarrassing incident into an educational occasion, revealed nonetheless some of the inherent problems of a "realistic," "authentic" portrayal of Nazi brutality and sadism. Goeth's random shooting of helpless inmates, and the hyper-realistic portrayal of victims being hit by his bullets, does indeed follow tropes and techniques employed in the countless police and war films set loose on the market for the alleged purpose of entertainment. No youth in present day America can take seriously the "graphic" depiction of death and violence in film, since it is part of a vast entertainment industry. On the other hand, so many youths in the United States are constantly exposed to actual violence on the streets that they cannot be expected to be moved by what they know is mere pyrotechnics. The connection between the reality of violence and its cinematic representation is possibly one of the most troubling aspects of contemporary American culture. While people shot in reality are said to die "just like in the movies," shootings in the movies both entertain and furnish examples for actual acts of violence on the street. Hence Spielberg's attempt to provide "graphic" evidence of the sadism of a Nazi concentration camp commander is qualified by the successful dissemination of images of violence by the film industry and is thereby "normalized" as part of a genre to which, of course, it ought not to belong (though in a paradoxical, perverse way it nevertheless does). The students who laughed because the Jewish woman shot by Goeth died in an insufficiently authentic manner were therefore comparing that scene both to other films where, presumably, people die more "authentically," and to their own very real experiences. As one of them said: "My man got busted in the head just like that last year."[8]

In a related sense, *Schindler's List* suffers from the difficulties that any film, not only Hollywood productions, confronts when attempting to recreate reality in a convincing, "authentic" manner. Though shot on location in black-and-white, and with an eye to fine details, the film cannot recreate an inhuman reality. We cannot blame it for not showing people actually being gassed, but only for showing them *not* being gassed; we cannot blame it for not showing the emaciated bodies of concentration camp inmates, but only for showing us the attractive, healthy naked bodies of young actresses whose shorn hair strangely resembles current fashions. It is precisely because of the inability of cinematic representation authentically to recreate a distorted reality that the claim of authenticity, and the sense of the viewers that they are seeing things as they "actually were," is so troubling. Possibly, the best way out of this dilemma is to condemn any representation of the Holocaust which attempts directly to confront what the Nazis called "the asshole of the world," where the actual process of dehumanization and murder was practiced on a daily basis. Thus one might argue that Lumet's *The Pawnbroker* (1965) dealt much more profoundly and sensitively with the question of trauma and memory among survivors than *Schindler's List*, or that Lanzmann's *Shoah* has shown the way to avoid the inevitable distortion and kitsch of conventional films dependent on plots and actors, sets and scripts. But if we believe that it *is* necessary to make cinematic representations of the thing itself, to show not only the forest grown over the death camp but also the death camp in operation, to record not only the survivors' memories but also the circumstances they remember, then we must accept the limitations of the genre and (some of) the price which may have to be paid. We cannot have it both ways. Indeed, as I will argue below, any representation of the Holocaust comes with a heavy price, and none can claim to be wholly free of bias, distortion, and the limitations of the conventions within which it operates.

It is therefore just as important to sketch out the parameters of the debate over *Schindler's List* as to discuss the film itself. Can fiction films be made on the Holocaust? Are documentaries a good alternative? Is memory, rather than either historical fact or fiction, the most immediate, sincere, and authentic element in Holocaust reconstruction? And if so, how can memory be represented in film, and at what price? Finally, how do the various cinematic options of representation relate to other media and means of representing the Holocaust, such as prose fiction, poetry, historical scholarship, memoirs and personal accounts, as well as visual displays in exhibitions and museums?

Assuming that we allow for the possibility of "authentic" fiction films on the Holocaust, one example which immediately comes to mind apart from *Schindler's List* is Holland's *Europa, Europa* (1991). Similarly based on a true story, and sharing the very same quality of being both "authentic" and at the same time too extraordinary to be true as representative of the fate of most Jews in the Holocaust, Holland's film was also relatively popular and owed its success to an adventurelike, fantastic, intense plot and the constant tension it creates between the unbelievable events it tells and the knowledge that at least as far as the protagonist was concerned they did indeed take place (more or less). In comparing the two films, however, it would seem that by and large *Schindler's List*, despite its damning Hollywood label and children's adventure movies director, manages to cope much better with the dilemmas of such cinematic fiction than the European-produced *Europa, Europa*, not only because it contains less kitsch and is more controlled in tone and content, but also because it dares to come much closer to the actual heart of the Nazi genocidal enterprise. Thus *Schindler's List* is less concerned with the incredible fate of a single individual and more (if insufficiently) concerned with that of the multitude of victims and the circumstances of their murder (or salvation). Schindler's Jews are doubtlessly exceptional, but they are far less exceptional than the Jewish lad who survives the Nazi onslaught, escapes from a Soviet training school, serves in a Wehrmacht unit on the Eastern Front, is educated in a Hitler Youth institution, and participates in the bloody Battle of Berlin, remaining both physically and mentally unscathed throughout his ordeal. Moreover, even more than is the case in Spielberg's film, *Europa, Europa* fully exploits the elements of this twentieth-century drama to create a heroic tale of ingenuity, imagination, courage and cunning, qualities which seem to distinguish this resourceful youth from his less gifted six million brethren. In this sense, too, we must therefore conclude that Spielberg's film is by far the less false and more honest rendering of individual fate in the Holocaust of these two "authentic" tales.

Because no cinematic representation of the Holocaust is likely totally to overcome the problem of audience familiarity with graphic violence in popular films, with the consequent diminution of the impact of Holocaust films employing the same techniques as *Dirty Harry* and *Full Metal Jacket*, we may either have to relinquish any attempt to represent the brutality of the Holocaust (say, by focusing on its bureaucratic aspects, as in the film *The Wannsee Conference*), or to search for ways to stress the truly unique element of the Holocaust, namely, the industrial killing of millions in the gas chambers. Indeed, the fact that those who wish to relativize (or deny) the Holocaust altogether attack precisely this aspect of the genocide of the Jews is only one more proof of its centrality in any representation of the event.

All this means, however, that there exists an inherent tension between exposure to the sheer brutality of the event and its trivialization, between complete ignorance of its course and scope and the dangers of partial or distorted knowledge, between a total distancing which breeds indifference and false objectivity, and a false familiarity which breeds an erroneous sense of understanding, between the abhorrence evoked by human degradation and suffering, and a perverse, pornographic curiosity about the limits of human depravity (as manifested, for instance, in Pasolini's *Salò*).

Can these tensions be overcome by perfecting a wholly different genre? Can documentaries, for instance, be used more effectively and truthfully than "authentic" fiction? In evaluating documentary films it must first of all be stressed that their quality depends both on the nature of the documentary material and on such factors as the selection, editing, and presentation of this material, as well as on the commentary which accompanies it, all elements which are extraneous to the document itself. Keeping these points in mind, we would have to admit that even Alain Resnais's justly celebrated *Night and Fog*, in spite of its many merits, suffers from numerous problems associated directly with the circumstances of its making (*not* its documentary material). The most glaring difficulty with this film is, of course, the complete absence of any mention of Jews as the main victims of the Nazi death camps. And, while Resnais's reasons for this lacuna may well have had to do with public sentiment in postwar France and his desire to make viewers understand the enormity of the

Holocaust without blocking it out by seeing it as an event which concerned only other, non-French human beings, this decision by the director (not at all related to the character of the documentary material he employed) does introduce a major distortion of the historical record in a film which is still categorized as a documentary and therefore an "authentic" representation of the past, a cinematic presentation of "objective" evidence. This distortion is also partly responsible for the lack of distinction in the film between concentration camps, forced labor camps, and death camps, since in reality it was their so-called biological identity which determined the inmates' location within the Nazi "concentrationary universe." Indeed, we might even say that Resnais's masterpiece, by presenting the Holocaust as a universal problem which ought to disturb each and every member of the human race, also makes it into an amorphous, almost ahistorical event, where neither perpetrators nor victims are clearly defined, where responsibility is so widely dispersed as to lose all significance, and where a looming sense of anxiety in the face of universal evil is not articulated into any specific call for practical action.

A major peril of documentaries is that they create an even greater illusion of portraying the past "as it really was" than such "authentic" fiction films as *Schindler's List* and *Europa, Europa*. Indeed, in the numerous discussions on *Schindler's List* and its historical veracity, it has often been implied that documentaries would be a much better way to learn about the past, especially *that* past. Yet the case of documentary film material about the Holocaust is highly problematic since the circumstances under which it was taken would very often strongly undermine its value as "objective" evidence. A newsreel filmed by a Wehrmacht propaganda company cannot be perceived as an objective representation of an event, whatever the claims of its makers. Films shot by Nazi film crews were clearly intended to present the victims of the regime as precisely the kind of subhumans German propaganda claimed them to be, so as to confirm the arguments of the Nazi leadership, as well as to create horror, disgust, fear, or detachment, but certainly not empathy in the German viewer. Similarly, amateur films also reflect the prejudices, morbid curiosity, or detachment from the victims characteristic of German personnel in Eastern Europe and the Soviet Union, and generally contain the same subtext as the official film material, namely, that since the victims have an unmistakably subhuman appearance, they doubtlessly deserve to be treated as such.[9]

Films made by the liberators inevitably represent the victims as horribly emaciated, only quasi-human creatures, and if they express sympathy for the human debris of Nazi racial policies, they do not arouse empathy. Rather, in accordance with the general propagandistic line of the Allies, the main aim of these films is to create hatred of the enemy and thereby to legitimize the war and motivate their soldiers at the front and the civilians in the rear. Consequently, when evaluating documentary films, we must bear in mind that both the selection of the material and, even more insidiously, the documentary film material itself, can often be just as biased as the "authentic" fiction; indeed, that in many cases, since it had been produced in the service of various propagandistic, ideological, and political ends, contemporary film material may be more biased, as well as more dangerous, precisely because it masquerades as an "objective" depiction of "reality." However much we may try to purge the documentary material from its polluting context, it will always retain some of the qualities which made it useful for those who initially produced it. Hence documentary films on the Holocaust are in constant peril of having a hidden subtext, perhaps unbeknown even to their makers, which may have a wholly contrary effect on the viewers from that hoped for and expected by those who produced them. Indeed, the detachment, revulsion, even anger, felt by modern viewers of documentaries employing Nazi cinematic representations of the victims may reflect much more the intention of the original German filmmakers than that of contemporary directors who inserted these film clips in their own movies.

We may therefore have to concede that documentaries on the Holocaust can be pernicious both because of their claim to veracity (based on the "original" film material they use) and our lesser ability to protect ourselves from that claim than when watching "authentic" fiction films, and because they dehumanize the victims (thanks to the nature of that "original" film material) and hamper our ability to empathize with them. Consequently, documentaries may have the adverse effect of desensitizing, even brutalizing the viewers and making them emotionally complicit in the crime by causing them to see the victims through the lenses of the perpetrators.[10] What then might be a better alternative? Can we turn to the memory of the Holocaust, rather than its "authentic" fictions or polluted documents?

Claude Lanzmann's *Shoah*, likely to remain the most important film made on the memory of the Holocaust, resists the kind of narrative deemed central to any Hollywood production, and scrupulously avoids using any documentary material from the period. Yet in spite of its remarkable qualities, *Shoah* suffers from some serious handicaps which are at least in part inherent to the genre. As Lanzmann himself has written, in making a film on the Holocaust one can either invent a new genre—which he believes he has done—or reconstruct, which to his mind is what Spielberg did. Reconstruction for him is akin to inventing archival documentation, whereas he would have refused to use even real documents (which he erroneously claims do not exist in any case). According to Lanzmann, Spielberg made a cartoon version of the Holocaust, filling in the blanks intentionally left empty in *Shoah*, whereas his own film is dry and pure, avoiding personal stories, and concerned not with survival but with destruction. His aim in making *Shoah*, says Lanzmann, was to create a structure, a mold, which could serve as a generalization of the (Jewish) people, that is, would encompass the destruction of the people as a whole. Spielberg, on the other hand, uses the destruction as a background for the heroic story of Schindler and fails to confront the blazing sun of the Holocaust. Hence, says Lanzmann, Spielberg's film is a melodrama, a work of kitsch. Implied in this analysis is not only that *Schindler's List* is the exact opposite of *Shoah*, but also that Lanzmann's film is the only possible cinematic rendering of the Holocaust.[11]

Yet Lanzmann's is a flawed masterpiece. As he notes in the above-cited interview, whereas the many viewers of *Schindler's List* known to have wept during the film obviously sought the release of catharsis which leads to pleasure, some who had refused to view *Shoah* might have been motivated by the inability to cry (that is, to "enjoy" the film) while watching it. In fact, of course, while *Schindler's List* has elicited all kinds of reactions, including laughter and derision, I have known many people who wept in *Shoah*, including myself. The point here is, however, that far fewer people have actually seen *Shoah*, both because it is emotionally horribly draining and because of its sheer length. I would assume that more people saw *Schindler's List* in the first month of screening than have watched *Shoah* since it was first released.

This is not, as such, a criticism of *Shoah*, but it does mean that the film's impact on the public was much more limited. Nor is *Shoah* as "dry and pure" as Lanzmann would like us to believe. For although it may not tell personal stories, *Shoah* is highly biased, and its biases are intensely personal, stemming directly from its maker's own national and ideological prejudices and finding expression in his style of interviewing, his editing technique, and the content of his comments. Lanzmann himself has admitted that he had eliminated numerous witnesses because they were too weak. In fact, it seems that he sought witnesses who were both strong enough to testify at some length and coherence, and weak enough to finally break down in front of the camera under the incessant pressure of his questions, thereby providing his viewers with that emotional release and personal touch he derides in Spielberg's film. Lanzmann is indeed a brutal interviewer, and though his technique is very effective and has made possible the production of an extraordinary film, it is also highly disturbing. For Lanzmann seems so obsessed with *Shoah* (both the film and the historical event), that the actual survivors serve him only as "documents," as living records, verbalized memories, not as human beings—hence the almost uncanny lack of empathy in a man who devoted much of his life to making a film on the memory of the destruction, and the mutilated lives of the saved, the last carriers of that memory.

Nor can we say that Lanzmann is seeking the "truth" of the Holocaust;

for his obsession with the complicity of the Polish population in the genocide (as well as its swift takeover of abandoned Jewish property and its amazing ability to erase the Jews from its memory) is matched by his relative lack of concern with the Germans and his almost total lack of interest in his own compatriots (in stark contrast to that other masterpiece of French documentary cinema, Ophuls's *The Sorrow and the Pity* [1969]). And because Lanzmann *is* very much concerned with memory, this last omission is especially striking in view of the role which the memory of Vichy (and its repression) has recently been shown to have played in postwar France.[12]

Finally, the main objection to Lanzmann's film must stem from his own apparent belief that his is the only possible film on the Holocaust. For whether we accept this statement or not (and it is difficult to see it as more than rhetorical), what is true is that only one *such* film can be made. *Shoah*, the film, is unique, for better or for worse. And if we believe that one must make more films on the Holocaust, then they will perforce have to be different, even if they do not reach the rank of masterpiece which Lanzmann's work, in spite of all the qualifications, richly deserves.[13]

One alternative to Lanzmann's enterprise which nevertheless shares some common features with it is the project of recording survivors' testimonies on videotape and depositing them in several video archives in the United States and Israel. These interviews lack the more overtly brutal aspects of Lanzmann's questioning (which tend to compromise the humanistic urge of his film), and are an even "purer" form of memory reconstruction in that they are not accessible to wide audiences. Indeed, these collections are an immensely important source for understanding both the reality and the memory of the Holocaust, as can be seen in a recent study by Lawrence Langer.[14] But in another sense, this is no alternative at all, since while we can say that *Shoah* was watched by relatively limited audiences, these videotaped interviews can only be perceived as oral documents to be used by scholars rather than as the kind of representations which would have any direct impact on the general public.

This brings me to alternative depictions of the Holocaust in other media or forms of representation.[15] By and large, it seems, the available modes of representation can be evaluated according to the same parameters I have employed regarding film, namely, fiction, documentary, and memory, to which we can add plastic visual display. Thus, novels, including such fictionalizations of authentic stories as Thomas Keneally's *Schindler's List*,[16] as well as to some extent poetry, fall into the category of fiction; historical scholarship and related disciplines dealing with the Holocaust (sociology, psychology, literary criticism, political science, and so forth), can be grouped under the category of documentary; memoirs and personal accounts belong to the genre of memory;

and museums provide a combination of public display of documents and the organization (as well as the creation, recreation, or fictionalization) of memory.

In the present context I lack the space to discuss the specific merits and problems of each of these genres. Suffice it to say that all of them seem to display many of the same characteristics as the different types of cinematic representation, both in the way they are perceived by the public and as far as their own inherent qualities are concerned. Thus we find a tendency to privilege memoirs or personal accounts over fiction, and scholarship over museums. Moreover, this ranking exhibits the same tensions we have seen above between limited exposure and distortion, imposed both by the nature of the medium and by the greater scope for bias and prejudice in the more popular genres.

Even more crucially, claims for "authenticity" or "realism" are in fact just as problematic in evaluating the relative importance of these genres as in the case of cinematic representation. Museums, which purport to present a dispassionate array of "authentic" artifacts, actually impose a more or less coherent and didactic narrative on their displays by means of their organization, selection, captions, and so forth. Yet the claim of displaying "real" objects often hampers museum visitors from uncovering the subtext that actually orders such plastic reconstructions of the past.[17] Survivors' memoirs too, quite apart from questions of authenticity, are not always free from melodrama and manipulation of emotions, as Naomi Diamant has shown, both the melodramatic mode and the plain style can be employed in "remembering" the same event.[18] Nor is historical scholarship to be seen (as it sometimes is, for instance, by film critics) as immune to prejudice and bias, quite apart from the built-in limitations of every historical text which impose on it a process of selection, evaluation, directions of inquiry, allegiances to subdisciplines, as well as personal interest and style. This does not mean that all historical writing would be wholly unreliable and suspect, but it does mean that some texts may contain a highly distorted or partial representation of the past while nevertheless adhering to the form of established scholarly practice. In this case too, the authority of the historian may play a role in popularizing distorted reconstructions of the past presented as true tales of events "as they really happened," often through exposure to the media of even more simplistic versions of the historian's original work. Hence the lay public is most likely to be exposed to those historical interpretations least likely to offer a reliable representation of the past, yet would be prone to take precisely such stories at face value because they would be presented as the culmination of scholarly research. For while contemporary historians are increasingly aware of the tenuous nature of their claims for objectivity, much of the public still maintains considerable faith in them as judges and interpreters of the truth, at least as far as the past is concerned.

By recognizing the limitations of historical scholarship (both as a source of objective truth and as a means for public enlightenment) on the one hand, and the general ignorance of the past among much of the lay public (even as regards such a crucial event in modern history as the Holocaust) on the other, it would seem to me that we cannot afford wholly to dismiss a relatively well conceived and produced, though flawed, cinematic representation of the Nazi genocide of the Jews which has managed to reach a far wider public than any other such venture since the television series *Holocaust* (1978). Indeed, the latter, though far inferior to *Schindler's List*, is a good example of the positive effect even mediocre films may have if they appear at the right time and in the right place. The impact of *Holocaust*, especially in Germany, can be said in retrospect to have been by and large salutary, in spite, or perhaps precisely because of the biting criticism of the German intelligentsia and the complaint that Hollywood had stolen Germany's history from the Germans.[19]

Moreover, since, on the one hand, we as scholars are rarely in a position to prevent the publication of novels, the making of films, and the establishment of museums concerning the Holocaust of which we may disapprove and since we do have an interest in creating a greater public awareness and knowledge of the Holocaust and other crimes against humanity, on the other, we would do well to try to influence the media by constructive criticism or involvement, rather than by outright dismissal of anything which does not quite meet our rather high standards.

For my own part, of all the Oscars recently awarded, both Spielberg's film and Oskar Schindler the man deserved it most. And as for Oskars, this brings to mind Günter Grass's Oskar Matzerath, the protagonist of *The Tin Drum*, and Volker Schlöndorff's cinematic version of the novel.[20] There are indeed some striking, almost bizarre similarities between the two characters. Both thrive only during times of war, terror, and hardship: Schindler makes a fortune and becomes a hero, Matzerath remains an eternally beautiful three-year-old whose appearance and glass-shattering voice protect him from all harm. Both are destroyed by peace and normalcy: Schindler fails in business, loses his fortune, drinks, and lives off "his" Jews, despised by his own countrymen; Matzerath is transformed into an ugly dwarf and ends up in an insane asylum. And yet, with all due respect to the literary genius of Grass and the cinematic gifts of Schlöndorff, I still prefer Oskar Schindler, the man and the film, if only because, when all is said and done, the man did save real people, and the film, in spite of all its faults, made an attempt to represent the evil of the time and the valiant efforts of one man to oppose it. The dwarf, Oskar Matzerath, whether in prose or on the screen, could only destroy. And, since he is only a metaphor, he was never much good at saving people anyway.

Notes

1. For a list, which does, however, include numerous films not dealing directly with the Holocaust, and for a discussion of these films, see Ilan Avisar, *Screening the Holocaust: Cinema's Images of the Unimaginable* (Bloomington: Indiana University Press, 1988).

2. See, e.g., John Gross. "Hollywood and the Holocaust," *New York Review of Books* 41, no. 3 (February 3, 1994), pp. 14–16. For similar and dissenting views by scholars and intellectuals, see, e.g., Fred Bruning, "Beyond Words." *Newsday* (December 20, 1993), pp. 50–51, 59; Philip Gourevitch, "A Dissent on 'Schindler's List,' " *Commentary* (February 1994), pp. 49–52; Janet Maslin, "Imagining the Holocaust to Remember It," *New York Times* (December 15, 1993), pp. C19 and C23.

3. For scholarly views on the limits of representation, see Saul Friedlander (ed.), *Probing the Limits of Representation: Nazism and the "Final Solution"* (Cambridge: Harvard University Press, 1992).

4. Primo Levi, *The Reawakening*, trans. S. Woolf (New York: Collier Books/Macmillan, 1987 [1963]).

5. Nor would most non-Israelis realize that many of the actors speak English with an Israeli accent, or simply speak modern Hebrew, shedding an ironic light on Spielberg's overt Zionist presentation of Israel as the logical conclusion and best means to avoid a repetition of the Holocaust, since the presence of contemporary Israeli actors in Nazi concentration camps reveals the potential vulnerability of all (even Israelis) to evil. For a sampling of the debate over the change of the melody in the Israeli media, see the weekly *Zeman Tel Aviv*, March 4, 1994. "Jerusalem of Gold" was replaced by "Eli, Eli" (My God, My God), a popular melancholy setting to music of the 1941 poem "To Caesarea" by Hannah Senesh, a Hungarian-born Palestinian volunteer parachuted into Nazi-occupied Hungary and executed by the Germans in 1944. This choice shifted the politics of the film's ending from the Arab-Israeli conflict to the Israeli-sponsored "heroic" aspect of the Holocaust, stressing not only resistance to the Nazis but also the reinvented, "normalized" Jews "made in Palestine," as the proper answer to gentile hatred and persecution. This revised ending of the Holocaust appears to have been more acceptable, because less controversial, to the Israeli public. On Senesh, see Leni Yahil, *The Holocaust: The Fate of European Jewry*, trans. I. Friedman and H. Galai (New York: Oxford University Press, 1991), p. 646; Tom Segev, *The Seventh Million: The Israelis and the Holocaust*, trans. H. Watzman (New York: Hill and Wang/Farrar, Straus and Giroux, 1993), pp. 87–88, 283–84.

6. Primo Levi, *The Drowned and the Saved*, trans. R. Rosenthal (New York: Summit Books/Simon & Schuster, 1988 [1986]).

7. Primo Levi, *Survival in Auschwitz: The Nazi Assault on Humanity*, trans. S. Woolf (New York: Collier Books/Macmillan, 1959 [1947]); *Paul Celan: Poems*, selected, introduced, and translated by M. Hamburger (New York: Persea Books, 1980); Jean Améry, *At the Mind's Limits: Contemplations by a Survivor on Auschwitz and Its Realities*, trans. S. Rosenfeld and S. P. Rosenfeld (New York: Schocken Books, 1986 [1966]).

8. See Kevin Weston, "Laughing Instead of Crying: Why Oakland Teens Had Disturbing Reactions to 'Schindler's List,' " *San Francisco Examiner* (Sunday, January 30, 1994), p. D2; Sandy Kleffman, "A Bid for Understanding after 'Schindler's List' Flap: Holocaust Survivors Offer to Speak to Castlemont Students," *San Francisco Chronicle / Bay Area and California / East Bay Edition* (Thursday, January 20, 1994), pp. A17, A19. I wish to thank Professor Anton Kaes for informing me of this incident and sending me the relevant material.

9. For some examples of such amateur films, see now the film *Mein Krieg*, directed by Eder and Kufus (1989–90). See also my review of the film in *American Historical Review* 97, no. 4 (October 1992), pp. 1155–57.

10. A good example is the problematic documentary *The Eighty-First Blow* (Israel 1975), directed by Haim Gouri, Jacques Ehrlich, and David Bergmann.

11. Interview with Claude Lanzmann by Daniel Heiman of *Le Monde*, published in a Hebrew translation in the Israeli weekly *Zeman Tel Aviv* (March 3, 1994), pp. 48–50.

12. Henry Rousso, *The Vichy Syndrome: History and Memory in France since 1944*, trans. Arthur Goldhammer (Cambridge: Harvard University Press, 1991).

13. For the text of the film, see Claude Lanzmann, *Shoah: An Oral History of the Holocaust*, English subtitles by A. Whitelaw and W. Byron (New York: Pantheon Books/Random House, 1985).

14. Lawrence L. Langer, *Holocaust Testimonies: The Ruins of Memory* (New Haven: Yale University Press, 1991).

15. See, most recently, James E. Young, *Writing and Rewriting the Holocaust: Narrative and the Consequences of Interpretation* (Bloomington: Indiana University Press, 1988). See also David G. Roskies, *Against the Apocalypse: Responses to Catastrophe in Modern Jewish Culture* (Cambridge: Harvard University Press, 1984); Alvin H. Rosenfeld, *A Double Dying: Reflections on Holocaust Literature* (Bloomington: Indiana University Press, 1980); Sidra DeKoven Ezrahi, *By Words Alone: The Holocaust in Literature* (Chicago: University of Chicago Press, 1980).

16. Thomas Keneally, *Schindler's List* (New York: Touchstone/Simon & Schuster, 1993 [1982]).

17. See, most recently, James E. Young, *The Texture of Memory: Holocaust Memorials and Meaning* (New Haven: Yale University Press, 1993); idem. (ed.), *Holocaust Memorials: The Art of Memory in History* (Munich: Prestel Verlag, 1994).

18. Naomi Diamant, "The Rhetoric of Holocaust Memory: The Melodramatic Mode and the Plain Style," unpublished paper delivered at Rutgers University, March 1994; idem., "The Boundaries of Holocaust Literature: The Emergence of a Canon" (Ph.D. diss.: Columbia University, 1992).

19. See especially Anton Kaes, *From Hitler to Heimat: The Return of History as Film* (Cambridge: Harvard University Press, 1989).

20. Günter Grass, *The Tin Drum*, trans. R. Manheim (Harmondsworth: Penguin Books, 1978 [1959]); *The Tin Drum*, Volker Schlöndorff (1979).

3 | The Cinema Animal

Geoffrey H. Hartman

As a film that conveys to the public at large the horror of the extermination, *Schindler's List* is entirely successful. The mass scenes are heart-rending: the liquidation of the ghetto, the enticement and deportation of the children from the camp, the mothers rushing the convoy, and later, the exhumation and burning of the bodies (a scene from hell). The scale is deliberately varied: from the brilliant opening, matching the smoke of the extinguished candle and the smoke of the locomotive, to Schindler's hilltop observation of the exterminating action, to the close-ups in the apartment buildings (the chaos of terror made physically painful to the viewer's eyes by hand-held, unsteady cameras, as if the eyes had to be punished for what they could not feel). Then back to the hilltop and the extraordinary glimpse of the little girl in the red coat wandering alongside and apart from the murders and roundups, as if on an ordinary kind of walk. Then the heartbreaking effort of the boy to find a hiding place, ending in the sewer. The sheer assault on the lifeworld of the Kraków Jews as well as on their persons could not be rendered more effectively than when the contents of the suitcases are emptied, first at the deportation center, where the spoliation is clear, then during the ghetto's liquidation, when even spoliation ceases to matter, and the contents and then the suitcases are contemptuously thrown over the banisters.

We have learned that technique is never just technique: it retains a responsibility toward the represented subject. This link of responsibility distinguishes Spielberg here. The difference between close-ups and long shots is utilized again and again: uncomfortably but tellingly we sometimes see the action as if through the telescopic sights of Goeth's (the Nazi commander's) murderous rifle. The imperative to make everything *visible* is not modified by such distancing; rather, the viewers' eyes are more fully implicated. We are made aware of our silent and detached glance as spectators removed in time and place. Neither the creator of this film nor its viewers can assert, like the chorus in the *Oresteia*: "What happened next I saw not, neither speak it."

Yet, as I realized later, the premium placed on visuality by such a film made me deeply uneasy. To see things that sharply, and from a privileged position, is to see them with the eyes of those who had the power of life and death. There is no convincing attempt to capture a glimpse of the daily suffering in camp or ghetto: the kind of personal and characterizing detail which videotestimony projects record through the "lens" of the survivors' recollections.

Nor is there an attempt to explore the behavior of the main protagonists. Spielberg has been commended for not making Schindler transparent or seeking to illuminate the mystery of his compassion. While we do not need or want an "explanation," both Schindler and Goeth remain stylized figures that fail to transcend the handsome silhouettes of the average Hollywood film. The madness of Goeth is made believable simply by the madness of the war and particularly this war against the Jews; and there is no conversion or turn in Schindler that is expressly highlighted. Seeing the brutal liquidation from the hilltop may have played its part; but it is only when "his" Jews are fated to be sent to Auschwitz that he shifts decisively from making money to spending his money to buy them back. The scene in the cellar between Goeth and Helen Hirsch, and in Goeth's house between Schindler and the drunken camp commander on the subject of power, are psychologically credible, but their frame remains a crude and deadly game of power.

Goeth's offhanded, as if casual murderousness, moreover, especially when he toys with sparing the young boy who has sinned against cleanliness (the neurosis is barely hinted at), can be perversely humanizing. Against our will, we are made to identify with the hope that something in this man is redeemable, and that the boy will be saved.[1] The pathology against the Jews, moreover, is always expressed in actions rather than words, as if no argument or introspection were needed. Only in defense of Schindler, imprisoned for kissing a Jewess, does Goeth trot out some garbage about the spell cast by those women, which betrays his own acted-out fascination with Helen Hirsch. The film's pace remains that of an action movie which tolerates no diversion except to increase suspense: it "clicks" from shot to shot, from scene to scene, with the occasional mechanical failure symbolizing a chance for human feelings to reenter the sequence.

Spielberg is always precise, with a special ability to translate history into scene and synecdoche. Yet his tendency toward stylization is both distancing and disconcerting. The wish to encompass, through the episode of "Schindler's List," the enormity of what happened in Kraków and Plaszów, leads to moments approaching Holocaust kitsch. The SS officer playing the piano during the liquidation of the ghetto, and the "Is it Bach? No, Mozart" comment of the soldiers who hear him, is an unnecessary touch; I feel the same about the scene with the "Schindler women" in the showers at Auschwitz, which is melodramatic and leaves the audience confused (like the terrified prisoners, in that crucial moment of uncertainty, when the lights go out) about the issue of disinfecting showers and gas showers. The episode, however, in which Goeth vaunts that he and his troops are making history, because the Jews who settled in Kraków six centuries ago will have ceased to exist by day's end, is important, and recalls Himmler's Poznan speech.

Poster effects, that make this very much a Hollywood film, will show through even more with the passage of time. While a certain flatness in the characters may be inevitable in a panorama of this kind, and strengthens the mass scenes and "actions" that convey so ferociously Nazi callousness and terror, the focus on Goeth on the one hand and Schindler on the other is too clean, like the killings themselves, which are quick and neat, though always shocking in their coldblooded nature. Two of the three endings of the film are also Hollywood: the farewell scene in the factory is stagey, and Schindler's breakdown (concerning his not having saved enough Jews: had he only sold his car, his gold Nazi pin, etc.) detracts rather than adds; the survivors walking en masse toward the sunset with "Jerusalem of Gold" sung by an angelic offstage chorus (in Israeli showings of the film, I understand the song was changed to "Eli, Eli"), while giving a certain comfort after all those scenes of mass victimization, is again Hollywood or fake Eisenstein. This sentimentality is redeemed only by the final sequence: it takes us out of docudrama, and presents the survivors, the Schindler remnant, together with the actors who played them, as they place a ritual pebble on Schindler's tombstone in the Jerusalem graveyard.

Claude Lanzmann takes a radical position in a comment on *Schindler's List*, writing that the Holocaust, "is above all unique in that it erects a ring of fire around itself. . . . Fiction is a transgression. I deeply believe that there are some things that cannot and should not be represented."[2] I too believe in the possibility of reticence: that there are things that should not be represented. Yet because our modern technical expertise is such that simulacra can be provided for almost any experience, however extreme, it is more today a question of *should not* rather than *cannot*. What should not be represented remains a moral decision; a choice that does not have to be aggravated by a quasi-theological dogma with the force of the Second Commandment.

It is true that the more violence I see on the screen, through real-time reporting or fictional re-creation (all history sooner or later returns as film, to use Anton Kaes's phrase), the more I rediscover the wisdom of a classical poetics that limited direct representations of violence or suffering, especially on the stage, and developed instead a powerful language of witness or indirect disclosure. The idiom of violence should not be routinized and become, as so often in the movies, an expectation, even a default setting. Though genius may breach any decorum and overcome our abhorrence, as Shakespeare does when he shows Gloucester's blinding on stage, it is clear that repeated depictions of *to pathos*, as Aristotle names those bloody scenes, will desensitize rather than shock, especially when art enters the era of mechanical reproduction. The Rodney King tape, shown over and over again, turns into an icon, a barely expressive metonymy.

In short, Spielberg's version of *Schindler's List* can be faulted on two counts. One is that it is not realistic enough. It still compromises with Hollywood's stylishness in the way it structures everything by large salvational or murderous acts. The stylishness, in fact, leads often to stereotype and visual cliché. But the second is that the very cruelty and sensationalism of the event, reconstructed through a spectacular medium, exerts a magnetic spell that alone seems able to convey the magnitude of the evil. Viewers of this powerful film are surely troubled by the question that Adorno has renewed concerning the pleasure we take in tragedy; or they may wonder how its spell, so close to voyeurism, could have been modified. The "ineluctable modality of the visual," with its evacuation of inwardness, fixates imagination more than the formulas of oral tradition. Artists have always, in one way or another, rebelled against the tyranny of the eye.[3]

A self-conscious commentary intruded into such a movie is no solution: it would merely have weakened its grip as docudrama, or postmodernized the film. Spielberg has created a fact on the screen, and the moral challenge passes to the viewers. Can we, either during the movie, or as those images recall themselves in the mind, become like the Perceval of legend, who must decide what to ask or not to ask of an extraordinary sight? There is no guarantee, of course, that the questions we ask—not only about how the Holocaust could have happened, but what is to be done now that it has happened—will be redemptive.

In the debate about this film the major issue becomes: What are the characteristics of an authentic depiction of the Shoah? "Authentic" is a heartfelt, yet slippery word. I will have to rephrase the question: How should we value a graphic, cinematic realism of Spielberg's kind, seemingly unconscious of itself (that it remains a fiction of the real) and which elides (except for the last scene) the passage of time and the relation of memory to reality?

To answer this question I seek the help of two other well-known films about the Holocaust. Claude Lanzmann in *Shoah* rejects all archival images or simulacra: he keeps the film in the present, the time of composition, reuniting survivors and the original (now deceptively peaceful) scene of their suffering. He animates that scene by an action of the survivors' own memory, and even—as in the case of Bomba, the Auschwitz barber—by using props to assist a painful return of the past. In this radical and principled work, the presence of the past is evoked primarily through human speech, through testimony; and so the film is anything but archival, or a historical simulacrum.

Lanzmann too is very much, in his presence, a part of this present. His questioning can become, not just with the perpetrators but also with the victims, a pressured interrogation. Occasionally this creates a problem. For he does not appear to be all that interested in the survivors' life or afterlife: the way their daily reality is still affected by a traumatic past. Instead, with relentless directorial insistence, he recovers and communicates every detail of *how* the "Final Solution" was implemented, every aspect of the death-machinery's working, of the technological Mammon that demands its sacrifice. That is the "reality" he brings home in all its technical and bureaucratic efficiency. Stunning, disconcerting, obsessive, and either hypnotic or tedious, *Shoah* is a film that does not entirely spare Lanzmann himself, who is shown to be—in the service of his cause—ironic, manipulative, and anything but likeable. To his credit, however, he does not seek to explain the obscene facts by a Marxist or any other thesis. "There is no Why here," he quotes (in a later comment on the film) a concentration camp guard's welcome, recorded by Primo Levi.

In Haim Gouri's trilogy that opens with *The Eighty-First Blow*, precisely what Lanzmann rejects is the very base of the representation. Reality is depicted exclusively through archival images. But individual memory does enter, through the voice-over of survivors who comment on the events—a tangle of voices with its own richness and variation, and in no simple way subordinated to the photomontage. These images and voices have to speak for themselves: though sequenced, there is no other effort to bring them into compositional time, which Lanzmann never departs from. Yet the director's didactic if invisible hand remains palpable. In *Flames in the Ashes*, for example, the part of Gouri's trilogy that deals with resistance, the issue of why Jews did not put up more fight is "answered" by footage of defeated Russian soldiers, columns of them stretching to the horizon in an endless line, utterly dejected, guarded by very few Germans, and scrambling abjectly, like animals, for cigarette butts or food.

Neither Gouri's nor Lanzmann's films are *primarily* about memory in its relation to reality. Although Lanzmann composes his film as an oral history, his interviews are used to reconstruct exhaustively and exclusively one aspect only—the most terrible one—of the Shoah: its end-phase, the "Final Solution," together with the technology and temperament that made it possible. Gouri's focus is more varied, less obsessive, but he must compose the visual track mainly in the "idiom" of the perpetrators, since most of the photos at his disposal (especially in *Flames in the Ashes*) were made by the Nazis themselves for propaganda or documentation.[4]

The very format of voice-over adopted in Gouri's trilogy is reminiscent of newsreels shown in the old movie theaters. Goebbels's propaganda machine exploited the format blatantly in such films as *Der Ewige Jude*. But in Gouri the excited and triumphant monologue of the announcer has given way to a spirited montage of voices. His documentary gains its integrity from the fact that it invents or reconstructs nothing. It struggles, rather, with a mass of received materials: utterances, images, musical score.[5] They are all "clichés." Gouri is symphonic, a conductor rather than a director; and though his emphasis remains on reportage, the structural gap between visual footage and voice-over makes the film both less unified in its realism and more interesting from a formal point of view. A picture, here, is not worth a thousand words but *requires* these words (the voices of the survivors, in their timbre as well as their message) to humanize it, to rescue it from voyeuristic hypnosis.

Yet Gouri never develops his technique in order to portray memory as either its own place, evolving its own stories or symbols, or in a competitive situation. The relation of cinematic image to voice-over (*voix-off*, the French say) is not problematized as in Alain Resnais's and Marguerite Duras's *Hiroshima, Mon Amour*. Different lifeworlds—that of the Japanese man and the French woman, that of the aftermath of the atomic bomb and the aftermath of the Nazi occupation—are juxtaposed in that film; while soundtrack and image are sometimes at odds. Today, as we recede from the original event, and identity—personal or collective—is increasingly based on publicized memories, there is bound to be an ever greater tension between different "cultures." These are now defined by what is rescued from oblivion or singled out for remembrance, by modes of representation, reception, and transmission.

However different their films, both Lanzmann and Gouri avoid an invasive technological gaze. We have become painfully aware of that gaze since Vietnam, Biafra, Somalia, Bosnia, Rwanda.[6] For it is no longer unimaginable that some of the terrible scenes reconstructed by Spielberg might have been filmed in real time—as if that present were our present—and piped almost simultaneously into our homes.[7] Those who watch *Schindler's List*, therefore, face the dilemma I have already mentioned. How do we respond to such sights? In our very impotence, do we protest and turn away, or find some other defense? Have we no choice but to demand that these representations be labeled unpresentable? How can we morally accommodate the fact that "what others suffer, we behold"?[8]

Schindler's List has not only achieved popular acclaim but is being prepared for widespread use in the schools. This suggests that all my reservations and questions have missed a very basic point: as the Greeks (though not the Hebrews) maintained, a clear picture of what is feared can moderate that fear.

It may be fundamentally affirming to "sing in the face of the object" (Wallace Stevens) as Spielberg incredibly seeks to do.

Yet even Spielberg cannot pass beyond the limits of realism. Though there is a bona fide attempt to follow the facts and to be accurate about the Jewish milieu depicted (how much his errors or compromises detract from the overall picture will remain in dispute), so much in the movie is structured like a fiction, so much is like other action films, though based on documented history, that the blurring between history and fiction never leaves us free from an interior voice that murmurs: "It is (only) a film." This happens not simply when the film is most vulnerable—when it is not about the Holocaust at all but stages a homoerotic psychodrama, scenes of tense mutual jockeying between Goeth and Schindler—but also when episodes like the liquidation of the ghetto force us into a defensive mode by the sheer representational power displayed. Visual realism can induce an "unreality effect." Hans Jonas is reported to have said that "At Auschwitz more was real than is possible."

Though Spielberg's gaze seems to me problematic, we should explore the questions it raises. And while I prefer Gouri's and Lanzmann's alternate modes of representation, almost the obverse of each other and more respectful than Spielberg of the action of memory and the issue of presentability, there is no need to insist dogmatically on a single type of "realistic" depiction. I want to describe briefly other exemplary modes, especially those that respect the action of memory.

In the case of Aharon Appelfeld (whose novels have not yet been filmed) memory is an absent presence. We are made to feel the scorching flame that animates his characters but we never see it consciously displayed as a haunting or unbearable force. We know something has displaced their life or basic trust or vital faith, yet memory's "fire," as Appelfeld calls it, is subject to a perpetual curfew.

His novels stand out, in fact, for not singing in the face of the object; he does not describe the Shoah directly, only the before and after. The survivor is often his theme, but not the specificity of Holocaust memory. He refuses the slightest hint of melodrama, focusing instead on the daily life of human beings who have difficulty living in this world after what they have gone through, yet cannot escape into political or religious mysticism. They want to do something with a life, their life, that was spared, but continue to feel guilty and out of focus.

Like Helga in *The Healer*, there is always a sick person who seems to take on herself the symptoms of an obscure illness; but that illness is intermittent, cut across by an extraordinary earthiness and a horizon where that earthiness is not opposed to faith. Yet there has been a fatal separation between faith and feeling, orthodoxy and assimilation. Jewish emancipation has not fulfilled Jewish needs. If we ask, given his characters' lack of orientation, where they are going, it is tempting to answer with Novalis: "Immer nach Hause," "Always home." That underlying nostalgia is too close to a death-drive.

A sense of spiritual waste emanates from Appelfeld's stories, exacerbated by the shiftless biological energy his characters display, and by strong, though discontinuous moments of physical pleasure in nature, in just being alive. There is no purposeful dying but also no rebirth. Yet it is rebirth that is at the horizon of all this aimless wandering. The irony in many Appelfeld novels, from *Age of Wonders* and *Badenheim* on, is that a post-traumatic condition, which requires no extreme effects of art to represent it, begins to resemble the human condition as a whole. So the insouciance or innocence of his assimilated Jewish characters (a trait that makes them sleepwalkers in an increasingly hostile environment) is not unlike that of camp inmates who have passed through the worst. Both groups display a hypnotic alertness, where everything is registered by the senses yet meaning and affect seem rarely to get through. A movie in their mind (which we cannot see) makes the survivors wander about restlessly, up and down, back and forth, ever wakeful though wishing to sleep it off. In the case of the assimilated, pre-Holocaust Jews, the restlessness seems to come from a haunting lack of memory: they are described as "ego floating on the surface of consciousness." For both groups, then, getting away from the past, its fullness or emptiness, is not enough: they crave a distraction—even an ecstasy—as deep as nature itself, or an anti-selfconsciousness principle as subsuming as art.

Often, therefore, Appelfeld evokes a magical but recuperative sleep, midway between amnesia and gestation. Of the youngsters who finally reached Israel, he writes: "After years of wandering and suffering, the Land of Israel seemed like a broad, soothing domain, drawing us into deep sleep. Indeed, this was our desire: to sleep, to sleep for years, to forget ourselves and be reborn."[9] An extended psychic absence is the necessary prelude for healing, for a rebirth that has a distinctly aesthetic dimension, in that empathy returns to what was previously merely observed.

"We must transmit memory," Appelfeld has written, "from the category of history to that of art." A question arises concerning that program: do his novels veil historical memory too much or do they save the specificity of art in an age of brutal realism? The problematic reaches beyond Holocaust-centered representations. A film like Resnais's *Last Year at Marienbad* is distinguished by its deliberate, stylized entanglement with the absence rather than presence of memory—with memory-envy. In its chill and elegant way, it parallels Appelfeld's distancing: a decisive event is presupposed, a virtual *lieu de mémoire* that cannot be brought to life, that refuses to become a living encounter.[10] Yet that there was, once, a place and a time of real encounter continues to exert its seduction. The French classicism of the film is, by way of both the sterile setting and the actors' deportment, a protest against another kind of seduction, that of contemporary realism. At the same time, it succeeds in starkly shifting the focus to a man and a woman who must perform their minuet with little to help them except a memory that is more unreal than real: memory here remains the mistress of illusions.

In a similar yet also startlingly different way, the German filmmaker Alexander Kluge refuses to allow the "forces of the present"—our programmatic realism—"to do away with the past and to put limits on the future." His movies come to terms with the past and its continuing pressure by incorporating images of ruined or deserted Nazi architecture. These negative *lieux de mémoire*, once glorified by Nazi films, serve as a reminder of the "eternity of yesterday." Symptoms of a fatal collective dream that has not really passed away, they play on in the *Kinotier*, the "cinema animal" (Kluge's phrase) we have become.[11]

What is to be done with that cinema animal: how can it be nurtured, but also trained? Memory and technology have become correlative themes. If, by a new fatality, everything returns as film, then not only is the present endangered as a site of experience, but also the past. The Soviet joke that "the past is even less predictable than the future" takes on a broader significance, one that encompasses us too. The authenticity of past and present are imperiled not only by Enlightenment philosophies of progress, which elide everything for the sake of the future, nor just by the selfishness of each Now Generation, but also by a subversive knowledge that information technology can infiltrate and mediate everything, so that our search for authentic or unmediated experience becomes both more crucial and desperate.[12]

That context strengthens the importance of a new genre of representation, the videotestimony, which is cinematic and counter-cinematic at the same time. Formally, videotestimonies make a double claim: they convey "I was there," but also "I am here"—here to tell you about it, to take that responsibility despite trauma and pain, despite the divide between present and past. The "I am here" is the present aware of the past but not seeking its grounding there—for it finds not a ground but a destabilizing abyss, a murderous ditch like the one victims were forced to dig for their own corpses. Thus the position of the Holocaust survivor expresses a much more difficult juxtaposition of temporalities than past and present. In the survivor, aware of new generations, aware of his own decimated community, truth and transmissibility enter into conflict. Some such tension has always existed: Gershom Scholem senses it in the veiled procedures of the mystic, and Walter Benjamin in the peculiar world of Kafka's imagination. But this time we know from photos, from film, from documents, very precisely what happened, and what makes the story so difficult to tell. The chilling facts, however, are not the only thing the witnesses seek to give, or what we want from them. Rather, their "I am here" balances the "I was there" and recalls the humanity of the victim who has to survive survival. There was life in death then, there is death in life now: how is that chiasmus to be honestly recorded?

It is here that technology both helps and hinders, and we see a new genre emerging. The video-visual medium has its hypnotism, but it becomes clear, when one views the testimonies, that its effect is, in this instance, more semiotic than hypnotic, that the medium both *identifies* and *differentiates* persons who have been through a wasting and dis-identifying experience. Every time we retrieve an oral history in this form, even when, tragically, it tells of Treblinka or Auschwitz, technology helps to undo a technology-induced sameness. For the more fluent we become in transmitting what we call our experience, the more similar and forgettable the experience becomes. What had previously to pass through the resistant channels of tradition is now mediated by a superconductive technical process that seems to promise absence of friction and equal time (equal light) for everyone. Hence a subversive feeling about the interchangeability and replication of experiences—a replication implicit in the technological means of their transmission.[13]

Testimonies are, as a genre, not limited to recording witnesses of the Holocaust: "testimonial video" is a more general contemporary phenomenon that links memory and technology in order to rouse our conscience and prevent oblivion. But the relation between memory and technology is especially problematic when the experience to be transmitted is traumatic. As I have indicated, the more technically adept we are in communicating what we call our experience, the more forgettable the latter becomes: more interchangeable and easily simulated. Yet Holocaust testimony, in particular, uses video to counter a video-inspired amnesia. A homeopathic form of representation is being developed.

While not exempt from error and unconscious fabulation (especially forty and more years after the events), these audiovisual documents allow occasional spontaneous access to the resurgence of memory as well as to significant *details* of daily life and death, which history as *histoire événementielle* displaces or passes by. Memory is allowed its own space, its own flow, when the interview is conducted in a social and non-confrontational way, when the attempt to bring memories of the past into the present does not seek to elide a newer present—the milieu in which the recordings took place. Since the period in which they will be viewed is not the period in which they were recorded, just as the period of recording is not the time of the original experience—a pattern challenged by "real-time" video, or "The Assault of the Present on the Rest of Time"—a temporal complexity is created very close to the dimensionality of thought itself, and which undermines the attempt to simulate closure, or any kind of eternity-structure.[14]

Let me give an example of that temporal complexity, inseparable from the rhythm of memory when expressed in words. In one of the Yale videotestimonies a woman tries to describe her state of confusion during a Nazi "action." She wraps her baby in a coat, so that it appears to be a bundle, and tries to smuggle it by a German guard who is directing the Jews to left or right. She says she holds the bundle on her left side, thinking she will rescue it that way; but that memory is already a confusion, showing the strain she was under in making choices. As she passes the guard, the baby, who is choking, makes a sound; the guard summons her back, and asks for "the bundle."

At that point in her story she utters a "Now," and creates a distinct pause. It is as if by that "Now" she were not only steeling herself to speak about what happened next, but seeking to recapture, within the narrative, the time for thought denied her in the rushed and crucial moments of what she had lived through. She goes on to describe her traumatic separation from the baby: she wasn't all there, she claims, or she was numb, or perhaps, she implies, she is imagining she had a baby—perhaps she has always been alone. Even Jack, her husband, she says, later on—slipping to another now-time as the camera pans to him (and for a moment we think she is saying that even with Jack she has remained alone)—even Jack didn't know her story, which she revealed to him only recently, though he too is a survivor. When, just before this moment, she admits she gave the officer the baby, she does not say "the baby" but "the bundle" (a natural metaphor, sad and distancing, yet still affectionate, perhaps a Yiddishism, the "Paeckel"): "He stretched out his arms I should hand him over the bundle and I hand him over the bundle and this was the last time I had the bundle."[15]

I remember in a shadowy yet haunting way a moment in one of Resnais's films (I believe it was *Muriel*, set in the period of the Algerian war and revelations of torture by certain elements of the French army), when a home movie is inserted, and the muteness of the medium seems to heighten our sense of the mutilation (physical, psychological, or both) inflicted on the woman who is its subject. Emptied of sound those scenes screamed all the more. I also remember them in black and white, and contrasting with the color film; but I may be wrong about that. The crude tape was like a play within a play, and I thought of the mime in *Hamlet*, that serves to catch the conscience of the king. Here as there the irruption of an archaic medium takes us out of the temptation to smooth over or aestheticize what happened. Breaking the frame suggests that a crude form of realism may be closer to the truth than its sophisticated version. Silenced memories live on silently.[16]

That Spielberg shoots in black-and-white has an archaizing effect and could have been a temporal distancing, but it seems post-color, so rich a tonality is achieved. Spielberg made the right choice; yet the film needed also an *internal* contrast to relieve what I have called its invasive technological gaze and to respect unglossy aspects, the graininess and haltings of memory. So Gouri, at the end of *Flames in the Ashes*, presents an epic array of photos, creased rather than glossy, and in a static flow of images quite unlike the film's erratic though fluent montage up to that point. But Spielberg seems always in a hurry, or in love with mimesis, with the motion and hugeness of a medium that has retained its magic, and which he stages, whatever the subject, for the sake of the child in us—for the children whose murder, though not directly shown, is his most terrible and poignant theme.

It is the child in the adult which remains Spielberg's theme even here: the abused and disabused child. Cinema addresses that sin against the child—not only, as in *Schindler's List*, by terrifying us with pictures of a mass infanticide, but also, in general, by reviving a structural link between the adult memory and the childlike imagination.[17] For our increased ability to recover the past through historical research or psychotherapy is abetted by technology's proficiency with simulacra. Yet Spielberg's art is not primarily retrospective, because the child and the adult differ as "cinema animals."

The child (in us) still learns through wonder; for young people, the past can never catch up with the future, with freedom, with possibility. Who can forget, in Spielberg's *Close Encounters of the Third Kind*, the boy's face when his toys spontaneously light up, start up, come alive? That mixture of innocence and wonder, of an expectant gaze that says "I always knew you were real, you were alive" is unforgettable. Whatever our age, when we enter the cave and become "cinema animals," we also reenter a realm of possibility. Our feelings are freed—even for the sinister subject, for a film like *Schindler's List*, which reconnects them with a knowledge we had desensitized or relegated to footnotes. But the adult, as distinct from the child, is a "cinema animal" also in a more disturbing way.

Now the ability to reproduce simulacra, or to think we *see* memories, to call them up and project them onto the wall of the cave, can make us their prisoner. They are no longer toys, companions, comforters, masks endearing rather than frightening, whose silent smiles or grins disclose, ever so intimately, a mysterious realm. In a society of the spectacle, strong images are what property or the soil is often said to be: a need of the soul. If the incidence of recovered memory seems to have increased dramatically in recent years, it may be that images of violence relayed hourly by the media, as well as widespread publicity on the Holocaust that leads to metaphorical appropriations (Sylvia Plath is a famous case), have popularized the idea of a determining trauma. It is understandable that many might feel a pressure to find within themselves, and for public show, an experience equally decisive and bonding, a sublime or terrible identity mark. The wound of absent memory may be greater than the wound of the memory allegedly recovered, and which, however painful, recalls a lost intensity, a childlike aura.

In a powerful and precise essay, "La mémoire trouée" or "The Memory That Is Full of Holes," the French writer Henri Raczymow speaks of a double vacancy that affects his identity as a Jew.[18] There is the loss of traditional Judaism, which Bialik captures in his poem "On the Threshold of the House of Prayer."[19] The Haskalah or Jewish Enlightenment had already created, before the war, a diaspora within the diaspora: many Jews could participate only intellectually and nostalgically in a communal life which, viewed from a threshold that was never crossed, seemed warm and appealing. This loss is made more rather than less acute by the realization that the mourned reality was a sentimental construct, and could not now be expressed except in fiction, or "by sewing scraps together." But the second loss for Raczymow's generation (for the children and grandchildren of the survivors) is what Nadine Fresco has called "the diaspora of ashes": the physical and cultural destruction of Jewish communities, especially in Eastern Europe.

Raczymow, whose family came from Poland, does not seek to impose his sense of an absent or ashen memory on anyone else. But the way he situates himself as a writer helps us to think through the fact that Spielberg too must be situated. There is no universal or omniscient point of view, however objectifying the camera-eye may seem to be. So the brilliance of *Schindler's List* reflects a specifically American kind of optimism. This optimism does not make a statement about human nature (presenting Schindler as a hero need not cancel out Goeth or atrocities never before depicted so vividly) but rather a statement about *film* as a technology of transmission which differs from *writing* as Raczymow conceives it.[20] For Spielberg the screen must be filled up; he brings to life what we know of the documented history—in that sense he does not "recover" memory at all but enables its full transmission as imagery. Raczymow, in contrast, both as a Jew and a writer, lives the paradox of having to express a double void, and becomes, in the words of Maurice Blanchot, "the guardian of an absent meaning":

> My books do not attempt to fill in empty memory. They are not simply part of the struggle against forgetfulness. Rather, I try to present memory *as* empty. I try to restore a non-memory, which by definition cannot be

filled in or recovered. In everyone there is an unfillable symbolic void, but for the Ashkenazic Jew born in the diaspora after the war, the symbolic void is coupled with a real one. There is a void in our memory formed by a Poland unknown to us and entirely vanished, and a void in our remembrance of the Holocaust through which we did not live. We cannot even say that we were *almost* deported.[21]

Notes

1. This insidious optimism is reinforced by the structuring theme of the film. J. Hoberman points out in a symposium on *Schindler's List* in the *Village Voice* (March 29, 1994), p. 31 that Spielberg chose a story in which the meaning of the camps' deadly selection ritual is reversed: "The selection is 'life,' the Nazi turns out to be a good guy. . . . "

2. *Manchester Guardian*, March 3, 1994, p. 15, translated from *Le Monde*.

3. In this and the next paragraph I anticipate my comments on "Holocaust Testimony, Art, and Trauma" (see *The Longest Shadow: In the Aftermath of the Holocaust* [Bloomington: Indiana University Press, 1996]).

4. An exception is footage of the Eichmann trial in Jerusalem, which deeply influenced him (see his *The Man in the Glass Booth*), as well as many of his compatriots.

5. In Alain Resnais's *Night and Fog*, one of the early (1955) if not the earliest attempt to work with archival footage (much of it familiar now, through that film), what one feels most is the dilemma: what can be done, morally, visually, with such atrocious images? In Resnais's "essay," then, scenes appear sometimes too composed, and the recited monologue that serves for voice-over too poetic, even if deliberately so.

6. " . . . this is what the white ones cannot understand when they come with their TV cameras and their aid. They expect to see us weeping. Instead they see us staring at them, without begging, and with a bulging placidity in our eyes." "I opened my eyes for the last time. I saw the cameras on us all. To them, we were the dead. As I passed through the agony of the light, I saw them as the dead, marooned in a world without pity and love." From the *New York Times* op-ed column of January 29, 1993, by Nigerian novelist Ben Okri.

7. According to journalist Richard Schickel, Spielberg said that he "wanted to do more CNN reporting with a camera I could hold in my hand"; he also reportedly told his cast "we're not making a film, we're making a document," *Time*, December 13, 1993, p. 75.

8. See Terrence des Pres, *Praises and Dispraises*. An unsparing use of archival footage can also, of course, raise that question, as in Resnais's *Night and Fog*. But this seminal movie intended to shock viewers out of their ignorance or indifference. Its assault on the viewer is only modified by an "essayistic" effect, achieved by Resnais's formal virtuosity of composition and Jean Cayrol's voice-over.

9. Aharon Appelfeld, "The Awakening," in Geoffrey H. Hartman, ed., *Holocaust Remembrance: The Shapes of Memory* (Oxford: Blackwell, 1994), p. 149. Also Appelfeld, *Beyond Despair*, introduction and Lecture One. In the case of survivor immigrants to Israel, the "sleep" was induced by a suppression from without as well as a repression from within: Zionist ideology had, on the whole, contempt for Old World Jews and insisted on refashioning them.

10. Appelfeld's American contemporary, Philip Roth, refuses to fast in the French way—which remains quite sumptuous—and does not give up anything of his own art and comic gift, because the Holocaust is not his theme. He manages to endow Anne Frank with an alternate life as Amy Bellette, the focus of Nathan Zuckermann's fanta-

sies in *The Ghost Writer*, just as he transposes Kafka into a Czech refugee who outlived his work and becomes an unknown Hebrew school teacher in New Jersey. See the fine article of Hana Wirth-Nesher, "From Newark to Prague: Roth's Place in the American Jewish Literary Tradition," in *What Is Jewish Literature?*, ed. H. Wirth-Nesher (Philadelphia: Jewish Publication Society, 1994).

11. See the presentation of Kluge's thought in "The Assault of the Present on the Rest of Time," *New German Critique* 49 (1990): 11–23.

12. Gertude Koch observes, in the *Village Voice* symposium (March 29, 1994), how even the "realism" of *Schindler's List* is mediated by film history: "he recycled every little slip of film that was made before to produce this film." She thinks Spielberg tricks us into believing—through this "rhetoric" which presents so powerfully what we seem to know or have actually seen before in other Holocaust movies—that it happened exactly like this. But this is a problem with every realistic film, although it can be argued that the stakes here are higher. I prefer to treat this problem as one concerning Spielberg's elision of the perspective of personal memory.

13. Critical thought, therefore, looks for residues of technology in every product, in case the truth has been modified to achieve transmissibility. The era of simulacra is necessarily an era of suspicion. Walter Benjamin is the literary source for these reflections, extended by Guy Desbord and Jean Baudrillard.

14. On testimonial video generally, see Avital Ronell, "Video/Television/Rodney King: Twelve Steps beyond *The Pleasure Principal*," in *differences: A Journal of Feminist Cultural Studies*, 4 (1992): 1–15.

15. Bessie K., Holocaust Testimony (HVT-205), Fortunoff Video Archive for Holocaust Testimonies, Yale University. See also Lawrence L. Langer, *Holocaust Testimonies: The Ruins of Memory* (New Haven: Yale University Press, 1991), p. 49.

16. Since writing this, I was able to see *Muriel* again. The home movie projected in the film is indeed silent, but it does not show Muriel's torture directly. Bernard (the French soldier who has returned from Algeria) narrates the abuse as a voice-over that accompanies images of the daily life of the soldiers, as they fight or train, mingle with civilians, mug for the camera. A powerful and typical Resnais counterpoint is created between two incompatible memories: a series of harmless images, picture postcards in motion, and a hauntingly absent—fantasized or covered up—reality. It is interesting to recall that this film, subtitled "Le Temps d'un Retour," and with a screenplay by Jean Cayrol, was released ten years after *Night and Fog*.

17. Historians like John Boswell in *The Kindness of Strangers* have begun to document the prevalence of infanticide. They make us aware how deeply the love of children is accompanied by a fear and resentment of them. Deborah Dwork, in *Children with a Star*, records the pain of children caught up in the Holocaust, but also the love that saved them, and establishes the importance of the oral history of child survivors. Judith S. Kestenberg's "International Study of Organized Persecution of Children" is creating an important archive. Finally I might mention Jean-François Lyotard's *Lectures d'enfance*, which are basically meditations on the *infans*: on the relation in the human being of the mute to the representable, a relation that can never satisfy a haunting "debt" contracted at birth.

18. Originally presented as "Exil, mémoire, transmission," and translated from "La mémoire trouée," *Pardès* 3 (1986): 177–82, as "Memory Shot Through with Holes," in *Yale French Studies* 85 (1994): 98–105.

19. The word "Beit Hamidrash" in Bialik's title means "House of Study" as well as "House of Prayer" and points to an integration which is among the things now lost.

20. The concept of writing, in Raczymow, is certainly influenced not only by the postwar "New Novel" (which he mentions) but by a longer genealogy that includes Mallarmé and Proust. The *cultural* revolt in French literature against realism—and often

within it—was more programmatic and consequent than in England and America. Moreover, several important authors, some Jewish, some not—they include Blanchot, Jabès, and Derrida—link the integrity of writing to its "Hebraic" questioning of (realistic) image-making.

21. Raczymow, *Yale French Studies* 85 (1994): 104.

4 | *Schindler's List* Is Not *Shoah*
Second Commandment, Popular Modernism, and Public Memory

Miriam Bratu Hansen

Iꜰ ᴛʜᴇʀᴇ ᴡᴇʀᴇ a Richter scale to measure the extent to which commercial films cause reverberations in the traditional public sphere, the effect of *Schindler's List* might come close to, or at least fall into the general range of D. W. Griffith's racist blockbuster of 1915, *The Birth of a Nation*. If we bracket obvious differences between the films (which are perhaps not quite as obvious as they may seem), as well as eight decades of media history, the comparison is tempting because a similar seismic intensity characterizes both Spielberg's ambition and the film's public reception.[1] Each film demonstratively takes on a trauma of collective historical dimensions; and each reworks this trauma in the name of memory and national identity, inscribed with particular notions of race, sexuality, and family. Each film participates in the contested discourse of fiftieth-year commemorations, marking the eventual surrender of survivor- (or veteran-) based memory to the vicissitudes of public history. While *Birth of a Nation* was not the first film to deal with the Civil War and its aftermath (there were in fact dozens of Civil War films between 1911 and 1915), the film did lay unprecedented claim to the construction of national history and thus demonstrated the stakes of national memory for the history of the present. And while *Schindler's List* is certainly not the first film to deal with the German Judeocide, Spielberg's story about a Sudeten-German Catholic entrepreneur who saved the lives of 1,100 Polish Jews asserts a similar place of centrality in contemporary U.S. culture and politics.

On the level of reception, both *Birth* and *Schindler's List* provoked responses from far beyond the pale of industrial-commercial culture, getting attention from writers, activists, and politicians who usually don't take films seriously; it thus temporarily linked the respective media publics (emergent in the case of *Birth*, all-inclusive in the case of *Schindler's List*) with the publics of traditional politics and critical intellectuals.[2] What is extraordinary about these two films is not just how they managed to catalyze contesting points of view but also how they make visible the contestation among various and unequal discursive arenas in their effort to lay claim to what and how a nation remembers—not an identical nation, to be sure, but distinctly different formations of a national public. As is well known, *Birth* was the first film to be given a screening at the White House (after which President Wilson's comment, "It is like writing history in lightning," became part of the legend), but it was also the first film to galvanize intellectual and political opposition in an alliance of Progressive reformers and the newly formed NAACP. As is likewise known, not all intellectuals protested: *Birth* became the founding text for an apologetic discourse on "film art" that for decades tried to relativize the film's racist infraction.[3]

Here, at the latest, my comparison turns into disanalogy. For can we compare the violent and persistent damage done to African Americans by *Birth* to the damage done, as some critics claim, by *Schindler's List* to the victims in whose name it pretends to speak? And can we compare the white and black, liberal and radical engagement for a disenfranchised community to the contemporary intellectual stance that holds all representations of the Shoah accountable to the task of an anamnestic solidarity with the dead? To what extent is the disjunction of the two films a matter of the different histories they engage and to what extent does it illustrate the profound transformation of public memory in contemporary media culture? What do we make, in each case, of the ambivalent effects of popular success? And how, finally, does popularity as such shape the critical accounts we get of the films?

In the following, I will try to trace some of the dynamics at work in the reception of *Schindler's List*. I regard the controversies over the film as symptomatic of larger issues, in particular the ongoing problematic of Holocaust remembrance and the so-called Americanization of the Holocaust, but also the more general issue of the relationship of intellectuals to mass culture, specifically to the media publics of cinema and television. I see both these issues encapsulated in the pervasive polarization of critical argument into the opposition of *Schindler's List* versus Claude Lanzmann's documentary *Shoah* (1985), as two mutually exclusive paradigms of cinematically representing or not-representing the Holocaust. This opposition, I will argue, does not yield a productive way of dealing with either the films or the larger issues involved.

I distinguish, roughly, among three major strands or levels in the reception of *Schindler's List*. First, there is the level of official publicity. Under this term I lump together a whole variety of channels and discourses, ranging from Spielberg's self-promotion and the usual Hollywood hype (culminating in the Oscar Award ceremony) to Presidential endorsements at home and abroad as well as government bannings of the film in some Near Eastern and Asian countries; from subsidized and mandatory screenings for high school students and youth groups to the largely adulatory coverage in the trade papers, the daily press, and TV talk shows.

The second, though by no means secondary, level of reception is the mercurial factor of popular reception. While this reception is no doubt produced and shaped by official publicity, it cannot be totally reduced to intended response. The distinct dynamics of popular reception comes to the fore in precisely those moments when an audience diverges or goes away from the film, when reception takes on a momentum of its own, that is, becomes public in the emphatic sense of the word.[4] This includes moments of failure, such as the much publicized irreverent reaction of black students at Castlemont High in Oakland.[5] It also includes the film's enormous success in Germany, which prompted endless discussions, letters to the editor, and the discovery of local Schindlers everywhere—a development one cannot but view with amazement and ambivalence. Methodologically, this aspect of reception is the most difficult to represent, for it eludes both ethnographic audience research and textually based constructions of possible spectatorial effects; yet it requires an approach that is capable of mediating empirical and theoretical levels of argument.

The third level of reception, on which I will focus here, is the vehement rejection of the film on the part of critical intellectuals. This includes both academics and journalists, avant-garde artists and filmmakers (among others, Art Spiegelman and Ken Jacobs in a symposium printed in the *Village Voice*), but also a fair number of liberal publicists (for example, Frank Rich, Leon Wieseltier, Philip Gourevitch, Ilene Rosenzweig) who voiced their dissent in middle-brow papers such as the *New York Times*, the *New Republic*, the *New York Review of Books* as well as Jewish publications such as *Forward*, *Tikkun*, and *Commentary*. Most of these critical comments position themselves as minority opinion against the film's allegedly overwhelming endorsement in the media, if not as martyrs in the "resistance" against popular taste ("there is little pleasure in being troubled by what so many have found deeply moving").[6] Accordingly, critical dissent is directed as much against the larger impact of the film—which Michael André Bernstein has dubbed "the *Schindler's List* effect"[7]—as against the film itself.

This response is no doubt legitimate and, in print at least, highly persuasive. For all I know, I might well have joined in, that is, had I seen the film in this country rather than in Germany. The kind of work the film did there, in light of a hopelessly overdetermined and yet rapidly changing "politics of memory," may arguably present a special case.[8] Seeing the film outside the context of American publicity, however, made me consider the film's textual work, if not independently of its intentions and public effects, yet still from a slightly displaced location in relation to both Hollywood globality and its intellectual critics. Let me say at the outset that it is not my intention to vindicate *Schindler's List* as a masterpiece (which would mean reverting to the *Birth of a Nation* debate). I think there are serious problems with the film's conception, and I could have done without much of the last third, when Oskar Schindler

(Liam Neeson), the opportunist, gambler, and philanderer, turns into Schindler, the heroic rescuer. But seen from a perspective of displacement, and considered from an intersticial space between distinct critical discourses and between disjunctive political legacies, the film did seem to have an important function, not only for empirically diverse audiences, but also for thinking through key issues involved in the representation of the Shoah and the problem of "public memory."[9] Moreover, in the way the film polarized, or was assumed to have polarized, critical and popular responses, the reception of *Schindler's List* threw into relief a particular pattern in the intellectuals' reactions to the film: they seemed to rehearse familiar tropes of the old debate on modernism vs. mass culture.

Before I elaborate on this pattern, and on what it occludes in the public as well as textual workings of the film, I will first outline the intellectual critique in its key points. The following summary distinguishes, roughly, among arguments pertaining to (a) the **culture industry** (in Horkheimer and Adorno's sense); (b) the problem of **narrative**; (c) the question of **cinematic subjectivity**; and (d) the question of **representation**.

(a) The first and obvious argument is that *Schindler's List* is and remains a Hollywood product. As such it is circumscribed by the economic and ideological tenets of the culture industry, with its unquestioned and supreme values of entertainment and spectacle; its fetishism of style and glamor; its penchant for superlatives and historicist grasp at any and all experience ("the greatest Holocaust film ever made"); and its reifying, leveling, and trivializing effect on everything it touches. In this argument, *Schindler's List* is usually aligned with Spielberg's previous mega-spectacles, especially *Jurassic Park*, and is accused of having turned the Holocaust into a theme park. Since the business of Hollywood is entertainment, preferrably in the key of sentimental optimism, there is something intrinsically and profoundly incommensurable about "re-creating" the traumatic events of the Shoah "for the sake of an audience's recreation" (Spiegelman).[10] Or, as J. Hoberman puts it so eloquently: "Is it possible to make a feel-good entertainment about the ultimate feel-bad experience of the twentieth century?"[11]

This critique of *Schindler's List* links the film to the larger problem of the Holocaust's dubious mass-media currency, recalling the ugly pun of "Shoahbusiness." The interesting question here is whether Spielberg's film is merely the latest culmination of what Saul Friedlander discerned, in films and novels of the 1970s, as a "new discourse about Nazism on the right as well as on the left," a discourse that thrived on the spectacular fusion of kitsch and death.[12] Or does *Schindler's List*, along with the success of the Holocaust Memorial Museum in Washington, D.C., mark the emergence of yet another new discourse? If the latter is the case, this new discourse, whose different dynamics the film might help us understand, will have to be situated in relation to other struggles over public memorializing concerning more specifically U.S. American traumata such as slavery, the genocide of Native Americans, and Vietnam.

(b) The second and more local argument made about the film's inadequacy to the topic it engages is that it does so in the form of a fictional narrative. One emphasis in this argument is on the choice of fiction (notwithstanding the film's pretensions to historical "authenticity") over nonfiction or documentary, a form of film practice that would have allowed for a different organization of space and temporality, different sound/image relations, and therefore different possibilities of approaching the events portrayed. Attendant upon the film's fictional form—with its (nineteenth-century) novelistic and historicist underpinnings—is the claim, supported by the publicity and Spielberg's complicity with it, that *Schindler's List* does not just represent one story from the Shoah but that it does so in a **representative** manner—that it encapsulates the totality of the Holocaust experience.[13] If that were the case, the film's focus on the heroic exception, the Gentile rescuer and the miracle of survival, would indeed distort the proportions and thus end up falsifying the record.

Related to this charge is the condemnation of the film's choice of a particular type of narrative, specifically, the **classical** mode that governed Hollywood products until about 1960 and beyond.[14] In a technical sense, this term refers to a type of narrative that requires thorough causal motivation centering on the actions and goals of individual characters (as opposed to the "anonymous" Jewish masses who were the object of extermination); a type of narrative in which character psychology and relations among characters tend to be predicated on masculinist hierarchies of gender and sexuality (in the case of *Schindler's List*, the reassertion of certain "styles of manhood" and the sadistic-voyeuristic fascination with the female body, in particular the staging of Amon Goeth's [Ralph Fiennes] desire and his violence toward Helen Hirsch, the Jewish housemaid [Embeth Davidtz];[15] a type of narrative in which the resolution of larger-order problems tends to hinge upon the formation of a couple or family and on the restoration of familial forms of subjectivity (Schindler as a super father figure who has to renounce his promiscuity and return to marriage in order to accomplish his historic mission, the rescue of Jewish families).[16]

A fundamental limitation of classical narrative in relation to history, and to the historical event of the Shoah in particular, is that it relies on neoclassicist principles of compositional unity, motivation, linearity, equilibrium, and closure—principles singularly inadequate in the face of an event that by its very nature defies our narrative urge to make sense of, to impose order on the discontinuity and otherness of historical experience. Likewise, the deadly teleology of the Shoah represents a temporal trajectory that gives the lie to any classical dramaturgy of deadlines, suspense, and rescues in the nick of time, to moments of melodramatic intensity and relief. There are at least three last-minute rescues in *Schindler's List*, leading up to the compulsory Hollywood happy ending. This radically exacerbates the general problem of narrative film, which Alexander Kluge has succinctly described as the problem of "how to get to a happy ending without lying."[17] The rescue of the Schindler Jews is a matter of luck and gamble rather than melodramatic coincidence; and although the story is historically "authentic," it cannot but remain a fairy tale in the face of the overwhelming facticity of "man-made mass death" (Edith Wyschogrod).[18] Critics of the film, notably Claude Lanzmann and Gertrud Koch, have observed that *Schindler's List* (like Agnieszka Holland's 1991 *Europa, Europa*) marks a shift in the public commemoration of the Shoah: the film is concerned with **survival**, the survival of individuals, rather than the fact of death, the death of an entire people or peoples.[19] If the possibility of **passing through Auschwitz** is the film's central historical trope, the implications are indeed exorbitant—though not necessarily, in my opinion, that self-evident and unequivocal.

Finally, as a classical narrative, *Schindler's List* inscribes itself in a particular tradition of "realist" film. This is not just a matter of Spielberg's declared efforts to ensure "authenticity" (by using authentic locations, by following Thomas Keneally's novel, which is based on survivor testimony); nor is it simply a matter of the film's use of black-and-white footage and imitation of a particular 1940s style. The film's "reality effect," to use Roland Barthes's phrase, has as much to do with the way it recycles images and tropes from other Holocaust films, especially European ones; but as a classical narrative, it does so without quotation marks, pretending to be telling the story for the first time.[20] As Koch argues, there is something authoritarian in the way *Schindler's List* subsumes all these earlier films, using them to assert its own truth claims for history ("MMM" 25–26). The question that poses itself is whether the film's citational practice merely follows the well-worn path of nineteenth-century realist fiction, or whether it does so in the context of a postmodern aesthetics that has rehabilitated such syncretistic procedures in the name of popular resonance and success. The more interesting question, though, may be to what extent this distinction actually matters, or in which ways the event of the Shoah could be said to trouble, if not challenge postmodernist assumptions about representation, temporality, and history.

(c) The third objection raised against *Schindler's List* pertains to the way it allocates subjectivity among its characters and engages the viewer's subjectivity in that process. The charge here is that the film narrates the history of 1,100 rescued Jews from the perspective of the perpetrators, the German Gentile Nazi turned resister and his alter ego, Amon Goeth, the psychotic SS commandant. As Philip Gourevitch asserts, "*Schindler's List* depicts the Nazis' slaughter of Polish Jewry almost entirely through German eyes."[21] By contrast, the argument goes, the Jewish characters are reduced to pasteboard figures, to generic types incapable of eliciting identification and empathy. Or worse, some critics contend, they come to life only to embody anti-Semitic stereotypes (money-grubbing Jews, Jew-as-eternal-victim, the association of Jewish women with dangerous sexuality, the characterization of Itzhak Stern [Ben Kingsley], Schindler's accountant, as "king of the Jewish wimps").[22] This argument not only refers to the degree to which characters are fleshed out, individualized by means of casting, acting, cinematography, and narrative action; the argument also pertains to the level of filmic narration or enunciation, the level at which characters function to mediate the film's sights and sounds, events and meanings to the spectator, as for instance through flashbacks, voice-over, or optical point of view. As psychoanalytic film theorists have argued in the 1970s and early '80s, it is on this level that cinematic subjectivity is formed most effectively because unconsciously.[23] If that is so (and let's for the moment, for the sake of argument, assume it is), what does it mean that point-of-view shots are clustered not only around Schindler but also around Goeth, making us participate in one of his killing sprees in shots showing the victim through the telescope of his gun? Does this mean that, even though he is marked as evil on the level of the diegesis or fictional world of the film, the viewer is nonetheless urged to identify with Goeth's murderous desire on the unconscious level of cinematic discourse?

(d) The fourth, and most difficult, objection to *Schindler's List* is that it violates the taboo on representation (*Bilderverbot*), that it tries to give an "image of the unimaginable."[24] If the criticisms summarized up to this point imply by and large that the film is not "realistic" enough, this critique involves the exact opposite charge, that the film is too "realistic." So, by offering us an "authentic" reconstruction of events of the Shoah, the film enhances the fallacy of an immediate and unmediated access to the past (the fallacy of historical films from *Birth of a Nation* to *JFK*)—by posing as the "real thing" the film usurps the place of the actual event. What is worse, it does so with an event that defies depiction, whose horror renders any attempt at direct representation obscene. Spielberg transgresses the boundaries of representability most notoriously, critics agree, when he takes the camera across the threshold of what we, and the women in the film "mistakenly" deported to Auschwitz, believe to be a gas chamber. Thus *Schindler's List*, like the TV miniseries *Holocaust*, ends up both trivializing and sensationalizing the Shoah.

The most radical proponent of this critique, Lanzmann, accuses *Schindler's List* of not respecting the unique and absolute status of the Holocaust: "unique in the sense that it erects around itself, in a circle of flames, a boundary which cannot be breached because a certain absolute degree of horror is intransmissible: to pretend it can be done is to make oneself guilty of the most serious sort of transgression."[25] The counter example of a film that respects that boundary and succeeds in an aesthetic figuration of the very impossibility of representation is, for both Lanzmann and other critics of Spielberg, his own film *Shoah* (1985). Lanzmann's film, as has often been pointed out, strictly refuses any direct representation of the past, whether by means of fictional reenactment or archival footage. Instead, the film combines interviews featuring various types of witnesses (survivors, perpetrators, bystanders, historians) to give testimony at once to the physical, sense-defying details of mass extermination and to the *"historical crisis of witnessing"* presented by the Shoah.[26] This crisis threatens not merely the project of a retrospective, anamnestic account, but the very possibility and concept of eyewitnessing and, by extension, the recording capacity of the photographic media. (This is why Lanzmann so radically distrusts Spielberg's untroubled accessing—or, as Lanzmann calls it, "fabrication"—of a visual archive: "If I had found an actual film—a secret film, since that was strictly forbidden—made by an SS man and showing how 3000 Jews, men, women, and children, died together, asphyxiated in a gas chamber of the crematorium 2 in Auschwitz—if I had found that, not only would I not have shown it but I would have destroyed it.")[27]

Lanzmann's argument, like the critique of *Schindler's List* in the name of *Shoah*, is bound up with a complex philosophical debate surrounding the Holocaust to which I cannot do justice here. Suffice it to say that the moral argument about the impossibility of representation—of mimetic doubling—is linked, via a quasi-theological invocation of the Second Commandment, to the issue of the singularity of the Shoah, its status as an event that is totally and irrevocably Other, an event that ruptures and is ultimately outside history. What matters in this context is the further linkage, often made concurrently, between the claim to singularity and the type of aesthetic practice that alone is thought to be capable of engaging the problematic of representation without disfiguring the memory of the dead. For the breach inflicted by the Shoah has not only put into question, irrevocably, the status of culture as an autonomous and superior domain (to invoke an often misquoted statement by Adorno);[28] it has also radicalized the case for a type of aesthetic expression that is aware of its problematic status—the nonrepresentational, singular, and hermetic *écriture* to be found in works of high modernism. *Shoah* has rightly been praised for its uniqueness, its rigorous and uncompromising invention of a filmic language capable of rendering "imageless images" of annihilation (Koch paraphrasing Adorno's *Aesthetic Theory*).[29] *Schindler's List*, by contrast, does not seek to negate the representational, iconic power of filmic images, but rather banks on this power. Nor does it develop a unique filmic idiom to capture the un-precedented and unassimilable fact of mass extermination; rather, it relies on familiar tropes and common techniques to narrate the extraordinary rescue of a group of individuals.

The critique of *Schindler's List* in high-modernist terms, however, espe-cially in Lanzmann's version, reduces the dialectics of the problem of repre-senting the unrepresentable to a binary opposition of showing or not showing—rather than casting it, as one might, as an issue of competing representations and competing modes of representation. This binary argument also rein-scribes, paradoxically, a high-modernist fixation on vision and the visual, whether simply assumed as the epistemological master sense or critically ne-gated as illusory and affirmative. What gets left out is the dimension of the other senses and of sensory experience, that is, the aesthetic in the more com-prehensive, Greek sense of the word, and its fate in a history of modernity that encompasses both mass production and mass extermination.[30] What gets left out in particular is the dimension of the acoustic, the role of sound in the pro-duction of visuality, especially in the technical media where sound has come to compensate for the historical marginalization of the more bodily senses. Yet, if we understand the Shoah's challenge to representation to be as much one of affect as one of epistemology, the specific sensory means of engaging this chal-lenge cannot be ignored. The soundtrack, for example, is neither the seat of a superior truth (as Lanzmann seems to claim for *Shoah*) nor merely a masked accomplice for the untruths of the imagetrack (as assumed in summary cri-tiques of the classical Hollywood film), but rather the material site of particu-lar and competing aesthetic practices.[31]

It is no coincidence that none of the critics of *Schindler's List* have com-mented on the film's use of sound (except for complaints about the sentimental and melodramatic music)—not to mention how few have actually granted the film a closer look. Although I share some of the reservations paraphrased above, I still would argue that *Schindler's List* is a more sophisticated, elliptical, and self-conscious film than its critics acknowledge (and the self-conscious-ness is not limited to the epilogue in which we see the actors together with the survivors they play file past Schindler's Jerusalem grave). Let me cite a few, brief examples that suggest that we might imagine this film differently, examples pertaining to both the film's complex use of sound and its structur-ing of narration and cinematic subjectivity.

To begin with the latter point, the complaint that the film is narrated from the point of view of the perpetrators ignores the crucial function of Itzak Stern (Ben Kingsley), the Jewish accountant, in the enunciative structure of the film. Throughout the film, Stern is the focus of point-of-view edits and reaction shots, just as he repeatedly motivates camera movements and shot changes.

Stern is the only character who gets to authorize a flashback, in the sequence in which he reponds to Schindler's attempt to defend Goeth ("a wonderful crook") by evoking a scene of Goeth's close-range shooting of twenty-five men in a work detail in retribution for one man's escape; closer framing within the flashback in turn foregrounds, as mute witness, the prisoner to whom Stern attributes the account. The sequence is remarkable also in that it contains the film's only flashforward, prompted by Schindler's exasperated question, "what do you want me to do about it?" Notwithstanding Stern's disavowing gesture ("nothing, nothing—it's just talking"), his flashback narration translates into action on Schindler's part, resulting in the requisitioning of the Pearlmans as workers, which is shown proleptically even before Schindler hands Stern his watch to be used as bribe. This moment not only marks, on the diegetic level of the film, Schindler's first conscious engagement in bartering for Jewish lives; it also inscribes the absolute difference in power between Gentiles and Jews on the level of cinematic discourse, as a disjunction of filmic temporality. Stern is deprived of his ability, his right to act, that is, to produce a future, but he can narrate the past and pass on testimony, hoping to produce action in the listener/viewer.

More often, temporal displacement is a function of the soundtrack, in particular an abundance of sound bridges and other forms of nonmatching (such as a character's speech or reading turning into documentary-style voice-over); and there are numerous moments when the formal disjunction of sound and image subtends rhetorical relations of irony and even counterpoint. This disjunctive style occurs primarily on the level of diegetic sound, in particular, speech. (The use of nondiegetic music in *Schindler's List* is indeed another matter, inasmuch as it functions more like the "glue" that traditionally covers over any discontinuity and sutures the viewer into the film.)[32] But the persistent splitting of the image track by means of displaced diegetic sound still undercuts the effect of an immediate and totalitarian grasp on reality—such as that produced by perfect sound/image matching in numerous World War II films or, to use a more recent example, Stone's *JFK*.

In the sequence that initiates the liquidation of the Kraków ghetto, disjunctive sound/image relations combine with camera narration that foregrounds Stern's point of view. The sequence is defined by the duration of an acoustic event, Goeth's speech that begins and ends with the phrase "today is history." The speech starts in the middle of a series of four shots alternating between Schindler and Goeth shaving, which briefly makes it an acoustic flashforward. Only in the fifth shot is the voice grounded in the speaking character, Goeth now dressed in a uniform, addressing his men who stand around him in a wide circle. In the shots that follow, the speech appears to function as a kind of voice-over, speaking the history of the ghetto's inhabi-

Fig. 4.1: Today is history;

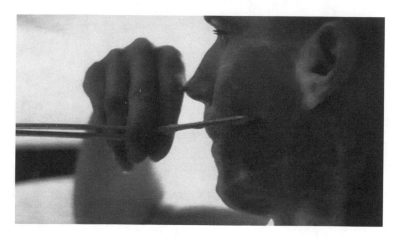

Fig. 4.2: —today will be remembered.

Fig. 4.3: —Years from now the young will ask with wonder about

Fig. 4.4: —this day. Today is history and you are part of it.
Six hundred years ago,

Rabbi's voice praying

Fig. 4.5: —when elsewhere they were put in the blame for the
black death, Casimir the Great

Fig. 4.6: —so-called, told the Jews they could come to

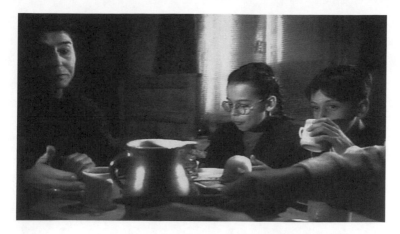

Fig. 4.7: —Kraków. They came, they trundled their

Mrs. Dresner's voice: a bit less

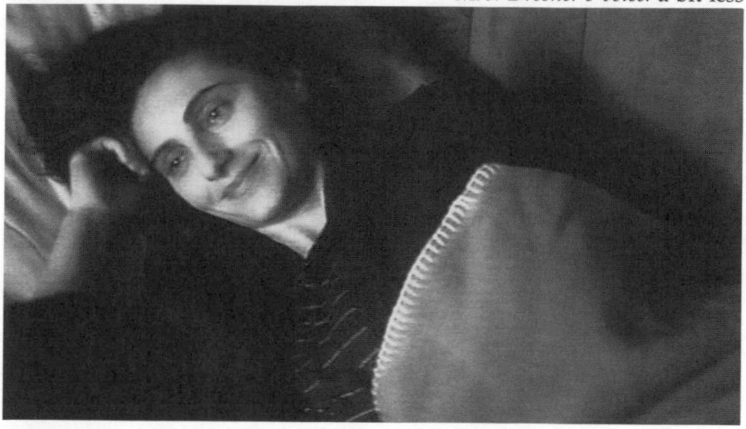

Fig. 4.8: —settled, they took hold, they

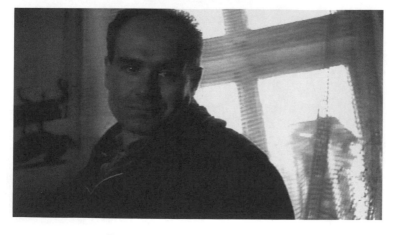

Fig. 4.9: —prospered; and business,

Fig. 4.10a: —science, education, the arts.

Fig. 4.10b

Fig. 4.11: They came here with nothing,

Fig. 4.12: —nothing,

Fig. 4.13: —and they flourished.

Fig. 4.14: —For six centuries, there has been a

Fig. 4.15: —Jewish Kraków; think about that. By this evening, those six centuries are a rumor;

Rabbi's voice fades

Fig. 4.16: —they never happened. Today is history.

tants and the imminent erasure of this history and its subjects. But the images of the living people we see—a rabbi praying, a family having breakfast, a man and a woman exchanging loving looks—also resist this predication. So does the voice of the rabbi that competes with Goeth's voice even before we see him pray, and it continues, as an undertone to Goeth's voice, into the subsequent shots of ghetto inhabitants (so that in one shot, in which we hear the subdued synchronic voices of the family at breakfast, there are actually three different layers of sound); the praying voice fades out just before the last sentence of Goeth's speech. Not coincidentally, all the Jewish characters shown in this sequence will survive, that is, they will, as individuals, give the lie to Goeth's project. What is more, nested into this sequence is a pronounced point-of-view pattern that centers on Stern and makes him the first to witness the ominous preparations. The act of looking is emphasized by a close-up of him putting on his glasses and turning to the window, and by the answering extreme high-angle shot that frames window and curtain from his vantage point. This shot is repeated, after two objective, almost emblematic shots (closely framed and violating screen direction) of rows of chairs and tables being set up by uniformed arms and hands, and then bookended by a medium shot of Stern watching and turning away from the window. The whole sequence is symmetrically closed by reattaching Goeth's voice to his body, thus sealing the fate of the majority of the ghetto population, the people **not** shown on the image track.

To be sure, the film's hierarchy of physicality and masculinity would never allow Stern to be seen shaving (as Schindler and Goeth are in the beginning of the sequence). But the structuring of vision on the level of enunciation establishes Stern as a **witness** for the narration, for the viewer, for posterity. By contrast, moments of subjective vision ascribed to Schindler, most notably the point-of-view shots that stage his two sightings of the little girl in the red coat, serve quite a different function, stressing character psychology rather than narrational authority. Stern's role as enunciative witness is particularly interesting in a sequence that does **not** involve optical point of view— the sequence in which Goeth kills Lisiek (Wojciech Klata), the boy whom he has made his personal servant. What is remarkable about this sequence is the oblique, elliptical rendering of the killing: we neither see Goeth shooting nor do we see the boy being hit; we only see his body lying in the background as Stern walks across the yard, and it is Stern's movement that motivates that of the camera. Even Stern's registering of the killing is rendered only obliquely, stressing the split between seeing and meaning, seeing and feeling characteristic of the concentration camp universe. Compared to the systematic way *Shoah* (in Shoshana Felman's reading) foregrounds the problematic of witnessing, such moments are perhaps marginal in *Schindler's List*, but they nonetheless deserve to be discussed in similar terms—as an aesthetic attempt to engage the extreme difficulty (though not absolute impossibility) of giving sensory expression to an experience that radically defies sense.[33]

Important as the close attention to the film's textual work is, it can only provide a weak answer to the fundamental objections raised by the film's intellectual opponents. Let me repeat that I am not interested in defending *Schindler's List* on aesthetic grounds (the aesthetic narrowly understood as relating to the institution of art and its mass-mediated afterlives). Nor am I suggesting that the film's use of sound and its overall narrational strategies are radical, unique, or original; on the contrary, most of these textual devices belong to the inventory of classical Hollywood cinema, from the mid-teens through the 1950s. Seen in light of the history of that institution up to and including commercial film production of the present, however, *Schindler's List* makes use of these devices in a relatively more intelligent, responsible, and interesting manner than one might have expected, for instance, on the basis of Spielberg's earlier work. The wholesale attack on the film not only erases these distinctions; it also misses the film's diagnostic significance in relation to other discourses, junctures, and disjunctures in contemporary American culture.

The point I'm trying to make is that the lack of attention to the film's material and textual specificity is itself a symptom of the impasse produced by the intellectual critique, an impasse that I find epitomized in the binary opposition of *Schindler's List* and *Shoah*. (Lanzmann's position in this regard is only the most extreme version of this opposition: "In [Spielberg's] film there is no reflection, no thought, about what is the Holocaust and no thought about what is cinema. Because if he would have thought, he would not have made it—or he would have made 'Shoah.' ")[34] It is one thing to use *Shoah* for the purpose of spelling out the philosophical and ethical issues of cinematic representation in relation to the Shoah; it is another to accuse *Schindler's List* of not being the same kind of film. For while *Shoah* has indeed changed the parameters of Holocaust representation, it is not without problems, aesthetic as well as political, nor is it sacrosanct.

More important, the attack on *Schindler's List* in the name of *Shoah* reinscribes the debate on filmic representation with the old debate of modernism vs. mass culture, and thus with binary oppositions of "high" vs. "low," "art" vs. "kitsch," "esoteric" vs. "popular." However, Adorno's insight that, to use Andreas Huyssen's paraphrase, ever since the mid-nineteenth century "modernism and mass culture have been engaged in a compulsive *pas-de-deux*" has become exponentially more pertinent in postmodern media culture.[35] "High" and "low" are inextricably part of the same culture, part of the same public sphere, part of the ongoing negotiation of how forms of social difference are both represented and produced in late capitalism. This is not to say that *Shoah*

Fig. 4.17: —*Lisiek*: I have to report, sir: I've been unable to remove the stains from the bathtub. *Goeth*: Go ahead, go on, leave. I pardon you.

Fig. 4.18

Fig. 4.19: —I pardon you.

Fig. 4.20

Fig. 4.21

Fig. 4.22

did not have to compete for funding in an unequal struggle with commercial cinema; nor that it did not have to fight for distribution and access. But once the film was released, especially in the United States, it entered the commercial circuit of the art film market and was praised by the same critics and in the same hyperbolic terms that celebrated *Schindler's List.*

Ironically, it could be argued, *Schindler's List* itself participates in the modernism/mass culture dichotomy even as it tries to overcome it. Here is where I would like to insert the concept of popular modernism (which I elaborate in greater detail elsewhere).[36] If we want to grasp the plurality and complexity of twentieth-century modernity, it is important to note the extent to which modernism was not just the creation of individual artists and intellectuals or, for that matter, avant-garde coteries, but also, especially during the interwar period, a popular and mass movement. I am thinking in particular of formations usually subsumed under labels such as Americanism and Fordism, but more specifically referring to a new culture of leisure, distraction, and consumption that absorbed a number of artistic innovations into a modern vernacular of its own (especially by way of design) and vice versa. It seems to me that Spielberg would like to go back to that moment—that he is trying to make a case for a capitalist aesthetics and culture which is at once modernist and popular, which would be capable of reflecting upon the shocks and scars inflicted by modernity on people's lives in a generally accessible, public horizon.

The reason I believe that something of that order is at stake has to do with the way *Schindler's List* refers itself to that great monument of cinematic modernism, *Citizen Kane.*[37] This argument is primarily based on striking affinities of film style—the self-conscious use of sound, low-key lighting, particular angles and compositions in frame, montage sequences, as well as the comic use of still photography early on in the film. If Spielberg tries to inscribe himself into an American film history pivoting around *Citizen Kane,* he also tries to revise the message—if one can speak of a message—of Welles's film. *Citizen Kane* traces the disintegration of its protagonist from a young man of lofty ideals to a monstrous figure of the specular, two-dimensional, and fragmented media culture he helped create. *Schindler's List* reverses the direction of this development. It presents us with an enigmatic character who starts out in the world of dazzling surfaces and glamor and who is repeatedly identified with the aesthetics of fashion, advertising and consumption. (In the scene in which Schindler proposes to Stern what is basically a highly exploitative scheme, Stern asks: "They [the Jewish 'investors'] put up all the money; I do all the work. What, if you don't mind my asking, would you do?" And Schindler replies: "I'd make sure it's known the company's in business. I'd see that it had a certain panache. That's what I'm good at. Not the work, not the work: the presentation!") But out of that cypher of a grifter-conman-gambler develops an "authentic" person, an integrated and intelligible character, a morally responsible agent. No doubt Spielberg himself has an investment in this redemptive trajectory; and if, as a number of critics have pointed out, the director strongly identifies with his protagonist, he does so in defense of a capitalist culture, of an aesthetics that fuses modernist style, popular storytelling, and an ethos of individual responsibility. Whether he succeeds in reversing *Citizen Kane's* pessimistic trajectory, that is, in disentangling Schindler—and the story of the Schindler Jews—from the reifying effects of mass-mediated, spectacular consumer culture, is an open question, depending as much on the film's longterm public effects as on textual critique.

But perhaps this question is beside the point, as is treating the opposition of *Shoah* vs. *Schindler's List* as if it were a practical alternative, a real option. For whether we like it or not, the predominant vehicles of public memory **are** the media of technical re/production and mass consumption. This issue is especially exacerbated for the remembrance of the Shoah in light of the specific crisis posed by the Nazis' destruction of the very basis and structures of collective remembering. (In contrast, with most of the "ordinary massacres" committed in the course of the German genocidal war all over Europe, the Shoah did not leave any communities of survivors, widows and children, not even burial sites that would have provided a link with a more "organic" tradition of oral and collective memory.)[38] In a significant way, even before the passing of the last survivors, the remembrance of the Shoah, to the extent that it was public and collective, has always been more dependent on mass-mediated forms of memory—on what Alison Landsberg calls "prosthetic memory."[39]

Much has been written about the changing fabric of memory in postmodern media society, in particular the emergence of new cultural practices (new types of exhibits, the museum boom) that allow the beholders to **experience** the past—any past, not necessarily their own—with greater intensity and sensuous immediacy (for example, at the United States Holocaust Memorial Museum).[40] We need to understand the place of *Schindler's List* in the contemporary culture of memory and memorializing; and the film in turn may help us understand that culture. This might also shed light on how the popular American fascination with the Holocaust may function as a "screen memory" (*Deckerinnerung*) in the Freudian sense, covering up a traumatic event—another traumatic event—that cannot be approached directly. More than just an ideological displacement (which it is no doubt as well), the fascination with the Holocaust could be read as a kind of screen allegory behind/through which the nation is struggling to find a proper mode of memorializing traumata closer to home. The displaced referents of such memorializing may extend to events as distant as the genocide of Native Americans or as recent as the Vietnam War. It is no coincidence that African American historians have begun using concepts developed in the attempt to theorize the Shoah, such as the notion of a "breach" or "rupture," to talk about the Middle Passage.[41]

Likewise, the screen memories of the Holocaust could be read as part of an American discourse on modernity, in which Weimar and Nazi Germany figure as an allegory of a modernity gone wrong.[42] The continued currency of these mythical topoi in the popular media may indicate a need for Americans to externalize and project modernity's catastrophic features onto another nation's failure and defeat—so as to salvage modernity the American way. This would give the American public's penchant for allegories of heroic rescue (elaborated in cinematic form by D. W. Griffith) a particular historical and political twist in that it couples the memory/fantasy of having won the war with the failure to save the Jews. In any case, if *Schindler's List* functions as a screen memory in this or other ways, the pasts that it may at once cover and traverse cannot be reduced to the singular, just as the Americanization of the Holocaust cannot be explained by fixating exclusively on its ideological functions.[43] That the film touches on more than one nerve, appeals to more constituencies than a narrowly defined identity politics would have it, could be dismissed as an effect of Hollywood's marketing strategies in the blockbuster era. But it could also be taken as a measure of the film's ability to engender a public space, a horizon of at once sensory experience and discursive contestation.

No doubt *Schindler's List* could have been a different film, or many different films, even as based on Keneally's novel. And different stories relating to the most traumatic and central event of the twentieth century will be and will have to be told, in a variety of media and genres, within an irrevocably multiple and hybrid public sphere. If *The Birth of a Nation* remains important to American history, it is not only for its racist inscription of the Civil War and Reconstruction periods; it is just as important for what it tells us about 1915, about the new medium's role in creating a national public, about the dynamics of cultural memory and public memorializing in a volatile immigrant society. *Schindler's List* comes at a radically different moment—in national and global history, in film history, in the history of the public sphere. To dismiss the film because of the a priori established unrepresentability of what it purports to represent may be justified on ethical and epistemological grounds, but it means missing a chance to understand the significance of the Shoah in the present, in the ongoing and undecided struggles over which past gets remembered and how. Unless we take all aspects—omissions and distortions, displacements and possibilities—of public, mass-mediated memory culture seriously, we will remain caught in the "compulsive *pas-de-deux*" of (not just) intellectual history.

Notes

1. The comparison was first suggested, in a somewhat different spirit, by Terrence Rafferty in the *New Yorker* 69 (December 20, 1993), p. 132. Rafferty praises the epic significance and "visionary clarity" of *Schindler's List* by invoking James Agee's reverie about *Birth* as "a perfect realization of a collective dream of what the Civil War was like, as veterans might remember it fifty years later, or as children, fifty years later might imagine it." Obviously, such a comparison asks to be turned against itself: see Philip Gourevitch, "A Dissent on 'Schindler's List,' " *Commentary* 97.2 (February 1994), p. 52.

For astute readings and suggestions on this essay, I wish to thank Homi Bhabha, Bill Brown, Michael Geyer, Alison Landsberg, and audiences at the University of Chicago, Harvard University, and the annual conference of the Society for Cinema Studies, March 1995.

2. Another example of such boundary-crossing publicity in the recent past is Oliver Stone's *JFK* (1992). My use of the term "public," like the distinction among various types of publicness, is indebted to Oskar Negt and Alexander Kluge, *Public Sphere and Experience* (1972), trans. P. Labanyi, J. O. Daniel, and A. Oksiloff (Minneapolis: University of Minnesota Press, 1993); also, see my foreword to this edition, pp. ix–xli.

3. See Janet Staiger, "*The Birth of a Nation:* Reconsidering Its Reception," in: Robert Land, ed., *THE BIRTH OF A NATION: D. W. Griffith, Director* (New Brunswick, N.J.: Rutgers University Press, 1994), pp. 195–213. For an earlier account, see Thomas Cripps, *Slow Fade to Black: The Negro in American Film, 1900–1942* (London: Oxford University Press, 1977), ch. 2. On the film's intervention in the contemporary political and ideological context, see Michael Rogin's excellent essay, " 'The Sword Became a Flashing Vision': D. W. Griffith's *The Birth of a Nation*," *Representations* 9 (Winter 1985), pp. 150–95. On the film's devastating and lasting effects on African Americans' cinematic representation and relation to film practice, see Manthia Diawara, ed., *Black American Cinema* (New York: Routledge, 1993).

4. See Alexander Kluge, "On Film and the Public Sphere," trans. Th. Y. Levin and M. Hansen, *New German Critique* 24–25 (Fall/Winter 1981–82), pp. 206–20.

5. Frank Rich, "Journal: 'Schindler's' Dissed," *New York Times*, 6 February 1994, section 4, p. 17; see also, "Laughter at Film Brings Spielberg Visit," *New York Times*, 13 April 1994, p. B11.

6. Michael André Bernstein, "The *Schindler's List* Effect," *American Scholar* 63 (Summer 1994), pp. 429–32; p. 429.

7. Bernstein, "The *Schindler's List* Effect," p. 429.

8. Michael Geyer, "The Politics of Memory in Contemporary Germany," in: Joan Copjec, ed., *Radical Evil* (London: Verso, 1996), pp. 169–200. See also Michael Geyer and Miriam Hansen, "German-Jewish Memory and National Consciousness," in: Geoffrey Hartman, ed., *Holocaust Remembrance: The Shapes of Memory* (Oxford: Blackwell, 1994), pp. 175–90.

9. See Geoffrey H. Hartman, "Public Memory and Its Discontents," *Raritan* 13.4 (Spring 1994), pp. 24–40. Hartman defines contemporary *"public* memory" in contradistinction to traditional *"collective* memory" (33). I am using the term in a more general and less pessimistic sense indebted to Negt and Kluge's theory of the public sphere (see note 2, above).

10. Art Spiegelman, in: J. Hoberman et al., "SCHINDLER'S LIST: Myth, Movie, and Memory," *Village Voice*, March 29, 1994, p. 27; hereafter abbreviated "MMM." See also Sean Mitchell's profile of Spiegelman, "Now, for a Little Hedonism," *Los Angeles Times, Calendar* section, December 18, 1994, pp. 7, 97–98; on *Schindler's List*, p. 98.

11. J. Hoberman, "Spielberg's Oskar," *Village Voice*, December 21, 1993, p. 65. See also Frank Rich, "Extras in the Shadows," *New York Times*, January 2, 1994, p. 4; and Leon Wieseltier, "Close Encounters of the Nazi Kind," *New Republic* (January 24, 1994), p. 42.

12. See Saul Friedlander's introduction to the volume of essays, edited by him, *Probing the Limits of Representation: Nazism and the "Final Solution"* (Cambridge: Harvard University Press, 1992), and *Reflections of Nazism: An Essay on Kitsch and Death* (1982), trans. Thomas Weyr (New York: Harper & Row, 1984), p. 13.

13. See Ora Gelley, "Point of View and the Narrativization of History in Steven Spielberg's *Schindler's List*," paper delivered at the Society for Cinema Studies annual conference, New York, March 1995.

14. David Bordwell, Janet Staiger, and Kristin Thompson, *The Classical Hollywood Cinema: Film Style and Mode of Production to 1960* (New York: Columbia University Press, 1985); David Bordwell, *Narration in the Fiction Film* (Madison: University of Wisconsin Press, 1985), ch. 9. The concept of classical cinema owes much to psychoanalytic-semiotic and feminist film theory of the 1970s; see Philip Rosen, ed., *Narrative, Apparatus, Ideology* (New York: Columbia University Press, 1986).

15. Ken Jacobs and Gertrud Koch, in "MMM," pp. 27–28.

16. Bernstein, "The *Schindler's List* Effect," p. 430; Geoff Eley and Atina Grossmann, "Watching *Schindler's List*: Not the Last Word," forthcoming, *New German Critique*.

17. Kluge, *Die Macht der Gefühle* (*The Power of Emotion*, 1983), film script and other materials published under the same title (Frankfurt a.M.: Zweitausendeins, 1984); see also Miriam Hansen, "The Stubborn Discourse: History and Story-Telling in the Films of Alexander Kluge," *Persistence of Vision* 2 (Fall 1985), p. 26. On the Hollywood convention of the always-happy ending, see David Bordwell, "Happily Ever After, Part Two," *The Velvet Light Trap* 19 (1982/83), pp. 2–7.

18. Edith Wyschogrod, *Spirit in Ashes: Hegel, Heidegger, and Man-Made Mass Death* (New Haven: Yale University Press, 1985).

19. Claude Lanzmann, "Holocauste, la représentation impossible," *Le Monde*, March 3, 1994, I, VII; "Why Spielberg Has Distorted the Truth," *Guardian Weekly*, April 9, 1994, p. 14; and Koch, in "MMM," p. 26.

20. Roland Barthes, "L'Effet de réel," *Communications* 11 (1968), pp. 84–89, trans. Gerald Mead, "The Realistic Effect," *Film Reader* 3 (1978), pp. 131–35. See also Barthes, *S/Z*, trans. Richard Miller (New York: Hill and Wang, 1974).

21. Gourevitch, "Dissent," p. 51. See also Jonathan Rosenbaum, "Gentile Persuasion," *Chicago Reader*, December 17, 1993, pp. 10 and 26–27; and Gelley, "Point of View."

22. Ilene Rosenzweig, *The Forward*, quoted in Frank Rich, "Extras in the Shadows," *New York Times*, January 2, 1994, p. 4; Donald Kuspit, "Director's Guilt," *Artforum* 32 (February 1994), pp. 11–12. Also see "MMM," p. 26.

23. See, for instance, articles by Christian Metz, Raymond Bellour, Kaja Silverman, Stephen Heath, and Laura Mulvey reprinted in Rosen, *Narrative, Apparatus, Ideology*. For a critique of the cine-semiotic concept of "enunciation," see Bordwell, *Narration and the Fiction Film*, pp. 21–26.

24. Gertrud Koch, "The Aesthetic Transformation of the Image of the Unimaginable: Notes on Claude Lanzmann's *Shoah*" (1986), trans. Jamie Owen Daniel and Miriam Hansen, *October* 48 (Spring 1989), pp. 15–24. Also, see Koch, *Die Einstellung ist die Einstellung: Visuelle Konstruktionen des Judentums* (Frankfurt a.M.: Suhrkamp, 1992), especially part 2: "Film und Faktizität: Zur filmischen Repräsentation der Judenvernichtung."

25. Lanzmann, "Holocauste, la répresentation impossible," p. 7. Lanzmann makes the same argument in his critique of the TV miniseries, *Holocaust*, "From the Holocaust to the *Holocaust*," trans. Simon Srebrny, *Telos* 42 (Winter 1979–80), pp. 137–43.

26. Shoshana Felman, "The Return of the Voice: Claude Lanzmann's *Shoah*," in: Felman and Dori Laub, M.D., *Testimony: Crises of Witnessing in Literature, Psychoanalysis, and History* (New York: Routledge, 1992), pp. 204–83.

27. Lanzmann, "Holocauste, la répresentation impossible," p. 7.

28. Theodor W. Adorno, "Cultural Criticism and Society," *Prisms* (German ed., 1955), trans. Samuel and Shierry Weber ([1967] Cambridge: MIT Press, 1988): "Cultural criticism finds itself faced with the final stage of the dialectic of culture and barbarism[:] to write poetry after Auschwitz is barbaric, and this corrodes even the knowledge of why it has become impossible to write poetry today" (one sentence in the original, three in the translation). See also Adorno's revision of this statement in *Negative Dialectics* (1966), trans. E. B. Ashton (New York: Seabury, 1973), pp. 362–63.

29. Gertrud Koch, "Mimesis and *Bilderverbot*," *Screen* 34.3 (Autumn 1993), pp. 211–22. See also Koch, *Die Einstellung ist die Einstellung*, pp. 16ff., 123ff., and "The Aesthetic Transformation of the Image of the Unimaginable."

30. It is this sense of the aesthetic which Benjamin tries to recover against and in view of the decline and perversion of the institution of art. See Susan Buck-Morss, "Aesthetics and Anaesthetics: Walter Benjamin's Artwork Essay Reconsidered," *October* 62 (Fall 1992), pp. 3–41.

31. James F. Lastra, *Technology and the American Cinema: Perception, Representation, Modernity* (forthcoming). See also Rick Altman, ed., *Sound Theory/Sound Practice* (New York: Routledge, 1992).

32. Cf. Claudia Gorbman, *Unheard Melodies: Narrative Film Music* (Bloomington: Indiana University Press, 1987); Hanns Eisler [and Theodor W. Adorno], *Composing for the Films* (New York: Oxford University Press, 1947).

33. Felman, "Return of the Voice."

34. Reported in Robert Sklar, "Lanzmann's Latest: After 'Shoah,' Jewish Power," *Forward*, September 30, 1994, p. 10.

35. Andreas Huyssen, *After the Great Divide: Modernism, Mass Culture, Postmodernism* (Bloomington: Indiana University Press, 1986), p. 24.

36. Miriam Bratu Hansen, "America, Paris, The Alps: Kracauer (and Benjamin) on Cinema and Modernity," in: Leo Charney and Vanessa Schwartz, eds., *Cinema and the Invention of Modern Life* (Berkeley: University of California Press, 1995).

37. Spielberg himself claims that he was neither inspired nor influenced by any fiction film when he was working on *Schindler's List* but only watched innumerable documentaries and sifted through piles of photographs. See Hellmuth Karasek, "Die ganze Wahrheit schwarz auf weiß: Regisseur Steven Spielberg über seinen Film 'Schindlers Liste,'" *Der Spiegel* 8 (1994), pp. 183–86; p. 185. In the same interview, however, he acknowledges having thought of "Rosebud" to capture the enigmatic distance, the lack of clear, intelligible motivation, with which he conceived of the Schindler character. See also Annette Insdorf, in "MMM," p. 28. Whether or not inspired by Welles, the relative restraint and withholding of interiority in Spielberg's construction of the Schindler character, at least during the film's first half, is in my opinion much preferable to the omniscient, unrestricted access we get to Schindler's feelings and thoughts in Thomas Keneally's novel on which the film is based.

38. "Per una memoria Europea dei crimi Nazisti," International Conference to Commemorate the 50th Anniversary of the 1944 Massacres Around Arezzo, June 22–24, 1994.

39. Alison Landsberg, "Prosthetic Memory: The Logics and Politics of Memory in Modern American Culture," Ph.D. diss., University of Chicago, 1996, especially ch. 4.

40. Andreas Huyssen, *Twilight Memories: Marking Time in a Culture of Amnesia* (New York: Routledge, 1995), especially chs. 1 and 12. See also Alison Landsberg, "The 'Waning of Historicity'?: A Closer Look at the New Media of Experience," paper delivered at the Society for Cinema Studies annual conference, New York, March 1995. For a brief survey of issues involved in American memorial culture, see Michael Kammen, *Mystic Chords of Memory: The Transformation of Tradition in American Culture* (New York: Knopf, 1991), pp. 3–14.

41. As recently Saidya Hartman, "Redressing the Pained Body," paper delivered at the Chicago Humanities Institute, February 1995. The term "breach" or "rupture" refers to Dan Diner, ed., *Zivilisationsbruch: Denken nach Auschwitz* (Frankfurt a.M.: Fischer, 1988). The first, quite controversial, attempt to conceptualize the trauma of slavery in terms of the Shoah is Stanley M. Elkins, *Slavery: A Problem in American Institutional and Intellectual Life* (1959; 2nd ed., Chicago: University of Chicago Press, 1968). More recently, see Paul Gilroy, *The Black Atlantic: Modernity and Double Consciousness* (Cambridge: Harvard University Press, 1993), pp. 213ff. Laurence Mordekhai Thomas, *Vessels of Evil: American Slavery and the Holocaust* (Philadelphia: Temple University Press, 1993) is a useful starting point but does not really engage with issues of representation and memory.

42. Michael Geyer and Konrad Jarausch, "The Future of the German Past: Transatlantic Reflections for the 1990s," *Central European History* 22 (September/December 1989), pp. 229–59. See also Zygmunt Bauman, *Modernity and the Holocaust* (Ithaca: Cornell University Press, 1989).

43. In the manner of, for instance, Peter Novick, "Holocaust Memory in America," in: James E. Young, ed., *The Art of Memory: Holocaust Memorials in History* (Munich: Prestel, 1995), pp. 157–63.

5 | Holocaust Others

Spielberg's *Schindler's List* versus Lanzmann's *Shoah*

Yosefa Loshitzky

ONE MEMORABLE IMAGE from Claude Lanzmann's *Shoah* eventually acquired the status of the film's visual "logo," or signature.[1] It is the smiling face of Henrik Gakowski driving a locomotive against the backdrop of a railroad sign proclaiming "Treblinka." He looks back to the imaginary wagons behind him and slashes his finger across his throat in a gesture of "warning." During the war this warning gesture was used by the Polish man, who worked for the Germans as a locomotive driver, to signal to the "ignorant" Jews crowded in the transport trains leading them to extermination what kind of fate awaited them. For Lanzmann, this image itself became the truth. Alongside it, he said, "historical footage becomes insufferable."[2] Almost a decade later a similar image was used in Steven Spielberg's *Schindler's List*. This time, however, the image of warning bore Spielberg's auteuristic vision. The performer of the warning gesture was not an old Polish man but a small child, and the disturbing ambivalence invoked by Gakowski's facial expression was replaced by an explicitly sadistic expression.[3] In addition, in Spielberg's film the trains full of Jews rumble not toward Treblinka but toward Auschwitz, "the most significant memorial site of the Shoah."[4]

Was Spielberg aware of the resonance created by these macabre images? Was he consciously using Lanzmann's iconic signature as an homage quotation? Or, perhaps, was he just "stealing" this powerful image and appropriating it for his own vision of the Holocaust? According to Gertrud Koch, Spielberg "recycled every little slip of film that was made before" to produce *Schindler's List*'s authoritarian quality, so as to position his film "at the end of film history."[5] If, indeed, we subscribe to Koch's thesis (which I do, for reasons that will become clear later), then Spielberg is not "innocent." He was fully conscious of the enunciative source of the quoted image. In any event, whether we have here an example of self-reflexive quotational practice (a postmodernist pastiche), an example of plagiarism, or even sheer ignorance on Spielberg's part regarding the source of the "original" image, the question of relationships remains a provocative one. If, indeed, Spielberg "stole" Lanzmann's visual signature, then we might well talk about a relationship of envy, based on an attempt to appropriate and assimilate one's object of envy. If, on the other hand, Spielberg used "Lanzmann's image" as an homage quotation, then we may talk about a relationship of pure admiration in which the master's influence is acknowledged. In fact, regardless of our preferred reading, the resonance between the two images points toward the complex relationship between the two films, both of which have already been canonized as the best films ever made on the Holocaust: *Shoah* in the domain of "documentary," and *Schindler's List* in the domain of fiction. Both films have a claim to be the last word on the Holocaust, a master narrative of the ultimate catastrophe endured by the Jewish people. Until Spielberg's film came out, however, *Shoah* was widely praised as a masterpiece and often proclaimed to be *the* Holocaust film. Thus, *Shoah* was the privileged site of debates about the representation of the Holocaust. It is no wonder, therefore, that even a "nondocumentary" film such as *Schindler's List* had either humbly to acknowledge Lanzmann's authority or to challenge it. This essay explores how, together, the two films generate a dialectics of Otherness by deconstructing some of their own binary oppositions.

Philosophical/Historical Tale versus Popular Tale

The public "aura" associated with *Shoah* and *Schindler's List* was, among other things, invoked by the cultural context of the films' production and the evocation of highly invested notions of Frenchness versus Americanness. Despite the mutual fascination/repulsion that these two cultures have historically sustained for one another, in the popular as well as middle-brow critical imagination Frenchness connotes sophistication, and intellectualism, while Americanness connotes populism, vulgarity, and low-brow entertainment. These evocative connotations go beyond the aesthetic dimension because they imply the traditional binarism of art/market–culture/commodity which obviously has far-reaching economic ramifications.

The national binarism invoked by the two films also reverberated in the realm of the public persona projected by the two directors. As a former leader in the French Resistance and a well-known journalist who worked with Jean-Paul Sartre as the editor of *Les Temps Modernes*, Lanzmann obviously has the halo of an intellectual. Furthermore, *Shoah* was based on a thorough process of historical research which continued for eleven years. Lanzmann taped 350 hours of interviews in fourteen countries so as to create what he called "a film of 'corroboration,' " in which the Poles say "the same thing as the Jews, and 'this is confirmed by the SS.' "[6] For Lanzmann—inspired by the historian Raul Hilberg, whose book *The Destruction of the European Jews* was used as a model for *Shoah*—the details are what matters. As André Pierre Colombat observes: "Hilberg's interviews always situate the film in a very precise historical chronology and framework. . . . Used in the final sections of each part of the film, they gather the disseminated testimonies heard in one general and clear historical interpretation."[7]

Claude Lanzmann's monumental nine-and-a-half hour film on the Holocaust was praised not only by critics and "free-floating intellectuals" but also by professional historians. The French historian Pierre Vidal-Naquet said of *Shoah*: "Writing is not the only historical mode. Why is *Shoah* a great work of history rather than a collection of tales? It is neither a novelistic recreation like *Holocaust*, nor a documentary—only a single document from the period is read in it, concerning the trucks at Chelmno—but a film in which men of today speak of the past. With Jewish survivors expressing themselves in a space that was once that of death, while trains no longer leading to the gas chambers roll on, and former Nazis sketch their past exploits, the witnesses reconstruct a past that was all too real; testimonial accounts overlap and confirm each other in the barest of voices and diction. We are, in brief, given absolute proof that the historian is also an artist."[8] Although, and perhaps because, no archival footage is presented in the film and Lanzmann instead presses Jews, Germans, and Poles to describe their Holocaust experiences before the camera, the film has been celebrated as the product of a vigorous and systematic historical method which transcends art in its consistent search for historical truth and transcends history through its melancholic beauty, rhythmic pace, and poetic images. Drawn from witnesses, survivors, and former Nazis detail by detail, the recollections unveil the terrible fate of the Jews against a background of moving trains and bureaucratic minutiae. Lanzmann's method of probing seemed cruel to some of the film's critics, but the survivors of the Holocaust all agreed to reconstruct painful events that many of them had tried to forget because they understood that part of the Final Solution was not only to do away with the Jews but also to obliterate all memory of them.

Lanzmann's eleven-year investment of intellectual, emotional, and physical energy resulted in a monumental biography of death, an oral history of the Holocaust as narrated by victims, perpetrators, and bystanders. While Lanzmann followed in the footsteps of Alain Resnais and Marcel Ophuls, who first probed the Nazi era and the European response to the Final Solution, he went far beyond them. Marcel Ophuls said of *Shoah*: "I consider *Shoah* to be the greatest documentary about contemporary history ever made, by far the greatest film I've ever seen about the Holocaust."[9]

Whereas Lanzmann is a professional journalist who uses film as a means to render rich and complex testimony on the Holocaust, Spielberg is a professional filmmaker—known as the most commercially successful director in movie history—for whom film is an end in itself. *Schindler's List* was for Spielberg a vehicle through which he received recognition both as a great filmmaker and as a reborn Jew. For Spielberg, as for other American Jews, the Holocaust has become central to the self-understanding of their Jewish identity. Hence Spielberg's road back to Judaism involved a cinematic voyage to the Holocaust, the new locus of Jewish identity in American public discourse.[10] *Schindler's List* thus merges Spielberg's much publicized rediscovery of his Jewish identity with the public's and critics' rediscovery of Spielberg as a reborn director. Consequently, *Schindler's List* functions as a redemptive rite of passage for Spielberg. It is a narrative of personal and collective redemption. Indeed, the sub-text of many reviews of *Schindler's List* is that the true wonder of the film is that Spielberg made it, not that it is a powerful depiction of the Holocaust in and of itself. It is as if in and through *Schindler's List* Spielberg is positioned against himself, directing against the grain, in order for Spielberg to transcend Spielberg.

As a self-made historian with journalistic training, Lanzmann created a film which, according to Vidal-Naquet, epitomizes a unique and nontraditional modus of historical writing. As a Hollywood popular storyteller, Spielberg, on the other hand, produced a classical Hollywood narrative. Whereas Lanzmann depicts a collective (yet individually distinctive) hero composed of a variety of Jewish victims, Spielberg, following the Hollywood model of the historical epic, chose an individual (and a nonvictim) to function as the protagonist of history. He thereby reaffirmed classical Hollywood narrative's psychohistorical approach to history in which the private story is accorded more weight than public history.

"The Fiction of Reality" versus "The Reality of Fiction"

To a large extent, we might argue, the binarism generated by *Shoah* and *Schindler's List* is the result of genre division. "Documentary and fiction, we are told, appear as different genres and cannot, some might say, be compared."[11] Indeed, journalistic accounts celebrated Spielberg's film as the finest nondocumentary film ever made on the Holocaust and *Shoah* as the best documentary ever made on the Holocaust. Yet these comfortable genre categories should not mislead us. Traditionally, documentaries have been viewed as superior to fiction films because of their pretense to monopolize the market of truth. Yet the cinematic institution's categories of "documentary" and "fiction" have continuously been thrown into crisis—especially since the emergence of cinema verité, which proved so influential in France from the late 1950s to the mid-1970s and to which Lanzmann's *Shoah* is indebted. Lanzmann, for example, described his film as a "fiction of reality,"[12] whereas Spielberg based his film on a "real story" and simulated many documentary traditions (including cinema verité features) in order to make the events of his film look more real.

Lanzmann's definition of *Shoah* as a "fiction of reality" echoes one of the more famous aphorisms coined by Jean-Luc Godard, which appears as a hand-written slogan in his film *British Sounds (See You at Mao)* (1969): "photography is not the reflection of reality but the reality of that reflection." Godard later modified this aphorism, defining cinema on many occasions as "the fiction of reality and the reality of fiction." Unlike the Rohmer/Bazin phenomenologi-cal approach, Lanzmann—like Godard—distrusts verisimilitude as a means of rendering reality. *Shoah*, to a certain extent, is influenced by the radical tra-dition of the May 1968 events, hence epitomizing Jean-Louis Comolli's ideal film, *le direct* (direct cinema), which extends the original conception of cinema verité. It is not a crude transformation of reality into cinematography, but rather a presentation of representation. It is a documentation of the process of producing events in front of the camera.[13] This explains why Lanzmann often called his witnesses the "characters" of the film. Moreover, Lanzmann edited their testimonies very carefully and staged certain scenes in search of a par-ticular "reenacting" of his original interviewees. In the cinema verité tradi-tion, the camera is used in these scenes as a valuable catalytic agent, a revealer of inner truth. As André Pierre Colombat suggests, "some witnesses become acting 'characters' in the film in agreement with a specific French sense of the word *repetition* (rehearsal)."[14]

The documentary/fiction dichotomy carries special implications for the representation of the Holocaust. The Holocaust has traditionally been con-ceived of as defying representation. This tradition evolved from the debates "that have revolved for several decades . . . around the question of an aesthet-ics after Auschwitz."[15] In these debates, triggered by Theodor W. Adorno's fa-mous dictum that after Auschwitz poetry could no longer be written, "silence" emerged as the least "obscene" aesthetic response to historical trauma. Of course, silence was used in these debates more as a trope marking the appro-priate boundaries of aesthetic reaction to the Holocaust (although in some cases it was both meant and read literally) than as an attempt at suppressing any expressive response to it. Documentary, due to its claim of direct access to reality and hence to "truth," was therefore a preferred genre for the represen-tation of the Holocaust. The widespread view of film as immanently the most mimetic of art forms, and the notion of documentary as a transparent window reflecting reality, accorded this genre a license to deal with the Holocaust in a nondistortive manner. This explains the privilege traditionally accorded to documentary in discourse on the representation of the Holocaust. Lanzmann's mistrust of documentary's claim to be "truer" than fiction guided his "fiction of reality," which challenges the boundaries of correctness imposed by the de-bate on post-Auschwitz aesthetics.

Although *Schindler's List* is a classical Hollywood film, it integrates into its narrative various devices traditionally coded as belonging to documentary modes. *Schindler's List* is a realistic film, as most Hollywood narratives are. Yet the realistic code of the film is recreated in documentary style. The scene which epitomizes the assimilation of the documentary code into the fictional narrative is the final scene when present-day Schindler Jews assemble in a line to place stones upon the real man's grave in Jerusalem. This is, in Simon Louvish's perceptive words, a "Lanzmannesque invasion of the actual into the simulation."[16] As the whole film is shot in black and white, this scene—shot in color against the dazzling, bright light of Jerusalem—stands out sharply. It conveys the impression of a "raw" slice of reality, contrasted with the over-stylized, nostalgic, black-and-white of the preceding footage. But even this seemingly original merging of fiction with documentary is part of a Hollywood tradition of the historical epic.

In fact, the assimilation of the documentary style into *Schindler's List* is part of the broader postmodernist aesthetics of the film. *Schindler's List* is a pastiche[17] of cinematic styles. The film bears the look of, to use Fredric Jameson's words, "the technological 'perfection' of the new nostalgia glossy-film product."[18] It is a visually spectacular and eclectic text, quoting from styles as diverse as film noir, German Expressionism, Italian Neorealism, World War II newsreels, and CNN news coverage. When Spielberg and cinematographer Janusz Kaminski chose to shoot in black and white, they conformed to a theory that this particular historical event could not be adequately rendered in color. Spielberg claimed: "I have no color reference for that period." Yet his expressive use of black-and-white is indebted more to cinematic traditions associated with black-and-white than to any claim of truth. In fact, black-and-white cinematography today has more the aura of "arty" glamor than a claim to formal authenticity. Contemporary codes of realism require color as the norm, while black-and-white is seen as a nostalgic, stylized, and artificial reference. This is also the reason why Spielberg used color for the closing scene. Its "authenticity" is indebted to the use of color and its being shot on location. Spielberg's use of black-and-white varies in relation to the cinematic style from which he is quoting. Thus, for example, the opening scene takes place in a cabaretlike milieu and is shot in dramatic contrasting black-and-white, which creates a chiaroscuro interplay of light and shadow associated with German Expressionism and film noir (in itself a highly stylized genre inspired by the visual iconography of German Expressionism).[19] These brilliant allusions to chiaroscuro lighting are influenced by the Hollywood studio film, particularly as realized in the work of Joseph von Sternberg, Orson Welles, and Max Ophuls. This highly evocative black-and-white is replaced by grainy black-and-white tonality, embedded with shades of grey in the "more realistic scenes" such as the liquidation of the Kraków ghetto, or the selection of running, naked women by Nazi doctors. These scenes embrace the "aesthetic of imperfect cinema,"[20] which renounces the perfection of Hollywood products by resorting to the low-quality (but highly authentic) images of newsreels and television news. Other scenes, in particular those representing everyday life in the Kraków ghetto or in Schindler's factory, invoke the style of Italian Neorealism, a movement associated with black-and-white depictions of life in Italy during and after World War II. Despite the diversity of styles integrated into *Schindler's List*, the final product (unlike the highly eclectic, "impure" films of filmmakers such as Pier-Paolo Pasolini, and Rainer Werner Fassbinder) does not render stylistic or ideological tensions and contradictions. To the contrary, the transition from one quotational practice to another is almost invisible. Following the tradition of the classical Hollywood narrative, the text never calls attention to itself as a complex, constructed text. Rather, one quoted style flows seamlessly into the next. It is very possible that the uninitiated spectator, the "naive reader," is not able to recognize, let alone deconstruct, the different stylistic codes embedded in the otherwise harmonious look of the film. It is left to the critic and the film scholar to accomplish the job.

Word against Image: Images of Absence, Images of Resurrection

Jim Hoberman opened his introduction in the *Village Voice* to excerpts from the roundtable discussion at the Jewish Museum on *Schindler's List* with the following clichélike truism: "In an age when even children understand that the image of an event transcends the event itself, *Schindler's List* is more than just a movie."[21] Lanzmann, however, rejected Holocaust images borrowed from archive footage, partly because he claimed that "it was not possible to determine which archive footage came from which camp, or which date. Film of Treblinka has come to be used as Auschwitz and vice versa. Lanzmann's obsession was to provide a precise and indeed pitiless verification of the events through their survivors' memories. The word was all; the picture, a means to an end . . . Steven Spielberg, at the opposite end of the scale, goes back to the old dramatic principle of narrative filmmaking: show, don't tell. The Holocaust will be painstakingly reconstructed, in all its horror and misery."[22]

Schindler's List's challenge to the traditional view of the Holocaust as confined to the realm of the unimaginable, a liminal zone of human comprehension bound by the "limits of representation," was to penetrate (cognitively and visually) this dark continent simply by imagining it. Demystifying the "heart of darkness," trying literally to reconstruct it through visual and oral representations, was something that had never been done before in mainstream cinema.[23] Spielberg was the first mainstream Hollywood Jewish filmmaker to break the taboo of explicitly imagining the Holocaust and the gas chamber as its ultimate sacred center and horrifying metaphor.[24] In essence, Spielberg violated the ancient Jewish biblical prohibition against creating images as it had been unconsciously resurrected in the moral taboo on representing the Holocaust. This violation culminated in what Terrence Rafferty describes as Spielberg's camera taking us "even further, straight into the heart of darkness: we follow the women who wound up at Auschwitz-Birkenau into the showers. . . . It is the most terrifying sequence ever filmed."[25] Spielberg's transgression of the taboo on imagining the Holocaust explains partially the enthusiastic reception of the film by critics and audiences alike, as well as the hostile responses on behalf of some Jewish intellectuals who perceived this violation as pornographic and desacralizing. The camera's penetration into the gas chamber was perceived by some as a violation of the Holy of Holies (*Kodesh Hakodashim* in Hebrew). Within this economy of scopophilic desire, *Schindler's List* provided an audience hungry for a spectacle of atrocity with the illusion of being there.

Spielberg attempted to rebuild Auschwitz as a movie set. Lanzmann, on the other hand, resurrected the Holocaust through the words of the witnesses and through images of absence, images of tranquillity and beauty at what were once sites of destruction. Lanzmann said, "If the film is a resurrection, it's because of how I was compelled to do it."[26] The achievement of *Shoah*, as Annette Insdorf points out, "is that it contains no music, no voice-over narration, no self-conscious camera work, no stock images—just precise questions and answers, evocative places and faces, and horror recollected in tranquillity."[27] Lanzmann's strategy is to make us "feel the difficulties of memory, the gap between reality and recollection." He forces us "to seek the images in our own minds."[28]

Whereas Lanzmann, as Gertrud Koch argues, "remains strictly within the limits of what can be imagined,"[29] Spielberg goes beyond imagination. This, as Yvette Biro perceptively observes, is "a vision of non-being."[30] Lanzmann's film never challenges "the limits of representation." There are no images of the extermination itself, and "its representability is never once suggested by using the existing documentary photographs that haunt every other film on this subject. In this elision, Lanzmann marks the boundary between what is aesthetically and humanly imaginable and the unimaginable dimension of the annihilation. Thus the film itself creates a dialectical constellation: in the elision, it offers an image of the unimaginable."[31] Lanzmann thus not only abandons the "succession of endlessly recycled déjà-vu images"[32] associated with Nazism, but he continues the tradition of conceiving of the Holocaust as defying representation. His subjective camera, as Koch points out, "never exceeds the limit; it takes us just far enough to allow us to sense, on the edge of imagination, the reality of the annihilation."[33] This is, of course, the absolute opposite to Spielberg's intrusive and penetrating camera, which goes right into the showers of the gas chambers—the most horrible, terrifying, and sacred space of Holocaust memory and a locus of denial for the assassins of memory.[34]

One of the unique features of *Shoah* is that "whenever something is narrated, an image (*Vorstellung*) is presented, the image of something which is absent."[35] Lanzmann called this process an " 'incarnation' of the truth 'in the present.' "[36] It is "this 'presence' of the place that Lanzmann uses as a basis for communicating to the audience the powerful evocation of horror in his film."[37] This dialectic of presence/absence with its preference of the word over the image implicitly critiques the privilege traditionally accorded to seeing in Western epistemology. As the film is first "based on what one should 'know' in order to understand what one 'sees,' words pronounced by the witnesses are of prime importance and are used as different sparks that give *Shoah* its first movements as the 're-presentation' of the Holocaust that it wants to be."[38] Lanzmann's critique of our image culture is quite challenging, given the fact that seeing controls the economy of cinema spectatorship. His preference of the word (an obvious choice for a journalist) is expressed through and in cinema, a medium associated with the moving image which has become the most privileged site of visual representation. Furthermore, this critique is made all the more difficult because film is, as Shoshana Felman points out, the "art par excellence which . . . calls upon *witnessing* by *seeing*."[39]

Shoah's dialectics of absent images reaches its climax in the scene when Jan Karski, the former courier of the Polish government in exile, refuses to remember and walks, literally, out of the frame, leaving the spectators to imagine what horrors are still unbearably vivid in a man's mind after thirty years. It is the image of the empty chair left behind this elegant, aristocratic-looking man which haunts the spectators' imagination, impelling them to reflect upon the void and the absence of Jewish culture from Europe and Poland in particular.

Shoah, as Simone de Beauvoir observes, "succeeds in recreating the past with an amazing economy of means—places, voices, faces."[40] The film's evocation of "involuntary memory" through places (the images of young forests and fresh grass at the former destruction sites in Poland) is in line with a great French tradition—the most well-known representative of which is Marcel Proust's novel *A la recherche du temps perdu*—of invoking memory through material objects. But not only memory is invoked through places. The shift of scenery from one type of landscape to another (such as the lush and peaceful green of the destruction sites in Poland, to the blue Mediterranean in Tel Aviv—where Avraham Bomba is interviewed—and the gray monumental

Washington Mall used as a backdrop for Jan Karski's interview) echoes the "Babel"-like effect created by the different languages used in the film.

While *Shoah* abandons the over-familiarity of recycled images associated with Nazism, relying entirely on talking-head interviews, *Schindler's List* reconstructs the past through the memory of other movies and images associated with the 40s. It is a film which invokes the memory of the Holocaust through the imaginary collective memory of the movies. Unlike *Shoah*, which invokes memory through the oral recollection of personal experience delivered by different witnesses and through the evocation of expressive faces and landscapes, the memory recaptured and "relived" through *Schindler's List* is not an "authentic," "reexperienced" memory but a cinema memory produced and recycled by the movie industry. The conscious reliance of *Schindler's List* on the constitution of film as a collective memory thus weakens the link between public memory and personal experience, a link that is so powerful in Lanzmann's *Shoah*. Although *Schindler's List* is based on a real experience, this experience (except in the last scene) is never subsumed into the narrative which favors reconstructed real-like images over evocative ones.

Conclusion: Victimhood, Heroism, and Redemption

One of the interesting points of comparison between *Shoah* and *Schindler's List* is related to the question of identification. What is each narrative's locus of identification? With whom is the spectator asked to identify? Who is the hero and who is the villain? Or to put it in another form: whose story is it anyway? At first this question might look trivial, if not irrelevant. After all, both are films on the Holocaust made by Jewish filmmakers whose commitment to the "Jewish cause" is beyond a shadow of a doubt. Yet a close textual and ideological analysis of both texts may reveal some unexpected latent meanings. The complexity of the dialectics of identification is particularly intriguing with regard to Spielberg's film. Why does the first studio film made on the Holocaust by a Jewish director frame the Holocaust as a moral tale of the "good" (though morally dubious) German? Why is the image of the hero of the Holocaust (hero in the sense of protagonist, as well as the good noble hero) fixed in the memory of movie-goers as that of a German and not a Jew? Spielberg's dialectics of identification seems to be quite complex, if not self-contradictory. It is fairly clear that "because Schindler has captured Spielberg's imagination, the director gives him the film."[41] The expository scene of the film, introducing Schindler to the spectator, vividly captures this fascination. There is a sense of the film's fetishistic delight in Schindler's dazzling (erotic?) paraphernalia: "the silk suit, the swaggering tie, the cuff-links, the gold Nazi pin, the bank notes that appear in his hand beneath the waiter's nose."[42] Liam Neeson, cast as Schindler, is, as David Thomson suggests, "all seduction." His "hollow panache, a flat sexy look, a connoisseur's calm,"[43] as well as his towering figure, all glorify him as a master-race prototype against a backdrop of "dwarfed" (literally and narratively) Jewish slaves. Indeed some criticism was leveled at Spielberg in response to what was perceived as the anonymity of the Jewish victims. Frank Rich in the *New York Times* criticized the film for portraying the Jewish characters as "generic." Spielberg, according to him, muted the atrocities by the anonymity of the film's Jews, who were neither individualized nor intimately characterized, as in Anne Frank.[44] Art Spiegelman goes even further and blames Spielberg for gentrifying "Julius Streicher's *Der Sturmer* caricatures."[45] Steven Buman, to give another example, claims that like *Sophie's Choice*, *Schindler's List* is a Christian narrative on the Holocaust. It is based on an archetypal opposition between good Christian slave owners and bad Christian slave owners. The Jews, in this narrative, are only a backdrop for Schindler's catharsis and redemption. In and of themselves, they are of no importance.[46] Uri Kleine, an Israeli film critic, discusses Spielberg's identification with Schindler in terms of an identification with power (and I would also add with prowess, given Schindler's reputation as a womanizer). Both Spielberg and Schindler gravitate proudly to the center of capitalism, and both attempt to redeem the easy money they have made through the performance of "a good deed." As Schindler was trying to save life through his capital, so Spielberg is trying to resurrect destroyed life through his capital.[47]

Spielberg's identification with Schindler as a locus of "good power" is conveyed also through his perverse identification with Jewish victimization. Before winning the Oscar for *Schindler's List*, Spielberg presented himself in many interviews as a victim of his success and equated his "victimization" with Jewish victimization during the Holocaust. "I've always been the victim of my own success," he said. "I have so many years of sort of the Good Housekeeping Seal of Approval stamped on my forehead, the way the Jews wore the star, you know, and I'm proud of it; the Jews were proud to wear the star as well."[48] One cannot help but be perplexed, if not revolted, by the perverse logic presented in this argument. Although here Spielberg expresses identification with the victims, and not the good German, his identification is problematic for several reasons. First, the disclaimer that the Jews were proud to wear the yellow star is a revisionist reading of the history of the Holocaust. It is more in line with the colonization of the symbols of the Holocaust by the American-born Jewish far-right than with any notion of historical truth.[49] Second, it points toward Spielberg's inability to identify with real victimization. Even when he expresses an identification with the victims, they must be proud victims. I should point out, however, that to a certain extent, what I describe as Spielberg's perverse dialectics of victimhood has to do with what Peter Novick calls "competitive claims to victimization"[50] which currently dominate American public discourse, a discourse which is increasingly being fragmented along lines of race and ethnicity.

Shoah, released almost a decade before *Schindler's List*, reveals, by contrast, a different frame of identification. The film projects Lanzmann's belief in German collective complicity and a compassionate and admiring look at the victims/survivors who are clearly individuated and humanized.[51] Both directors, however, submit the experience of the Holocaust to the Zionist perspective, which sees the creation of the State of Israel as a process of secular redemption. Both narratives, to use Saul Friedlander's words in a different context, "suggest a mythic link between the destruction of European Jewry and the birth of Israel—i.e. catastrophe and redemption—which in turn, give a new dignity to the Jews of the Diaspora, as victims or survivors."[52] *Shoah* concludes with an interview with Simha Rottem (known as "Kajik") at the Lohame Haghettaot Kibbutz Museum (Ghetto Fighters' Kibbutz) in Israel. Kajik, who was sent by the surviving ghetto fighters to Aryan Warsaw to contact Itzhak Zukerman (Antek), relates his experience of going back to the ruined ghetto. Reflecting on this experience he says: "I didn't meet a living soul. At one point I recall feeling a kind of peace, of serenity." And he adds: "I said to myself: 'I'm the last Jew. I'll wait for morning, and for the Germans.' " Shot in Israel, approximately forty years after the Warsaw ghetto revolt, this highly tragic sentence provides the redemptive closure to *Shoah*. Yet, this redemptive closure is engraved with an apocalyptic awareness. Perhaps, the film implicitly suggests, Jewish history has not ended yet and another catastrophe is waiting just outside the "closed" door. Spielberg's film, on the other hand, suggests total and complete redemption. Its moving ending, shot in Jerusalem, shows the real "Schindler's Jews," accompanied by the actors personifying them, as an expanded tribal family united by its indebtedness to its two patriarchs: "the good German" and "the good American-Jewish director." The potential of this appeal for amnesty (to the murderers) and against amnesia remains to be seen.

Notes

1. This image in fact appears on the cover of the book *Shoah: An Oral History of the Holocaust* (New York: Pantheon Books, 1985), which is the complete text (in English) of the film with a preface by Simone de Beauvoir.

2. André Pierre Colombat, *The Holocaust in French Film* (Metuchen, NJ: Scarecrow Press, 1993), p. 335. For a further discussion of this scene, see Colombat, pp. 335–36.

3. Although Lanzmann read Gakowski's expression as sadistic, he also acknowl-

edged the ambivalence he felt toward this old Polish man who "carries a true open wound that will not cure" (quoted in Colombat, *The Holocaust in French Film*, p. 336).

4. Deborah Dwork and Robert Jan van Pelt. "Reclaiming Auschwitz," in *Holocaust Remembrance: The Shapes of Memory*, ed., Geoffrey H. Hartman (Oxford: Blackwell, 1994), p. 232.

5. Gertrud Koch in *"Schindler's List*: Myth, Movie, and Memory," *Village Voice* 39, no. 13 (March 29, 1994), p. 25. These are excerpts from a roundtable discussion of *Schindler's List* which was held at the Jewish Museum in New York City in March 1994.

6. Quoted in Annette Insdorf, *Indelible Shadows: Film and the Holocaust* (Cambridge: Cambridge University Press, 1989), p. 253.

7. Colombat, *The Holocaust in French Film*, pp. 331–32. A different view is presented by the literary critic Shoshana Felman in her famous article on *Shoah*. According to her the historian Raul Hilberg is presented in the film not as "the ultimate authority on history" but as *"one more* witness. . . . Though the filmmaker does embrace the historical insights of Hilberg, which he obviously holds in complete respect and from which he gets both inspiration and instruction, the film also places in perspective the discipline of history as such, in stumbling on (and giving us to see) the very limits of historiography." Felman quotes Lanzmann himself, who said at Yale that *Shoah* is not a historical film but "it is something else . . . the whole process of the film is a philosophical one." See Shoshana Felman, "Film as Witness: Claude Lanzmann's *Shoah*," in *Holocaust Remembrance*, p. 97.

8. Pierre Vidal-Naquet, *Assassins of Memory: Essays on the Denial of the Holocaust*, trans. Jeffrey Mehlman (New York: Columbia University Press, 1992), p. 111.

9. Quoted in Insdorf, *Indelible Shadows*, p. 254.

10. For a further discussion of the role of the Holocaust in American Jewish identity, see Peter Novick, "Holocaust Memory in America," in *The Art of Memory: Holocaust Memorials in History*, ed. James Young (Munich and the Jewish Museum, New York: Prestel, 1994), pp. 159–65.

11. Simon Louvish, "Witness," *Sight and Sound* 4, no. 3 (March 1994), p. 14.

12. Quoted in Colombat, *The Holocaust in French Film*, p. 313.

13. For a discussion of this issue see Yosefa Loshitzky, *The Radical Faces of Godard and Bertolucci* (Detroit: Wayne State University Press, 1995), pp. 43–44.

14. Colombat, *The Holocaust in French Film*, p. 324.

15. Gertrud Koch, "The Aesthetic Transformation of the Image of the Unimaginable: Notes on Claude Lanzmann's *Shoah*." *October* 48 (Spring 1989), trans. Jamie Owen Daniel and Miriam Hansen, p. 15.

16. Louvish, "Witness," p. 15.

17. For Fredric Jameson, pastiche is a typical postmodernist strategy "amputated of the satiric impulse" which characterizes parody as its modernist counterpart. Fredric Jameson, "Postmodernism, or the Cultural Logic of Late Capitalism," *New Left Review* 146 (July–August 1984), pp. 64–65. Lanzmann's aesthetics, on the other hand, is modernist in its minimalism and asceticism.

18. Fredric Jameson, *Signatures of the Visible* (New York: Routledge, 1990), p. 9.

19. The double motif—a trope typical of both German Expressionism and film noir—is presented through the characters of Schindler and Goeth, who stand apart as the angel and devil, the extremes of human ambivalence. Frequently, the film's brilliant recourse to chiaroscuro lighting either illuminates them as two extremes (one is lighted, the other is in dramatic shadow) or challenges the spectator's perception of who is who.

20. Jameson, *Signatures of the Visible*, p. 219.

21. Jim Hoberman, *"Schindler's List*: Myth, Movie and Memory," p. 24.

22. Louvish, "Witness," p. 12. *Shoah* is unique among films on the Holocaust in its total eschewal of archival footage. As Insdorf points out: "The truths he is after are not necessarily in the photographs captured by German cameras" (*Indelible Shadows*, p. 252). It is often forgotten that most of the visual material we have of the period was shot by the Germans, hence representing the victims from the point of view of the oppressors.

23. Of course, many fiction films on the Holocaust have tried to depict the concentration camp universe. A film such as *Seven Beauties* (1975) by Lina Wertmuller resurrected the camp universe. However, as a black comedy, invested with anarchistic spirit, its portrayal of this universe never claimed the discourse of the real. The television miniseries *War and Remembrance* had a scene in the gas chamber.

24. A testimony to the power of the notion of gas in post-Holocaust Jewish consciousness is the reaction of the Israeli public to the threat of chemical warfare and the use of gas masks during the Gulf War. For a further discussion of this issue, see Brenda Danet, Yosefa Loshitzky, and Haya Bechar-Israeli, "Masking the Mask: An Israeli Response to the Threat of Chemical Warfare," *Visual Anthropology* 6, no. 3 (1993), pp. 229-70. It is no accident that Claude Lanzmann, who was in Israel during the war, spoke out against the government's policy of *havlaga* (restraint) precisely because of the memory of the Holocaust. In fact, *Shoah* is Lanzmann's second film in his trilogy on "Jewish power" (or lack of it). The first film of this trilogy is *Pour Quoi Israel?* (1973). The third, *Tzahal* (1994), is about the IDF (Israeli Defence Forces). It premiered in Paris on October 2, 1994.

25. Terrence Rafferty, "A Man of Transactions," *New Yorker* (December 20, 1993), p. 132.

26. Quoted in Insdorf, *Indelible Shadows*, p. 252.

27. Ibid., p. 254.

28. Louvish, "Witness," p. 15.

29. Koch, "The Aesthetic Transformation of the Image of the Unimaginable," p. 21.

30. Yvette Biro, "The Unbearable Weight of Non-Being," *Cross Currents* 6 (1987), p. 75.

31. Ibid., p. 21.

32. Anton Kaes, "History and Film: Public Memory in the Age of Electronic Dissemination," *History and Memory* 2, no. 1 (Fall 1990), p. 121.

33. Koch, "The Aesthetic Transformation of the Image of the Unimaginable," p. 22.

34. This controversial scene was criticized by some as reinforcing arguments of Holocaust deniers. After all, there was no gas in the shower. Furthermore, the scene (recalling the famous shower scene in Alfred Hitchcock's *Psycho* [1961]) provides the foundation for a new genre of, to use Idith Kurtzweil's suggestive term, "Holocaust Horror." See Idith Kurtzweil, "*Schindler's List*," *Partisan Review* 2 (Spring 1994), p. 203.

35. Koch, "The Aesthetic Transformation of the Image of the Unimaginable," p. 21.

36. Quoted in Colombat, *The Holocaust in French Film*, p. 305.

37. Ibid., p. 314.

38. Ibid., p. 315.

39. Felman, "Film as Witness," p. 92.

40. Simone de Beauvoir, preface, to Lanzmann, *Shoah*, p. iii.

41. David Thomson, "Presenting Enamelware," *Film Comment* 30, no. 2 (March-April 1994), p. 46.

42. Thomson, "Presenting Enamelware," p. 45.

43. Ibid., p. 47.

44. Frank Rich, "Extras in the Shadows," *New York Times*, January 2, 1994, (Late New York Edition), sec. 4, p. 9.

45. Quoted in *"Schindler's List*: Myth, Movie and Memory," p. 26.

46. Steven Buman, "Hhote, Haesed, Vehayeshuha Hanotzrit" (sinner, grace, and Christian redemption), *Hadoar*, March 4, 1994, pp. 13–16, a debate on *Schindler's List* (in Hebrew).

47. Uri Kleine, "Haish lelo Sfekot" (The man without doubts), *Ha'aretz*, March 11, 1994, p. 68 (in Hebrew).

48. Quoted in Toni Shales, "The Man at the Top of 'Schindler's List,' " *Washington Post*, December 15, 1993, p. B1.

49. The yellow star was appropriated as their symbol by the ultra-racist right in Israel (the *Kach* movement and *Kahana Hay*), which emerged out of the rise in America of Meir Kahane and the Jewish Defense League.

50. Novick, "Holocaust Memory in America," p. 161. Novick refers here to the tension existing today between African Americans and American Jews. To a certain extent *Schindler's List* has become a locus of debate between these two groups.

51. I am not ignoring, however, the controversy and the ethical questions associated with Lanzmann's interviewing techniques, which were criticized by some as being cruel to the victims.

52. Friedlander, "Memory of the *Shoah* in Israel," in *The Art of Memory*, p. 152. In fact, that mythic narrative has become the official narrative in both Israeli and American discourse on the Holocaust. For a further discussion of this mythic link in Israeli and American memory culture of the Holocaust, see James Young, *The Texture of Memory: Holocaust Memorials and Meaning* (New Haven: Yale University Press, 1993). See in particular the chapters on Israel and the United States.

6 | But Is It Good for the Jews?
Spielberg's Schindler and the Aesthetics of Atrocity

Sara R. Horowitz

> Aujourd'hui, je ne suis pas sûre que ce que j'ai écrit soit vrai. Je suis sûre que c'est véridique.
> [Today, I am not certain that what I have written is true. I know it is accurate.]
>
> —Charlotte Delbo, *Aucun de nous ne reviendra* [None of Us Will Return]

> Now I know it really happened.
>
> —woman, overheard exiting a theater showing *Schindler's List*

Oprah winfrey, U.S. television's most popular talk show host, declared on national television that the mere act of seeing *Schindler's List* has made her "a better person" as she chastised her audience for not having made time to see it. Christine Todd Whitman, governor of New Jersey, mandated special screenings of Spielberg's film as an antidote to racism and anti-Semitism in her state. Viewers with little prior interest emerge from the theater convinced that the Holocaust "really happened"; some even express interest in reading or viewing survivor testimony. One rabbi, steeped in the historical, literary, and cinematic representations of the Shoah, confessed to me that, viewing Spielberg's film, he had wept for the first time over murdered Jews of Europe and "could finally mourn."

Inherent in this almost universal acclaim for Spielberg's *Schindler* is an acceptance of the film's truth claims, indeed an acceptance of the film as a discourse of the real. In filming Thomas Keneally's historical novel, Spielberg has created a historical movie—that is, a movie as and about history. Both the novel and the film take artistic license in presenting events researched by Keneally and affirmed by historians. Thus, like Keneally's novel (or "non-fiction novel," the term his publisher employs)[1] Spielberg's *Schindler* utilizes a fictionalized vehicle to convey historical information. Although Keneally invents dialogue for his characters and Spielberg compresses events, imagines conversations, and invents confrontations, both artists accurately reconstruct the trappings and settings of the Nazi genocide. The painful attention to detail asserts the historical truth of the story depicted.

As a historical movie, a close kin to docudrama, Spielberg's *Schindler* occupies a ground at once historical and imaginative, a composite of fact and fiction, or "faction." So construed, like most historical films, Spielberg's eludes evaluation according to either historical rigors or aesthetic standards. Although historical films lay claim to history, artistic license is invoked to explain discrepancies from historical fact: It *is*, after all, a movie, it must engage its audience. Correspondingly, although an artistic representation, the film places itself beyond "mere" aesthetic judgment: But that's how it happened.

I suggest instead that a historical film be answerable on both aesthetic and historical grounds. Spielberg's feature film, of course, is not the first imaginative representation of the Nazi genocide. Similar to Shoah fiction, *Schindler's List* is an enactment of memory which attempts cinematically to represent atrocity and survival. The present study interrogates the assumptions inherent in Spielberg's historical film about verisimilitude and reality, as well as the implications about the history, art, and memory of Nazi atrocity. Following Saul Friedlander's insistence on "probing the limits of representation" of Nazi atrocity—that is, thinking deeply and critically about the emplotment and aesthetics of historical and imaginative Holocaust narratives[2]—this essay will examine the film in light of the generic conventions and tropes it employs or refutes, and its implicit conversation with other imaginative depictions of the Nazi genocide. The essay focuses on the film's figuring of Jews, and in particular the eroticization of the Jewish woman victim, as well as the concretization of good and evil (and the "good" and "bad" Germans) in the characters of Schindler and Goeth. I will conclude by examining the ethical implications of the epic film genre.

Schindler: Do I have to invent a whole new language?
Stern: I think so.

When Itzhak Stern, Schindler's Jewish accountant, faces deportation to Auschwitz, Schindler attempts to reassure his right-hand man. In return for the faithful service and expertise that helped build Schindler's fortune, the war profiteer promises a letter of introduction to the commandant at Auschwitz, asking that Stern receive "special treatment." Stern blanches at the mention of a term (*Sonderbehandlung*) which, in Nazi jargon, has acquired a meaning synonymous with murder. Schindler quickly clarifies the benign meaning of his words and demands with a trace of frustration, "Do I have to invent a whole new language?" Stern responds, "I think so."

What is this "new language"? In survivor writing and in the critical discourse about Holocaust representation, the Shoah is frequently discussed as precipitating a crisis in representation: first, because the death taint of Nazi jargon has irretrievably corroded language and symbolic expression; second, because the experience of horror and genocide remains in some sense outside the boundaries of language. Even in the midst of testimony, survivors repeatedly tell listeners and readers that they cannot find the means to adequately convey remembered experience. Primo Levi, for example, complains in his memoirs about Auschwitz that "our language lacks words to express the offense, the demolition of a man";[3] Charlotte Delbo reflects, similarly, "The words do not have the same meaning."[4] This struggle to depict and own the contents of one's memory reveals something about the nature and magnitude of the atrocities of genocide, and about trauma, survival, and memory.

The creation of a "new language" after Auschwitz has occupied writers struggling to represent the Nazi genocide in narrative and in art. In an afterword to *The Painted Bird*, Jerzy Kosinski's autobiographically based novel about a child victim of atrocity during the Third Reich, the author explains that his novel explores the " 'new language' of brutality and its consequent new counter-language of anguish and despair."[5] The boy protagonist of Kosinski's novel passes through a period of muteness before recovering the power of speech which will enable him to bear witness. The passage through the tormented speechlessness of atrocity to a speech saturated with the experience of horror resonates with Paul Celan's "Bremen Speech." In his now famous address, Celan describes speech as going "through its own lack of answers, through terrifying silence, through the thousand darknesses of murderous speech," in order to "resurface, 'enriched' by it all."[6] The boy's struggle against speechlessness self-consciously signals the author's effort to forge this "new language" out of which to construct a Holocaust narrative.

While the cinematic Schindler learns from his grim accountant that the enactment of genocide generates and demands a "new language," Spielberg does not invent a new cinema. Instead, he transforms Keneally's novel into an epic, relying on the conventions of the historical feature film, especially visual verisimilitude. In a sense, the choice to reproduce the conventions of a historical movie without interrogating the limitations of the genre precludes Spielberg's *Schindler* from achieving the masterwork status many viewers have ascribed to it.

The historical feature film, like the historical novel, presents itself as a transparent medium through which one may witness the workings of history. To achieve this, the filmmaker may invent, contrive, stage or reenact scenes, so long as these scenes conform to the known historical facts. While one could evaluate the truth claims of a documentary film by the authenticity of the film footage presented—are the interviews, the original film footage, what they claim to be?—historical films and docudramas assert authenticity on the basis of factual accuracy and verisimilitude. The painstakingly accurate reconstructions of the Kraków ghetto, of the camps at Plaszów and Auschwitz, for example, invite the viewer to imagine that one is looking at the Holocaust itself, or at a film taken at the time. The close resemblance to the topographies represented help assert the claim that the scenes depicting Oskar Schindler, Amon Goeth, and others also closely resemble reality.

The black-and-white, hand-held cinematography of *Schindler's List* reinforces the truth claims of the film. The film seems "old," suggestive of genuine documentary footage. This accounts for the many viewers for whom Spielberg's film conclusively "proved" the existence of the Holocaust. At the same time, because the film is not really old and genuine but merely filmed "as if" it were so, it makes a false claim to authenticity, much like a contemporary family momentarily donning Victorian garb for a sepia-tinted photo whose truth claims may be readily punctured and debunked. As in the "vintage" contemporary photo, *Schindler*'s verisimilitude rests on the two-dimensional surface of things. Spielberg's film mistakes and misrepresents the nature of the Holocaust. The detailed attention to minutiae in reconstructing the appearance of the Kraków ghetto veils the flatness of the film's depiction of ghetto life and death. In one scene, ghetto Jews cluster around a fire, complaining that they have no money, no time to "organize a thought." To the dismay of a wealthy couple accustomed to their spacious, luxuriously appointed apartment in what has become the Aryan section of Kraków (anyplace not in the ghetto), their shared ghetto quarters are bleak and crowded. Missing from the film is a sense of the daily attrition of hunger, disease, the numbing omnipresence of death, the "filthy louse" that even Adam Czerniakow, eldest in the Warsaw ghetto, complained of finding on his shirt, details which inform other filmic representations of ghetto life, for instance, Alan Adelson's *Lodz Ghetto*. The film gives no sense of how the self becomes eroded and ultimately displaced by the extremities of hunger—how the ghetto inhabitant becomes "90 percent your stomach and a little bit you," as Leyb Goldin describes himself in his ghetto diary.[7] From the privileged distance of contemporary American Jewry, the European Jewish community is idealized nostalgically and also flattened, without the sense that emerges so strongly from ghetto diaries of class, religious, and ideological differences among Jews, and of the vitality and diversity of Jewish culture.

Ultimately, of course, verisimilitude—no matter how successful—is not reality but artifice posing as reality. When this "as if" posture goes on uninterrupted by a self-conscious moment, the film presses its claim for historical truth simply by virtue of being film. Especially with films representing the Shoah, this unproblematized transparency—an illusion created by elaborate staging—has dangerous undertones. Staged—that is, falsified—film images played an important role in facilitating and justifying the Nazi genocide in German newsreels. A filmed version of Theresienstadt, for example, elaborately set up to resemble an idyllic village for Jews, occludes the real camp, which remains unseen by the camera lens. Emanuel Ringelblum and Adam Czerniakow describe intricately staged newsreels that Nazi camera crews filmed in the Warsaw ghetto. "Every scene is directed," Ringelblum observes in his diary.[8] Such a powerful and pernicious use of staged documentaries renders problematic a film whose truth assertions rest on verisimilitude. In view of the intensive and innovative use of film as a Nazi propaganda vehicle, Holocaust film needs to be suspicious of its own power to dramatize, to persuade, and to substitute celluloid representations for genuine events.

Spielberg's film gestures back to other cinematic representations of the Holocaust by means of ample quotations of previous films, particularly films which broke new ground. For example, Spielberg depicts heaps of luggage whose contents the ghetto Jews sorted into massive piles of glasses, shirts, shoes, gold teeth, and other objects. The items belonged to Jews deported from the ghetto and murdered. The scene evokes Alain Resnais's documentary *Night and Fog*, one of the first Holocaust documentaries, where similar mounds evoke the grisly death of Jews in the death camp. As in Resnais's film, the heaps of possessions stand in for the corpses of their owners, providing a bearable metonymic representation of atrocity. Similarly, as the train carrying women from Schindler's factory nears Auschwitz, a Polish onlooker in a field beside the track draws his finger along his throat in a gesture representing death, a moment imported from Claude Lanzmann's *Shoah*. The scene in the shower at Auschwitz reproduces in tone and mood the shower scene at a Nazi brothel in Zbynek Brynuch's *The Fifth Horseman Is Fear*, a consonance whose implications I shall return to later.

Spielberg's use of filmic quotations suggests not only that *Schindler's List* participates in a long tradition of Holocaust films, but that it is the culmination of these prior attempts to represent the Holocaust cinematically—suggests, in other words, that the present film functions as a master narrative for the murder of the Jews of Europe. The black and white cinematography reinforces the sense of a "serious" rather than an "entertainment" film.

At the same time, however, the conventional historical movie is extraneous to the production of history, undercutting *Schindler*'s claim to seriousness. At best—that is, when flawlessly accurate—the "faction" of the historical feature film conveys information already uncovered by and known to historians, to an audience who can receive it only in a less demanding, less rigorous format. Film thus becomes the vehicle for transmitting the already known, already interpreted, always redundant and superfluous. A movie *about* history is a diminished form of representation, educational only in the limited sense of presenting a soft version of history, but not in the sense of stimulating critical thought. By basing his cinematic choices on the unproblematized conventions of fictionalized history, Spielberg unwittingly undermines the film's claims *as* history, thus trivializing film's potential.

This is not to say that filmic representations of the Shoah need be only gilded illuminations of factual casebooks. To accomplish something other than transmitting the already known, film—like fictional narrative—may interrogate the way we think of history, enabling viewers to see something not noticed before, to think differently or more deeply. Unlike historical feature films—movies *about* history—whose closure and transparent representations leave the viewer resolved, films *as* history or films that think history leave viewers unsettled. Rather than teaching a set of facts derived and imposed from outside, feature films—like fictional narrative—can examine the ways in which people perceive, remember, and reconstruct the events they live through, recollect, and record. Not merely illustrations or enactments of sets of historical facts arrived at elsewhere, feature films may themselves be the working out of historical meanings.

Schindler to Rabbi: You should be preparing for the Sabbath.

In filming the Holocaust, *Schindler's List* reproduces negative stereotypes of Jews, whose victimization serves as the arena for Oskar Schindler's spiritual transformation. The film opens with an image of the sanctification of the Jewish Sabbath through the lighting of Sabbath candles and the intoning of the benediction over wine, the *Kiddush*. The candles burn down, literalizing the term Holocaust as an offering to God wholly consumed by flames. Thus the candles symbolize the extinguishing of European Jewish life and the burning of Jews in the crematoria. The smoke from the extinguished candle blends into the smoke of a train bringing displaced Jews to Kraków station. The Jews of Europe are emblemized by the flame of the Sabbath candles, and the extinguishing caused by the Holocaust is later reversed imagistically by the lighting of Sabbath candles in Schindler's Czechoslovakian factory—reversed by Schindler's act of saving Jewish lives.

This initial emblemizing of the Jews as Sabbath candles signals to viewers that *Schindler's List* will be a film about religion, or a religious film, specifically a film about Judaism. The pair of scenes in which the Jewish Sabbath is sanctified bracket the Nazi genocide, marking its beginning and its ending. But, apart from serving as icons of Eastern European Judaism, viewed externally and nostalgically, the ritual acts and objects of sanctification are not given any depth or Jewish meaning. A Jewish spiritual crisis is neither precipitated nor resolved in *Schindler's List*; unlike Elie Wiesel's *Gates of the Forest* or André Schwarz-Bart's *Last of the Just*, Spielberg's film does not chart the Jewish victim's struggle with the Jewish God. Instead, the film turns out to be about Christianity, transforming Schindler into a prodigal son and ultimately into one of the Christ-like saviors that populate Spielberg's films. *E.T.*, for example, is replete with Christological references. The alien humanoid who proves himself more-than-human comes to earth from a "home" beyond the skies (heaven) to redeem humans from a bleak, valueless life devoid of loving connections because humans cannot save themselves. Similarly Schindler, whose face is backlit, illuminated, or framed with a halo, and who looks on his Jews from above, rescues the powerless, death-bound Jews. Schindler saves "his" Jews—whom he calls "my people"—physically and redeems them spiritually.

The double presence of Jewish ritual objects and recitations masks the marginality of Judaism as religion. The insignificance of Judaism is further affirmed by a second pair of scenes associated with sacred ritual, the two church scenes. In the first, Schindler makes initial contact with Jewish black marketeers and smugglers; in the second, he renews contact with his estranged wife and promises fidelity. The first church scene opens on a group of Jewish men meeting in a church to conduct black market transactions. The scene evokes the anti-Semitic canard of Jews desecrating sacred Christian ritual and space. Entering the sanctuary, the Jews dip their fingers into holy water, then transact illegal business deals. As the Jews obtain rare and expensive items, such as silk shirts, chocolate, and hosiery, the film reproduces the anti-Semitic stereotype of the crafty, canny, well-connected Jew, as promulgated in the *Protocols of the Elders of Zion*.

The first church scene resonates with the New Testament's multiple descriptions of Jews defiling the Temple and Jesus' consequent need to purify the holy space by throwing out the Jewish money changers (Matt. 21:12–13, Mark 11:15–17, Luke 19:45–46). Jewish readers understand this to imply that Jesus interrupts and displaces traditional modes of Jewish worship. The money changers, after all, facilitated the purchase of sacrificial doves. Christian readers, on the other hand, see in this a prohibition against doing business on hallowed ground: "You shall not make of my house a house of trade" (John 2:16). Historically, the image of the Jewish money changer whose presence defiles sacred space conflates with the Jew as money lender, with the troping of the Jew as materialistic and avaricious. Jewish attachment to money over attachment to God, to nation, or to other people is repeatedly portrayed in Nazi propaganda newsreels and feature films, such as *Jud Süss*. *Schindler's List* reinforces the stereotype of the money-grubbing Jew by repeatedly focusing on rich Jewish families. During the forced move to the Kraków ghetto, the camera takes us into the opulent home of wealthy Jews; the woman exits wear-

ing a fur coat. Later, as the ghetto is liquidated (a euphemism for the deportation and murder of its Jewish inhabitants), a Jewish family hastily wraps its
ample cache of diamonds in bread and consumes it.

In the film, Jews partake of Christian sacred ritual, such as holy water,
and violate sacred Christian space. This desecration resonates with the widespread anti-Semitic folk belief that Jews steal and defile the Eucharist. Similarly, the physical traits of Jewish men in Spielberg's film correspond with the
image of the Jew in folk culture. The longstanding stereotype of the Jew in
the European imagination as puny, short, pushy, and dirty, physically marks
the Jewish male. These characteristics distinguish him from Christians. What
Hitler referred to as the Jew's "alien" face proved the Jew's unassimably alien
status. These real and imagined physical differences comprised an important component of modern anti-Semitism, providing visible "racial" markers
which substitute for the invisible physical mark of circumcision.

In the popular imagination, this visible difference between Jew and Christian, or Jew and Aryan, is reinforced by the "secret language" of the Jews,
which separates them not only physically but also linguistically from the
dominant culture.[9] When Stern brings Jewish investors to meet with Schindler
in the latter's limousine, the Jews huddling in the back seat could be straight
out of a Nazi propaganda poster on eugenics and racial science. One appears
apelike, with a large jaw covered in stubble. Disheveled, large-nosed and un-
kempt, the Jews contrast negatively with Schindler's clean good looks, as the
short stature of Jews contrasts repeatedly with Schindler's towering height.
Spielberg films the Jews through the rear-view mirror so that Schindler's gaze
becomes the viewer's gaze. The Jews mutter in Yiddish, the "secret" language
of Eastern European Jews. In European popular belief, the evocation of this
secret Jewish language becomes a trope for the otherness of the Jew.

Schindler to Helen Hirsch: It's not that kind of kiss.

The opening scene of *Schindler's List* depicts the ritual Sabbath candles
without the presence of a woman or a woman's voice. In traditional Judaism,
the woman of the house inaugurates the Sabbath by lighting Sabbath candles
and intoning a blessing. Both rabbinic literature and Jewish folk culture
strongly associate candles with the Jewish woman—especially the Jewish
mother—such that the candles become an emblem for Jewish womanhood. In
Spielberg's film, viewers see the candles but hear a male voice reciting the *Kiddush*, the sanctification of the Sabbath over wine, an act traditionally performed by the man of the house. The subsuming of the female voice by the
male, and the consequent melding of specifically male and female ritual acts—
acts which serve as gender markers in traditional Judaism—is endemic to the

film on two levels: the occlusion of the female behind the male, and the feminization of the Jewish male. The women in *Schindler's List*, whether Jewish or Aryan, exist only as a locus of male struggle and desire. At the same time, the film's Jewish men transmute into the category of women when in relation to Aryans, notably Goeth and Schindler.

Just as the film reproduces the stereotypical image of the puny and aggressive Jewish male, it presents the Jewish woman as the alluring dark beauty in the mode of Rebecca of Sir Walter Scott's *Ivanhoe*. In Nazi propaganda, her visual loveliness veils a hidden racial repulsiveness. The Jewess tempts Aryan men into the crime of miscegenation, whose monstrous offspring make visible the Jewess's real ugliness. In imagining a Jewess who tempts men into liaisons with dangerous consequences, this prevalent image depicts Jewish women as agents of their own sexual violation and projects onto them male desire. *Schindler's List* adeptly exposes this mixture of attraction, fear, and revulsion through the relationship between Amon Goeth and Helen Hirsch and through the comments of Schindler's cellmate, who warns that "Jewish girls . . . cast a spell on you."

At the same time, however, *Schindler's List* also eroticizes the Jewish female victim of Nazi atrocity. As the film enacts the progress of genocidal brutality, sexuality becomes linked with violence. The repeated representation of brutality acted out on the bodies of women evokes a common trope of Holocaust films, the eroticized woman victim. Figured in an unproblematized manner in such films as *Sophie's Choice* and *The Night Porter*, and critiqued in films such as *Angry Harvest*, the trope reaches its most extreme form in pornographic paperback novels which utilize the camp setting and the relationship between Nazis and female inmates as the occasion for the playing out of sadomasochistic fantasies.[10] In Spielberg's film, during the long sequence involving camp commandant Amon Goeth and Helen Hirsch, a beautiful camp inmate pressed into service as his personal maid, *Schindler's List* titillates the viewer with the suggestion that Helen Hirsch, already marked for death, will be sexually violated as well before the genocide is completed.

Goeth's pathological brutality is revealed in two scenes with women—one with Helen Hirsch, one with Goeth's Aryan mistress—by means of a displaced sexual transaction. Beginning with the intimacy of a manicure and ending in Goeth's beating of Helen, the sequence between the commandant and his maid explicitly links sexuality with violence. After the manicure scene, where Goeth becomes visibly aware of the physical nearness and femaleness of Helen's body, he follows her into the cellar, which serves, apparently, as her living quarters. As Goeth catches sight of her and she fills the camera's gaze, Helen is clothed in an inexplicably wet shift which clings to her breasts. The audience thus participates in Goeth's erotic gaze. Like Goeth, the viewer is meant to desire Helen's body, visually sexualized by the wet clothing. As Goeth's desire resolves in a physical beating, the audience participates in a voyeurism which encompasses both sex and brutality, with the victimized Jewish woman as its object.

The appeal to the audience's voyeurism is repeated in the shower scene at Auschwitz, a scene pornographic both for its depiction of terrified, naked Jewish women and for its use of the gas chamber to provoke the viewer's sense of suspense. In Resnais's *Night and Fog*, the camera probes this dark center of genocide years after the final killing. Aware of the magnitude of horror and sheer human misery of the place, Resnais's narrator momentarily pauses. "You have to know to look," he says quietly, before explaining what the camera reveals: fingernail marks left on the gas chamber ceiling by the death-struggles of its victims.

Unlike Resnais, however, Spielberg's camera does not hesitate but follows the victims right into the gas chamber. Spielberg can do this, of course, because the gas chamber turns out not to be a gas chamber at all but a real shower room, benignly cleansing the women with a fine spray of water. The protracted scene uses the historical memory of mass murder to manipulate viewers; the women fearfully await the suffocating fumes of Zyklon B and the audience wonders whether it will view real killing. Since in any case *Schindler's List* would not show actual gassing but only a staged representation, the audience is permitted to anticipate viewing the ultimate atrocity. Until its moment of resolution in the film, the gas/shower sequence titillates with the promise of a kind of kinetic wax museum of horrors. The anticipated enactment of genocide is thrilling because it is forbidden and at the same time permitted because it is artifice.

So intent on exploiting the admixture of horror, nudity, and life-and-death suspense of the gas/shower scene, the film makes a gross miscalculation. While Spielberg repeatedly explains that he filmed *Schindler's List* to affirm his Jewish heritage and the historical truth of the Holocaust, the film's treatment of the phenomenon of the gas chamber seemingly confirms not the testimony of Holocaust survivors but the claims of Holocaust deniers that the Nazi genocide never occurred.

In an earlier scene set in the women's barracks at Plaszów, a young woman repeats the rumors she has heard about gas chambers at Nazi killing centers. When the other women refuse to believe in the existence of such unimaginable death machinery, Mila defends herself. She has merely communicated, not affirmed, what she has heard. "I didn't say I believed it. I said I heard it." Of course, Mila agrees, the rumors could not be true. Any Jew who could possibly know about such killings—anyone who had been inside a gas chamber, she further explains—"wouldn't be around to tell of it." Mila's reasoning resonates with the argument of Holocaust deniers. French philosopher Jean-François Lyotard explains the contention of revisionist Robert Faurisson as follows:

> To have "really seen with his own eyes" a gas chamber would be the condition which gives one the authority to say that it exists. . . . Yet it is still necessary to prove that the gas chamber was used to kill at the time it was seen. The only acceptable proof . . . is that one died from it. But if one is dead, one cannot testify that it is on account of the gas chamber. . . . In order for a place to be identified as a gas chamber, the only eyewitness I will accept would be a victim of this gas chamber; . . . there is no victim that is not dead; otherwise this gas chamber would not be what he or she claims it to be. There is, therefore, no gas chamber.[11]

By representing the claims of the Holocaust deniers within what purports to be a historically accurate film and a master-narrative of sorts, Spielberg sets up the expectation that *Schindler's List* will strongly refute those claims. Nothing of the sort occurs. Instead, the film ends up affirming the arguments of the deniers. In light of the debate in the Plaszów barracks, the spray of shower water which finally allays both the women's fear that they will perish and the audience's fear that they will witness this murder, also seemingly refute the reality of the gas chamber.

The shower scene provides another occasion for the camera to eroticize the Jewish female body. The nude bodies beneath the jets of water gesture to a visually similar scene in Brynuch's Czechoslovakian feature film, *The Fifth Horseman Is Fear*. In Brynuch's shower scene, a group of Jewish women prepare themselves to "service" soldiers in a Nazi brothel where the film's male protagonist comes to find his sister. The camera lingers on the faces and bodies of the women. Slow, fluid, and softly lit, the scene is markedly different from the rest of the film in mood, tone, and lighting. Moreover, its depiction is superfluous to the development of the film's plot. Indeed, after the film's completion, the shower scene was inserted at the insistence of producer Carlo Ponti, in hopes of making the film more marketable. Thus, both the contents of the scene and the circumstances of its production reveal it as yet another instance of the eroticization of the female Holocaust victim.

The ambivalence of Goeth's attraction to Helen, and the vulgar comment of Schindler's cellmate about intercourse with Jewish women ("Did your prick fall off?") reveal the film's awareness of the complicated trope of the eroticized Jewess in the popular imagination. But the film's critique of the trope, inherent in the intimate brutality of Goeth's beating Helen, is undercut by the film's own imagistic linking of eros and violence. The association of sexuality with atrocity implicates not only the Jewish woman but the Aryan woman as well. The everyday pathology of Goeth's murderous urges are frequently enacted in a sexually charged atmosphere, most notably in the presence of his mistress. For example, while a selection takes place in the *Appellplatz* below, Goeth sits bare-chested for his physical examination. Not without irony, the film depicts Goeth's physician chiding the commandant for being "too fat" while starving Jews jog past Nazi doctors hoping to be judged healthy enough to be utilized as slave labor. Goeth talks of the need to "make room" for "new shipments" by killing substandard Jews. Throughout this contemplation of murdering Jews, Goeth's mistress caresses his bare chest. Thus, Goeth's sexual potency depends on his health and his power to kill.

The film pursues this connection in the sequence where Goeth stands bare-chested on his balcony, randomly firing at Jews with his rifle. The camera cuts from the commandant to the naked woman lying in his bed, to Goeth shooting, to the Jews below, to his mistress. Finally Goeth struts into the bedroom, aims the rifle at the woman, then urinates into a toilet. The series of images links killing to masculinity. Goeth aims his rifle at his mistress, making the weapon into the equivalent of a penis. Instead of discharging from his rifle and shooting her, he moves past her and urinates. The sequence equalizes the acts of shooting, fornication, and urination. On an obvious level, the scene underscores the casualness of death and the seaminess of Goeth's character. At the same time, it asserts an equivalence among Jews, his mistress, and the toilet, all repositories for Nazi effluvia. Atrocity is enacted with semen, urine, or gunshot. Such an equation suggests a critique of war, or fascism, or Nazism, on the basis of patriarchy or male sexuality. In *Male Fantasies*, Klaus Theweleit links racism and fascist terror with the fear of woman as other. His study of the images of woman in the writing of officers of the Frei Corps, German volunteer armies after World War I, implicates real and imagined brutality toward women in the construction of masculine identity and male bonding.[12] But Spielberg's film does not advance such a critique; rather, it simply absorbs and reproduces these images of women and violence, without knowingly interrupting or interrogating their production.

In *Schindler's List*, women remain in some sense outside the war between Nazis and Jews. Ultimately the film's erotic economy blurs the difference between the Aryan women who fornicate with Goeth or Schindler and the Jewish women whom the men may desire, fantasize, even shoot, but may not know carnally. Shooting becomes the cinematic equivalent of sex. The mistresses of the Aryan protagonists have no life, no personality beyond their sexual function, just as Jewish women have no life beyond the camps. Not only does this comparison blur the real—the historical—differences between Jewish and Aryan women, but it occludes the fascist concept of the ideal woman and the German glorification of Aryan motherhood.[13] The film depicts woman as morally inert; like Jews, she seemingly represents a natural category, reifying stereotypical images of gender and race.

Since *Schindler's List* sets up shooting as the cinematic equivalent of sexual penetration, Jewish men become women—that is, helpless and violated. The Jewish men on screen are consistently shorter, weaker, narrower, more slight than the Aryan men whom they live to serve (they live literally because they serve). The effeminized Jewish male contrasts sharply with the virile and lusty Aryan male. The film thus effaces Jewish manhood, already negated by the contemporary American popular perceptions of the Jew out of which the film emerges. Indeed, contemporary American culture problematizes Jewish male virility, figuring Jewish men as sexually insecure and inadequate (for example, Miles, the Jewish producer on television's *Murphy Brown*), or as overcompensating with sexual aggression (as in some of the plays of Neil Simon).

Schindler's List unfolds as a contest of Aryan manhood, with women and Jews as the proving ground. In the film's first sequence involving Schindler, he impresses important Nazi officials and solidifies useful connections over the bodies of scantily clad showgirls. The film alternates between cuts of a key Nazi officer's lustful gaze and the showgirls' legs. When a photographer snaps a photo of Schindler, the Nazi officer, and his girlfriend, the Nazi shifts in front of the woman. The move effectively blocks her out of the shot so that only he and Schindler appear in the photograph. This suggests that Nazism is strictly a male enterprise. Indeed, Aryan women function in the film almost exclusively as objects of lust. Not until the Auschwitz sequence do we see SS women.

The film posits two contesting models of manhood—Schindler and Goeth. The film asks, What is a real man—the sadist or the savior? The male character's relationship to women not only asserts his virility but also serves as a marker for his corruption or innocence. The contrast between Goeth and Schindler is brought out by the scene each shares with Helen Hirsch in the cellar at Plaszów. Although Goeth desires her, wishes "to reach out and touch you in your loneliness," and although he has utter control over her life and death, he cannot bring himself to act on his desire. Instead, following the film's equation of sex and violence, he beats her. Schindler, on the other hand, listens compassionately to her narrative of suffering. In contrast to Schindler's succession of mistresses, Helen's face glows angelically, the backlighting creating a halo around her face. Finally he kisses her forehead, not sexually but chastely. "It's not that kind of kiss," he reassures her.

Throughout the film, Jews praise Schindler's goodness: "They say you are good." The film revolves around the paired issues of Schindler's goodness and his manhood, initially posed oppositionally. Finally these two aspects conflate when he gives Helen "not that kind of kiss." While neither Schindler nor Goeth violate Helen sexually, Schindler's chaste kiss affirms that, unlike the commandant, he views her as a "person in the strictest sense." Schindler's version of manhood wins out over Goeth's because, the film suggests, to be a real man is to be good.

However, Schindler's chaste kiss veils, rather than interrupts, the eroticization of violence, revealing a moral confusion at the center of the film. Since in Nazi ideology, Helen Hirsch is "not a person" because she is Jewish, Goeth's refusal to rape her confirms his status as a loyal Nazi. Goeth's beating of Helen is interpolated with cuts of Schindler kissing a series of sexually attractive women, including a beautiful Jewish camp inmate. Women, because they are women, are also not persons "in the strictest sense of the word." Schindler's prison confession, "I kissed a Jewish girl," merely shifts the Jewish woman from one category of nonperson to another. Nonetheless, Schindler's willingness to act out his desire on the body of a Jewish woman marks him as good in the film's moral economy, while Goeth's refusal to rape Helen marks him as evil.

Stern to Schindler: The list is an absolute good.

Ultimately, however, chastity rather than promiscuity becomes the barometer of goodness. We witness Schindler's spiritual metamorphosis by observing the transition in his sexual relationships. As Schindler becomes more "good"—more authentically Schindler—he kisses chastely rather than demandingly and finally promises fidelity to his wife. Thus, Schindler proves his manhood through the enactment of Christian virtue. This further conflates the atrocity done to Jews with the eros of violence. It also, problematically, makes genocide and fornication into moral equivalents.

What makes Schindler "good"? The life-giving list, Stern tells him, is "an absolute good." After transporting the Jews on the list to the safety of the new factory in Czechoslovakia, Schindler goes to church. This second church scene counterbalances the earlier one where he attempts to set up business contacts with Jewish black marketeers. Before, he deliberately sat alongside Jews, partaking of their defilement of sacred space. Now, he sits behind his wife, who prays. Instead of profaning the sacred, he renews the sacraments of marriage: "No doorman or maitre d' will ever mistake you." He promises fidelity. As the war ends, Schindler addresses the Jews massed below him, those whose earthly salvation is assured, and makes the sign of the cross. Schindler, in other words, becomes fully Christian, the embodiment of "absolute good."

Schindler's spiritual awakening enables him not only to save the lives of Jews but apparently to save them spiritually as well. In the factory, he berates the rabbi for transgressing the Sabbath. "What day is this? Friday? . . . You should be preparing for the Sabbath." The restoration of Jewish faith through the vehicle of the believing Christian occludes the long history of Christian anti-Semitism in Europe, a history which facilitated the enactment of Hitler's Final Solution. The (kosher?) wine Schindler unaccountably provides for the sanctification of *Kiddush* masks the historical instances of blood accusations in Europe, where Jews were massacred on false charges of substituting Christian blood for sacramental wine. In *Schindler's List*, the Sabbath candles burn anew in Schindler's factory. The Jew becomes a Jew—adopts the emblem of the Jew—only when the Christian becomes a Christian. Judaism, in other words, is redeemed through Christianity.

After liberation, Schindler asks for three minutes of silence to mourn the dead. Holocaust narrative repeatedly invokes the trope of the mute witness, the survivor silenced by loss, by atrocity, by trauma, by the sheer meaningless-ness of horror. Spielberg's Jews, however, do not remain silent. Rather than risk a representation of the mute witness, or of the utter incomprehensibility of the Shoah, Spielberg chooses to relinquish the filmic possibilities for genuine reflection—the blank screen, for example, that Abraham Ravett utilizes in his memorial film, *Everything for You. Schindler's List* quickly displaces the invoked silence with a recitation of the *Kaddish*, the traditional mourner's prayer. Nei-ther the film's Jews nor the audience may participate in a silent commemora-tion, in a silence commensurable with the unspeakableness of the atrocity inflicted on the Jews of Europe.

The film's reinstitution of the verbal icons of Judaism occurs in a sequence markedly different from earlier segments of the film. Previously, pseudodocu-mentary sequences suggested that the camera had simply been left rolling as history unfolded. Through its placement at personal interchanges fraught with historical significance, the pseudodocumentary conveys both the imper-sonality of history and an intimacy with its key players. However, from the arrival at the Schindler factory in Czechoslovakia, the scenes are visibly staged, played for emotional manipulation through speechifying and theatri-cality rather than for verisimilitude. Of course, the earlier sequences are also elaborately structured to manipulate the audience. But in the Czechoslovakia sequence the conventions shift from pseudodocumentary to the sentimental epic, the mode already imbedded in the earlier verisimilitude. It is in this con-text that *Schindler's List* reintroduces Jewish ritual.

The easy and sentimentalized resumption of Jewish ritual practice ignores the effect of the Holocaust on contemporary Jewish theology. Marking the be-ginning and end of genocide with a representation of Jewish ritual practice—the sanctification of the Sabbath—the film posits a closure to the catastrophe, hiding the rupture caused to the continuum of Jewish history and thought. I am not suggesting that the Shoah left Judaism culturally and religiously defunct. Indeed, as Allen Mintz, David Roskies, and others have argued,[14] Judaism has struggled to absorb the memory of Jewish catastrophe into collective consciousness, narrative, and sacred ritual. However, reaching across history, Judaism has been indelibly marked, just as the survivor has been marked, by the encounter with genocide. In seamlessly weaving the before and after, *Schindler's List* effaces the presence of the Shoah in contemporary Jewish life and thought.

In discussing theology and ethics after the Holocaust, Irving Greenberg suggests that "no statement, theological or otherwise, should be made that would not be credible in the presence of the burning children."[15] If so, then the rekindled Sabbath candles should evoke not only the liberation of Jewish practice from genocidal oppression, but also the burning of Jewish bodies in the concentration camp crematoria, an association the film evokes in its early cut from candle smoke to train smoke. Brought into the later Sabbath scene, the association of Jewish ritual and Jewish deaths should complicate the scene, weighting the triumphalism with irretrievable loss. Instead, in service to the sentimental moment, the intonation of the Sabbath sanctification functions only to cap Schindler's spiritual transformation, affirm his largesse, and reassure the audience that nothing has been lost.

The film contains a nugget of popular American Jewish theology: after the ashes of Auschwitz, the birth of Israel. The morning after Schindler's midnight departure from his Czechoslovakian factory, the Schindlerjuden learn that the entire world hates Jews. Told, improbably, by a Russian soldier that they can go neither east nor west, the liberated Jews realize that the only safe haven is Zion. Ostensibly in search of food, the Jews crest the Czechoslovakian horizon, with the line of people extending from one edge of the screen to the other. The Czechoslovakian landscape becomes any landscape. To the strains of Naomi Shemer's hit song of the Six Day War (1967), "Jerusalem of Gold," the black-and-white film turns into color, marking the movement from past to present. Czechoslovakia transmutes into Jerusalem, implying that the only place for a Jew after the Holocaust is Israel and that the rebirth of Zion redeems the catastrophe. In an American film by a Jewish American director, the unproblematized reproduction of this political-religious ideology, even in popularized form, posits a distance between the endangered Jews of Europe whose only refuge is Israel, and the American (secular) Jews who comprise part of the film's audience and who thrive in safety elsewhere. While it expresses horror at atrocity and pity for Shoah victims, the film essentially "others" the survivor. *Schindler's List* posits a distance not only between the contemporary American Jew and the Jew of Europe but between the contemporary American and the Israeli Jew. The continuity of Jewish life and culture, depicted on screen solely as a Zionist phenomenon, frees the American Jew from living out

Jewish destiny, just as the easy resumption of Jewish ritual frees the secular Jew from acknowledging the complexities of post-Holocaust theology. Ultimately the American Jew—along with the rest of the viewing audience—identifies with the Aryan Schindler who, from a position of greater security, rescues the less fortunate European/Israeli Jew.

As the film sets up the final sequence—the homage at Schindler's grave site—the Schindlerjuden arrive in Israel because they can go nowhere else. The absence of an American refuge is consonant with the prevailing Zionist interpretation of Jewish history, which views Diaspora life as untenable for Jews anywhere. Michael Berenbaum, director of the U.S. Holocaust Memorial Museum, has stated that, as Americans come to view the Jewish past, they inevitably Americanize it—that is, give its events an "American" meaning in the civic arena.[16] What American uses has Spielberg made of Israel? While the camera portrays the Schindlerjuden of the past as aging and invalid in the present, the image of the virile and handsome Schindler is never displaced. Although a legend on screen informs the viewer that after the war Schindler failed at business and marriage, the film preserves the visual image of Schindler in his prime, not only physically but morally and spiritually.

Elsewhere Spielberg has said that he modeled his Schindler on his mentor and father surrogate, Steve Ross, head of Warner studios. Liam Neeson, the actor who plays Schindler, studied home movies of Ross to learn his mannerisms. While Otto Preminger's *Exodus* constructed a new Jew by imaginatively linking the American Jew with the virile Israeli soldier, *Schindler's List* imagines the American Jew onto the Aryan savior. Thus *Schindler's List* distances the American Jew not only from the old Jew of Europe, but also from Israel, which exists in the film solely as a place for Holocaust survivors and cemeteries—a repository, in other words, of Jewish memory. In the film's reconstruction of the Nazi genocide, many of the European Jews actually speak with an identifiably Israeli accent, thus further conflating the old Jew with the Israeli. Like the culture of the European Jew Israel is viewed sentimentally and nostalgically. But Jewish life is redeemed ultimately in America through identification with and emulation of the successful Christian.

Schindler: Stop the train.

The sentimentality of Spielberg's film repeatedly deflects audience attention from the catastrophe it represents. *Schindler's List* is a feel-good Holocaust film, and not because Schindler ultimately saves the lives of 1,500 Jews. The film consistently draws our attention away from the on-going atrocity and genocide, a deflection masked by the brutality enacted on screen. In the Kraków ghetto early in the film, Stern saves a history and literature professor from transportation. By directing the audience to feel relief at the survival of the man whom the camera has individualized, the film hides the unspeakable tragedy of the anonymous, doomed Jews on the transport trucks. In the Auschwitz sequence, the sheer force of Schindler's will rescues the women mistakenly sent to the camp rather than to Schindler's Czechoslovakian factory. Refusing the commandant's offer of the "next shipment" of women due at the camp, Schindler pays dearly to redeem the women whose faces the audience has come to recognize. From this triumphant negotiation, the camera cuts to the Schindler men, watching the return of their women. The sequence of scenes disallows a recognition that in the economy of the Nazi genocide, the rescue of one "shipment" seals the doom of the other. The unyielding death quota does not diminish Schindler's accomplishment. The film's effacement of it, however, softens the unrelenting nature of atrocity during the Holocaust and the moral complexities of survival that Primo Levi refers to as the "gray zone."

Similarly, in a scene meant to convey Schindler's bold canniness and to presage his altruistic transformation, the industrialist rescues Stern from a train bound for Auschwitz. "Stop the train," he calls, and, indeed, the train stops. And so Stern does not die. The sequence invites the audience to feel relief and joy at the successful rescue of Schindler's accountant. To revel unambivalently in the triumph of Schindler's cleverness, the audience is directed to forget the death-bound human cargo on that train. Their doom serves only to set up Stern's good fortune.

In *Act and Ideology*, Berel Lang insists that the Holocaust generates a "moral discourse—discourse not about moral issues, but *as* moral."[17] Ultimately, although Spielberg's *Schindler* is about morality, it is not a moral film. The filmmaker's unexamined use of the epic genre limits the moral complexity of the film. The old-fashioned epic film revolves around an extraordinary central figure who, even if flawed, changes the course of human events. The epic genre individualizes the exceptional man, but the everyday people remain insignificant and interchangeable. The myriad extras are undifferentiated, stereotypical. The epic always resolves tidily, and its neat closure tells the viewer not to look beyond the film, beyond the borders of the screen. But to be a moral discourse, Holocaust film must propel its viewers out of the film—back into history and out into the present, then back into the film to interrogate the representation and the phenomenon.

Part of the neatness of the epic consists in affirming the ultimate rightness of what transpires. Why did some people survive and others perish? The depiction of victims and survivors in *Schindler's List* suggests that survivors have earned their survival; by implication, then, the film blames victims for their own death. The young boy saved from Goeth in the camp merits survival. He is shown earlier hiding a Jewish woman under the stairs during the liquidation of the ghetto. Later, after the theft of a chicken at the Plaszów camp, a Jewish inmate is randomly shot on the Appellplatz. The quick-thinking boy has the presence to whimper, point to the corpse, and say, "He did it." We know, of course, from survivor testimony and other witnessing that randomness and luck determined who would live. Indeed, Goeth's sniping from his balcony exemplifies the randomness of death. But all of the film's Schindlerjuden survive because they were clever or good or brave or loyal or beautiful. I don't mean to suggest that survivors were not all of these; but others were, as well, and perished anyway. The effect of justifying each act of survival is to reassure the audience of the rightness of the workings of history, and to diminish the outrage at the senseless and brutal murder of millions of people. Goeth's shootings portray the arbitrariness of death, but during the Holocaust, living was random, measured against a backdrop of pervasive death.

Schindler's List is a narrative of heroics whose two central personalities, Schindler and Goeth, vie for primacy. These two larger-than-life figures represent the struggle of absolute good against absolute evil, the angelic against the demonic. Schindler's extraordinary altruism redeems not only his Jews but also Schindler himself. Goeth, on the other hand, kills for the joy of it. The commandant is so evil that the audience cannot comprehend but can only condemn him. Missing from the film is the banality of evil—the daily enactment of atrocity and genocide which permeated even the intimate recesses of its perpetrators' lives. Goeth's psychopathology is a matter of historical record. However, Spielberg's choice to develop *Schindler's List* as a contest between the incomprehensibly good and the incomprehensibly evil prevents the film from developing a complicated sense of the Nazi perpetrator. Just what allows ordinary people to commit extraordinarily brutal acts? What facilitates what Robert J. Lifton refers to as the coexistence of the killer self and the decent self?

The demonization of the Nazi through the outrageously evil Goeth frees viewers from questioning their own possible collusion with racism or prejudice. The antipodal balance between the industrialist and the commandant gives the audience only two alternatives, hence easy release from self-examination. Since we cannot be the demonic Goeth, we surely must be Schindler. The film thus permits the audience a pose of moral superiority without necessitating moral engagement.

Given the sharp impact *Schindler's List* has had on its viewing public, and the surge of popular awareness of the Holocaust, I feel deeply ambivalent about articulating my own critical observations. With the exception of Holocaust deniers and anti-Semitic regimes, only a handful of intellectuals and scholars, and a few Holocaust survivors, have publicly voiced objections to the film. Discussing the film with students, relatives, and neighbors who have felt profoundly moved, I find difficulty voicing my reservations. Criticizing the deep fabric and texture of the film in front of people moved to tears and beyond seems an act of profound insensitivity. Yet to agree with the effusive praise heaped on the film—to agree, for example, that seeing *Schindler's List* of itself makes one a better person, or that it is a flawless representation of the Holocaust—I find equally difficult. Allowing *Schindler's List* to stand as a master-narrative of the Holocaust seems ethically irresponsible.

Is *Schindler's List* an important film? Yes, by virtue of its popularity. Spielberg's film may well be the one vehicle by which many Americans come to learn of the Holocaust. For this audience, the film's version of Holocaust suffering will stand unrefuted by other sources. In addition, some viewers may not know any Jews personally. The film's reproduction of anti-Semitic stereotypes—the greedy, crafty, ugly Jew—may likely be the image they retain. In his study of prewar Germany, George Mosse points out that negative folk images of Jews not only provoked anti-Semitic behavior but also determined the way German Jews constructed their identity and personality. In conscious or unconscious opposition to the predominant stereotypes, German Jews repudiated the "bad" image of the Jew by projecting it onto Eastern European Jews. They adopted the values and norms of the dominant culture, espousing "Germanic ideals of looks and behavior."[18] The extent to which the visual markers of the Jew as "other" unknowingly recur in Spielberg's film is a barometer of the pervasiveness of these images today and their assimilation not only into American culture but into the self-image of American Jews.

The racist and sexist tropes reproduced by the film still exist today. At the very least, a moral discourse about the Shoah ought to interrupt and interrogate those tropes. Perhaps, too, a Holocaust film needs to stand in humility in the face of unspeakable horror, rather than accommodate itself to the hubris of the epic.

From the start, the viewer recognizes Goeth as the villain, Schindler as the hero. The dichotomy places the audience outside the film, admiring one man, condemning the other. The audience is never implicated in the moral economy of the film, never prodded to examine its own social and political ethics. Upon receiving the Academy Award for *Schindler's List*, Spielberg observed, "May we all have Schindlers in our lives!" Perhaps. More to the point would be a request that we all behave like Schindler when circumstances demand and that we attack the underlying attitudes that necessitate a Schindleresque rescue.

Notes

1. Simon & Schuster categorizes Keneally's book as fiction, describing it as "a factual account done with fictional techniques" or a "non-fiction novel," according to Sarah Lyall, "Book Notes," *New York Times*, 9 March 1994, p. C21.

2. Saul Friedlander, ed., *Probing the Limits of Representation: Nazism and the "Final Solution"* (Cambridge: Harvard University Press, 1992).

3. Primo Levi, *Survival in Auschwitz: The Nazi Assault on Humanity*, trans. Stuart Woolf (New York: Collier, 1969), p. 22.

4. Charlotte Delbo, *Aucun de nous ne reviendra* (Paris: Editions de Minuit, 1970), p. 60.

5. Jerzy Kosinski, *The Painted Bird* (Boston: Houghton, 1976), p. 256.

6. Paul Celan, *Collected Prose* (Manchester: Carcanet Press, 1986), p. 34.

7. Leyb Goldin, "Chronicle of a Single Day," trans. Elinor Robinson, rpt. in *The Literature of Destruction*, ed. David G. Roskies (Philadelphia: Jewish Publication Society, 1988), p. 425.

8. Emanuel Ringelblum, *Notes from the Warsaw Ghetto*, trans. Jacob Sloan (New York: McGraw Hill, 1958). See also Adam Czerniakow, *The Warsaw Diary of Adam Czerniakow*, ed. Raul Hilberg et al., trans. Stanislaw Staron et al. (New York: Stein & Day, 1979).

9. The very word "barbarian" evokes the incomprehensible "ba ba" of foreign speakers, asserting that otherness is conveyed through language. In Lanzmann's *Shoah*, Polish farmers recollect hearing from passing trains the guttural and incomprehensible "ra ra" of Jewish speech.

10. For a discussion of pornographic uses of Nazi imagery, see Catherine Itzin, "Entertainment for Men," *Pornography: Women, Violence and Civil Liberties* (Oxford: Oxford University Press, 1992), pp. 27–53.

11. Jean-François Lyotard, *The Differend: Phrases in Dispute*, trans. Georges Van Den Abbeele (Minneapolis: University of Minnesota Press, 1988), p. 4.

12. Klaus Theweleit, *Male Fantasies*, vols. 1 and 2 (Minneapolis: University of Minnesota Press, 1987 and 1989). See also Sander Gilman's discussion of the connections between the fear of woman, of the racial other, of death, in *Difference and Pathology: Stereotypes of Sexuality, Race, and Madness* (Ithaca: Cornell University Press, 1985).

13. See, for example, the Nazi documents reproduced in *Nazi Culture: A Documentary History*, ed. George Mosse (New York: Schocken, 1966), pp. 30–47, and Claudia Koonz, *Mothers in the Fatherland: Women, the Family and Nazi Politics* (New York: St. Martin's Press, 1987), pp. 1–18 and 51–90.

14. See, for example, Allen Mintz, *Hurban: Responses to Catastrophe in Hebrew Literature* (New York: Columbia University Press, 1984), and David G. Roskies, *Against the Apocalypse: Responses to Catastrophe in Modern Jewish Culture* (Cambridge: Harvard University Press, 1984).

15. Irving Greenberg, "Cloud of Smoke, Pillar of Fire: Judaism, Christianity, and Modernity after the Holocaust," in *Auschwitz: Beginning of a New Era? Reflections on the Holocaust*, ed. Eva Fleischner (New York: Ktav, 1977), p. 23.

16. Michael Berenbaum, *After Tragedy and Triumph: Modern Jewish Thought and the American Experience* (Cambridge: Cambridge University Press, 1990).

17. Berel Lang, *Act and Idea in Nazi Genocide* (Chicago: University of Chicago Press, 1990), p. xii.

18. George Mosse, "The Image of the Jew in German Popular Culture," *Germans and Jews: The Right, the Left, and the Search for a "Third Force" in Pre-Nazi Germany* (Detroit: Wayne State University Press, 1987), p. 75.

7 | The Image Lingers
The Feminization of the Jew in *Schindler's List*
Judith E. Doneson

Toward the finale of Steven Spielberg's film *Schindler's List*, as the Catholic German Oskar Schindler prepares, with his Jewish assistant Itzhak Stern, his list of Jews to be saved, Stern looks at Schindler and proclaims: "The list is an absolute good. The list is life." Schindler and his catalogue of human survivors bring to mind the Good Samaritan, whose image in Christian art is of one who aids a traveler "robbed, stripped, and left by the side of the road half dead," forsaken by other passersby. The Samaritan fixes the traveler's wounds, brings him to an inn, and takes care of him, thereby earning the praise of Jesus Christ as one who knows the meaning of mercy.[1] And so did Oskar Schindler take care of "his Jews," as he called them, regardless of his motives, during a period when most of the world had abandoned them.

We do not question the existence of "Righteous Gentiles," Oskar Schindler being prominent among them, as those non-Jews are called who endeavored to rescue or assist Jews during the Holocaust. Their numbers, however, were small, the cold statistic of six million Jews annihilated offering proof. Yet if one were to examine the myriad of fiction films exploring the Holocaust that have appeared since the end of World War II, irrespective of country of origin, it might appear that goodness infiltrated Europe during this evil era, for a majority of these films portray, in some manner, Christians/gentiles attempting to save the lives of weak, passive Jews.

In fact, the prevailing vision that informs Holocaust films is rooted in a popular theology that views the Jew as condemned eternally for rejecting Jesus as the Messiah but whose continuing existence is necessary as witness to Christian doctrine as well as to test the qualities of mercy and goodness incumbent upon good Christians. This takes shape in the alliance of the weak, passive, rather feminine Jew being protected by a strong Christian/gentile, the male, signifying a male-female relationship. It is generally a benevolent, symbiotic coupling based on the stereotype of the meek female dependent upon the strong male and the need both have for each other. The relationship exists on two levels: one depicts the Christian/gentile in his attempts to rescue the weak Jew; the other reflects a sexual attitude whereby the male Christian saves a female Jew because he loves her. We rarely witness this cinematic coupling manifest itself in a racial manner despite the fact that racist thinking often did perceive the Jew as having a feminine nature, and a residue of racial ideology is observed in these films.[2]

Schindler's List is among the few films that does illustrate an uncompromising but cliched racial view of the Jewish temptress; at the same time, it does not deviate from earlier patterns established in similar films that tend to feminize the Jew. In fact, Steven Spielberg's film embraces the traits that define this Christian/male-Jewish/female model as it continues to weave its course into the present.

Stereotypes, Sander Gilman reminds us, coexist in uncounted numbers, never to die. They may recede from the center of perception, and at any given moment, seemingly contradictory models may operate simultaneously. But each age continues to use bits and pieces of the existing images, though they may be restructured to appear new and unique.[3] And so it is with Jewish imagery in Holocaust films, ostensibly altered and changed from a different age, yet persistent in the analogous motifs that help to form a picture of the Jew in the collective mind.

In order to distinguish the feminine stereotypes which concern us, we must examine the Jew in one aspect of his historical dress—that of the "other," the "outsider." It was during the nineteenth century in Europe that the division of labor between the sexes and ideals of respectability, especially the distinction between vice and virtue, normal and abnormal, forced awesome challenges on the population.[4] At this juncture, serious accusations of confusing gender were aimed at the Jews. For instance, Jews, like women, were considered to be hysterical and nervous.[5] Additionally the nineteenth century viewed both women and Jews as passive rather than active.[6]

Otto Weininger, a Viennese Jew who converted to Christianity, was a chief exponent of this gender duality; he made the confusion of sex roles the cutting edge of his racism and anti-Semitism.[7] The major thrust of Weininger's influential study *Sex and Character* is based on the fundamental differences between sex and character. Every human being is a combination of male and female elements. Man is the positive, productive, logical, conceptual, ethical, spiritual force capable of genius, while woman is the negative element, incapable of any of these virtues. In Weininger's view, a woman of the highest standard was immeasurably beneath a man of the lowest standard.[8]

Within this vision of low esteem in which he held women, Weininger included the Jew. As there is no real dignity in women, observed Weininger, so what is meant by the word "gentleman" does not exist among Jews. Jews are soulless. Both women and Jews were thought to be innately nervous; they suffered fits of hysteria. Manliness, however, meant normalcy, self-control, and harmony of the body and mind. Those who were not manly must be regarded as diseased. It must be emphasized that Weininger found many learned physicians who confirmed his philosophical disposition toward Jews.[9]

On the theological level, Weininger believed Christianity to be heroism at its highest point and Judaism the extreme of cowardliness.[10] In somewhat contradictory fashion, however, for a man who viewed the world in polar opposites, Weininger also saw Judaism not necessarily as an extreme. The Jew is "neither very good nor very bad, with nothing in him of either the angel or the devil."[11] He is, then, in the theological sense, in limbo, that place, according to Gertrude Grace Sill in *A Handbook of Symbols in Christian Art*, which is found in the lower part of the earth, close to hell, where reside, among others, unbaptized souls.[12]

And that is where we find the Jew in the earliest representations of the Holocaust in film following the termination of World War II—in perennial limbo, in a defective state—that of Jewishness. In a more benevolent mode than racist theory might allow, this cinematic Jew is neither devil nor angel, neither heathen nor Christian. He is, simply, "Jew," devoid of the attributes of valor and nobility, the prince of weakness.[13]

Remarkably, *Schindler's List* in 1993 echoes the first fiction films appearing on the Holocaust. Both the Polish film *The Last Stop* (1948) and the Czech film *The Distant Journey* (1949) were filmed in black-and-white, a more obvious selection in that era, but both films were also filmed on location: *The Last Stop* at Auschwitz and *The Distant Journey* at Theresienstadt. Wanda Jakubowska's *The Last Stop*, in fact, employed survivors of Auschwitz in the actual filming. But however these films resemble each other stylistically, it is the similarity in their content that beckons us. Though filmed at Auschwitz, *The Last Stop* has only one central Jewish character. The additional Jews in the film are in the background, marching silently into the gas chambers. The champions of the film are political prisoners planning a rebellion at Auschwitz. Martha, the Jewess, is brought into the resistance—made a hero—by the gentile organizers. In *The Distant Journey*, the main character, Tony Klein, a non-Jew, risks his life to save his Jewish wife and her family by entering the Theresienstadt ghetto. The strong, gentile male is the savior of the feminine Jew, in this instance, for the sake of love.

This interchangeable model continues in various shapes. In the American film *The Diary of Anne Frank* (1959), the Franks hide together as a family and are sustained by their Dutch Christian saviors. In the Italian film *Kapo* (1960), a Jewish girl sells her soul to the Nazi devil by becoming a kapo, a concentration camp overseer, and only receives salvation through the love of a Russian prisoner of war. In the Czech film *The Shop on Main Street* (1965), Tono is tormented by his Catholic conscience over whether or not he has the courage to save the

Jewish Mrs. Lautman. None of the Jews in this Slovak town do anything to help themselves. In the French film *Black Thursday* (1974), Paul tries to fulfill his Christian duty and his role as a male protector in his efforts to save the Jews; but the Jews refuse to listen and so they are deported from Paris. In the American-British joint production *Voyage of the Damned* (1976), the German captain, somewhat reminiscent of Oskar Schindler, protects his cargo of Jews, who set sail from Germany on the ship *St. Louis* as if on a cruise until they are refused entry into Cuba and the United States, which turns them into hysterical and frightened refugees. In the American film *Julia* (1977), the Jewish Lillian writes plays and goes to the theater while her gentile friend Julia risks her life in Europe on behalf of the resistance. These are but representative examples of an inventory of films dealing with the Holocaust that restates the portrayal of the Jew as a weak, feminine character in need of protection by the strong, male, Christian/gentile. *Schindler's List* makes no attempt to shatter this mold.

Steven Spielberg is fearless in his undertaking to interpret the Nazi persecution of the Jews. From slave labor, to arbitrary beatings and murders, to the liquidation of the Kraków ghetto, to the "selections" at Auschwitz, to the cremation of Jewish bodies at the Plaszów concentration camp, Spielberg attempts to transform his camera into a recorder of history. But whose history is it? As in Raul Hilberg's classic *The Destruction of the European Jews*, Spielberg has shown us the Holocaust largely from a German perspective. (Excluding personal belongings, we do not recall any visual signs of a Jewish presence in Kraków, such as distinctly Jewish institutions or even a synagogue apart from the mosaic of broken Jewish gravestones used as a road in Plaszów.) Throughout the action, the Jews are seen primarily as compliant victims of this history.

Renowned psychologist Bruno Bettelheim continually reinforced this image of the Jew as a weak, passive victim. One of the main ideologues expounding the position that the behavior of the Jews during the Holocaust helped contribute to their destruction—his ideas rooted in Anne Frank's Diary and the play and film that followed—Bettelheim closed his final work prior to his 1990 suicide by reiterating his theories on Jewish passivity during the Holocaust.[14] Employing the Frank family as representative, Bettelheim argued that living life as usual under unusual circumstances, hiding as a family unit with no planned escape route, or offering no resistance is what led to the annihilation of millions of Jews. In Bettelheim's opinion, "A certain type of ghetto thinking has as its purpose the avoidance of taking action. It is a type of deadening of the senses and emotions, so that one can bow down to the mujik who pulls one's beard, laugh with the baron at his anti-Semitic stories, degrade oneself so that one will be permitted to survive."[15]

Certainly, the category of Jews Bettelheim describes populates *Schindler's*

List. For instance, throughout the movie, Spielberg utilizes a technique that is meant to signify factual history: At intervals, he presents a written chronology of events that are occurring. Thus, early in the film we read that in September 1939, the German forces defeat Poland and Jews are ordered to relocate and register. The camera focuses on a full-bearded rabbi in a fur hat and long black robe—at first glance, a Roman Vishniac photograph come to life—strolling gracefully with his family, as if on a Sunday jaunt, toward a table to register with the Nazis. Just like that. The scene expands as crowds of Jews simply sign-up—as directed.

In another "historical" paragraph, we read that a Jewish council, the *Judenrat*, comprised of twenty-four elected officials, was established to carry out Nazi orders. The notion of actual elections is questionable, unless officials were retained who had been elected prior to the war as a means of self-government within the Jewish community. The message, though, is consistent: There was Jewish compliance in carrying out Nazi orders. (The complexity and function of the Jewish councils is certainly not evident in the film.)[16] And in yet another historical note, we are informed that the deadline for entering the newly established Jewish ghetto is March 20, 1941. The camera then reveals masses of Jews burdened with their belongings languidly winding their way across a bridge toward their new home. The prevailing component in the preceding samples is that there was passive compliance with the Nazis by the Jewish population of Kraków.

On a more individual level, we are shown Nazi soldiers cutting off the beard of a complaisant religious Jew, evoking similar images the Nazis themselves filmed for anti-Semitic purposes; or wealthy Jews negotiating with Schindler over whether or not to back him in his enterprise—business as usual, as Bettelheim might see it. Of course, we must not forget the Jews operating in the black market who are able to procure sardines and silk for Schindler, or Marcel Goldberg, the member of the Jewish police force cooperating with the Nazis, who must be bribed by Schindler in order to save Jews. Even the female engineer who supervises building construction at Plaszów takes her work for the Nazis so seriously that she loses her life.

Finally, we might recall two incidents that speak to a Jewish reluctance even to assist their fellow Jews. In the first instance, while still in the ghetto, a Mrs. Dresner boldly claims that she is not going to hide like an animal. Another woman informs her that there are lots of places to hide. Then, when the ghetto is liquidated by the Nazis and Mrs. Dresner and her daughter search desperately for a place in which to conceal themselves, the same woman who told her to find a refuge refuses her entry into her secret hideaway; she will take only her daughter. As Mrs. Dresner flees alone, she is confronted by a boy of perhaps nine wearing the badge of the Jewish police, who is ready to turn her over to the Nazis. Suddenly he notices her daughter, who refused to hide without her mother, walking down the stairs. At that moment, he decides to help them, but only because he is fond of the daughter. In this instance, the little boy, Adam, functions in the role of the gentile-male in that he has been given power over other Jews by the Nazis; he is willing to save Mrs. Dresner and her daughter solely because of his feelings for the daughter.

In the second situation, which parallels the first, there is a deportation in the Plaszów concentration camp. The Jewish children scatter. One little boy, desperate for a place in which to conceal himself, jumps into a receptacle of human waste, only to be told that he cannot stay—there is no room.

The emphasis, then, is not only on the passive nature of the Jews but also on their unheroic behavior toward one another. Apart from Itzhak Stern, Schindler's Jewish assistant, there is not one Jew who exhibits even a hint of valor. *Schindler's List* perpetuates the image of a weak, feminized Jew, the passive figure so negatively described by Otto Weininger, and later, Bruno Bettelheim, at the expense of truth. For indeed, what is missing in the film of *Schindler's List* is the other half of history—the Jewish response to their destruction. Elements of this, we might note, such as the Jewish resistance movement, are mentioned in Thomas Keneally's novel, on which the film is based.[17]

Briefly, the ghetto in Kraków was not simply an area, as one segment of the film intimates, where once-active Jews stood in the cold warming themselves over a fire—waiting. In fact, the ghetto had its own infrastructure. There were three hospitals, a home for the elderly, an orphanage, workshops, synagogues. And there were underground activities focusing on education and assisting those in need. An underground newspaper was published. A Jewish fighting organization, the ZOB, was formed, carrying out many acts of sabotage outside the ghetto, the most notorious being an attack on a café in which several Germans were killed.[18]

Since there are no references to resistance and organization within the ghetto, the Jews remain the perfect victims—weak, ineffectual, incapable of helping themselves—the stereotype of women. If someone strong, fearless, and virile—an Oskar Schindler—does not act on their behalf, they are doomed. This, of course, makes the role of Schindler all the more meaningful—he is the foil par excellence to the Jews, yet he is nothing without them. The Jews need Schindler; Schindler needs the Jews.

This best expresses itself in the relationship between Oskar Schindler and Itzhak Stern. The dichotomy is established in their first meeting. Stern informs Schindler: "I must tell you, I'm a Jew." Schindler retorts: "And I'm a German." While the major thrust of the film is the battle between the Germans and the Jews, Schindler and Stern, instead of engaging in hostility, become the "odd couple." *Schindler's List*, in fact, is a film of German-Jewish couples: Schindler and Stern, Germans versus Jews, Goeth and Helen, Schindler and "his" Jews. Indeed, in Kraków, a major city in Poland, we barely see a Pole. Certainly, we meet no Polish characters of any consequence: There is the little girl who cries "good-bye, Jews"; a young boy who, when a train passes en route to Auschwitz, mimes the slashing of his throat, indicating the Jews will die; and the scene in church with the religious Poles praying while Jews carry out black market activities. At some level, the film wants to inform us that during this tragic era in their history, in a Christian nation, the Jews were alone. The film is so focused on its purpose, one of its primary strengths, that we are forced to comprehend the intense obsession of the Nazis—apart from Schindler—to destroy all of the Jews—men, women, and children. Now, Itzhak Stern functions in the film only through his relationship to Oskar Schindler. He exists under no other circumstances. He has no family. No friends. No confidants. Yet Stern did have a wife who was with him throughout the war.[19]

In the film, though, he is alone. His purpose is to aid in the creation of the larger-than-life hero, Schindler. He evolves into the woman behind the successful man. He cooks, he cleans, he washes clothes; in other words, he runs every aspect of Schindler's business. Of course, Schindler is also alone—and dependent. An inveterate womanizer, his wife, too, though we do meet her, is out of the picture until the conclusion. He has the power, the persuasive charm, the background to deal with the Nazi command. But he relies upon Stern to maintain him. And, as usually happens in such relationships, the one with the power and charm gets the credit. It is only during their private moments that Schindler can be soft to Stern and Stern can speak his mind. We see this when Stern, working temporarily for the Plaszów camp commander Amon Goeth, meets Schindler in secret and implores him not to let things fall apart. As Stern says: "I worked too hard."

Their coming together is reminiscent of an old-fashioned, arranged relationship. Schindler wants Stern. Stern must acquiesce. At first, Stern is hesitant, shy, afraid to speak his mind. He shows his feelings by refusing to drink with Schindler. But, the marriage is made. He cannot back out. Then, as he learns to understand Schindler, his fondness for him develops until one day, Stern truly cares about him. They consummate their relationship when Stern readily shares a drink with Schindler.

Schindler is also of two minds. He wants Stern to fulfill his needs, in this case, for money and power. Stern satisfies him, but in so doing, also helps his people, or Schindler's Jews. The motivations that ultimately lead Schindler to save his Jews and lose his fortune, or when that exact moment occurs in the film—some suggest during the liquidation of the Kraków ghetto—seem meaningless. The fact is, he does it. But in the context of the film, his evolution takes place under the gentle coaxing and prodding of Stern.

Stern brings in the one-armed worker to thank Schindler. Schindler feigns anger. But when the man is later murdered by the Nazis, Schindler is truly enraged. They killed one of his Jews, he tells the Nazis; he was important to the war effort. This is not avarice speaking. It is a humane response. In the film, it is his affiliation with Stern that prompts his humanity to surface. It is the feminizing factor in his life, one with a soul attached to it (rather than a one-night stand) that sparks the internal struggle within Schindler that leads to the valiant rescue of his Jews. The symbiosis of the relationship is validated: Stern—and the Jews—need Schindler to survive; Schindler needs the Jews to bring to the fore a compassion that has been lying dormant.

The association between Schindler and Stern—Schindler and the Jews— is undoubtedly benevolent. The connection between Plaszów commandant Amon Goeth and Jewess Helen Hirsch, whom Goeth chooses as his house- keeper, on the other hand, is rooted in racist ideology. There is nothing subtle in their relationship. For Goeth, Helen embodies the Jewish temptress—seduc- tive, dark, forbidden—in his case, by law. This is surely a perverse vision in that Helen is consumed by fear, not a desire to seduce—even for survival. That, of course, makes her all the more intriguing to Goeth—she is both temptress and slave. He wants her; he knows he cannot have her; but he owns her.

In the scene in which Goeth defends Schindler to another Nazi for kissing a young Jewish girl at his birthday party, Goeth slips into his racist character. He tells the officer that the girl was quite beautiful; that these women cast a spell on you, like a virus—like typhus. Goeth says that Schindler should be pitied for getting this virus—not punished. There is nothing Christian, noth- ing kind, in Goeth's opinion of the Jewish temptress. It is simply a verbal re- iteration of a common Nazi stereotype.

At one juncture, however, Helen does kindle a desire buried deep inside Goeth, one that, for an instant, detaches him from the stereotype, almost pro- voking him to appear human. In this instance, their relationship fits the model of the weak, feminine Jew being protected by the strong, male Christian. Schindler speaks to this when he attempts to comfort Helen in her basement hideout. He informs her: "He [Goeth] enjoys you so much he won't let you wear the star. He doesn't want anyone to know you're a Jew." Still, the moment she comes too close to igniting that spark, though unintentionally, Goeth with- draws, calls her a bitch, and slaps her repeatedly. Nonetheless, it is the spell of Goeth's unconsummated fascination with Helen that saves her life.

Whereas Schindler's contact with Helen in the basement, even his gentle- ness in explaining Goeth's behavior toward her, informs us that the myth of Schindler as savior has invaded his own perceptions. When he first confronts a frightened Helen in the cellar, he assures her: "Do you know who I am. I'm Schindler." He has become the embodiment of a holy shrine: Touch him and you are saved. The woman who implores him to save her parents by bringing them into his plant knows this. "Everyone knows no one dies here," she pleads. And with a bribe to Marcel Goldberg by Schindler, the couple is transferred from Plaszów to Schindler's plant.

The film's final scenes leave no doubt that Oskar Schindler is indeed a holy man. As Schindler's Jews and their progeny march over a hill, into the present, to the Christian cemetery on Mount Zion in Jerusalem where Schindler is buried, one by one they place small rocks on Schindler's grave until the inscription on his gravestone is surrounded by loose stones. It is customary in Jewish tradition to place a stone, or a piece of grass, on a grave, a sign to the departed that he or she has had a visitor. Visit the grave of the recently deceased Lubavitcher Rebbe at the Old Montefiore Cemetery in Queens, New York, or the grave of the Maharal of Prague or the Ari in Safed, Israel—all famous rabbis in Jewish history, *tzaddikim*, the Hebrew word for "righteous ones"—and you will see a sight similar to that of Schindler's last resting place: gravestones adorned with pebbles and notes imploring the holy departed to grant their wishes, answer their prayers, serve as an emissary between themselves and God. For the Jews in the film, Schindler appears as such an anointed figure. Having failed in business, except during the war, and at his marriage, Oskar Schindler found success through his relationship with a group of Jews fated for destruction.

The opening scene in *Schindler's List* is the kindling of a pair of Jewish Sabbath candles as a man in Eastern European dress recites the prayer over the wine. The candle flames burn lower and lower until they are obliterated. One of the closing shots in the film is of Schindler's grave, with its cross in the center, as the camera pulls back on Mount Zion to encompass the monastery or church to which the burial grounds belong and the larger cross attached to the edifice looming against the deep blue sky. This is the only shot we see of Jerusalem. In one of the historical paragraphs written on screen, we are informed that in 1958, Yad Vashem (the main memorial in Israel to the destroyed Jews as well a research center for scholars of the period from throughout the world), declared Oskar Schindler a "Righteous Gentile." Yad Vashem, with its monuments to gentile as well as Jewish heroes, is never viewed. This suggests an adherence to the relationship that has been portrayed throughout *Schindler's List*, that of the weak, feminine Jew being protected by the strong, male Christian/gentile—even in Jerusalem.

The final shot in the film, just prior to the credits, is of Schindler's stone-laden grave, where a hand places a rose on his monument. The camera draws back to show the Christian cemetery filled with crosses as we read on the screen: "In memory of the more than six million Jews murdered." Is this a condemnation of Christianity? For how could so many Jews have been murdered if Christians were following their creed during the war? Or does it mean to honor Christian martyrs like Schindler who did help Jews survive? Either way, it does not alter the thrust of the film, one that refuses to let go of an image that lingers throughout a majority of the films dealing with the Holocaust. Rather, it lends emphasis to the notion that Jewish survival depends upon Christian benevolence. It extends the stereotype of the weak, feminized Jew into the present.

Let us not forget that a historical film is as much about the present as it is about the past.[20] Only then can we realize that *Schindler's List*, in adhering to its feminized image of the Jew, speaks to a truth we may have thought obsolete with the rise of the Jewish State. As the war ends, Schindler, a Nazi after all, is forced to abandon his Jews so he and his wife can flee the approaching liberating armies. The following morning, the Jews awaken as a lone Russian liberator approaches.

Itzhak Stern asks him if there are any Jews left; where can the survivors go? The Russian answers: Don't go east; they hate you there. And, he counsels, he would not go west either. He then points toward a hill and asks, but really advises, if that is not a town over there. At this juncture, the camera captures hundreds of Jews coming over the mountain on their way to Schindler's grave in Jerusalem. The implication, coming from the Russian, is that Jews no longer belong in Europe. Go over there, in the distance, to your own Jewish state.

Heeding his advice, the Jews march over the hill to the tune of "Jerusalem of Gold." This is a song that was popularized during the Six Day War in 1967 when Israel, surrounded by Arab nations ready to wage a war many believed the small state would lose, instead won an incredible victory. The repercussions of this war, however, led to the Israeli army becoming an occupying force, most notably over Palestinian refugees. The consequences of the victory belong in a historical/political framework. Had Israel lost that war, however, the state might have been liquidated. By winning, it tarnished its image as David versus the Goliath of Arab nations. It became simple to compare the Palestinian situation to that of the Jews during the Holocaust. Israeli soldiers were likened to Nazis. Seemingly, many preferred the image of the weak, endangered state over the victorious one.

Therefore, in a contemporary context, we discern an ambivalent tone in *Schindler's List* regarding the Jewish state. The Russian seems to be offering a Zionist solution, but he really maintains that Jews belong with Jews. "Jerusalem of Gold" is a moving melody that suggests a time of danger that became a celebration but then turned into a political morass. And the cross on Schindler's grave combined with all the crosses in the Christian cemetery? Perhaps an insinuation that the memory of Jewish destruction should serve to remind Israel that a more Christian attitude toward its neighbors ought to be forthcoming. Politics aside, the intent might be that too strong a Jewish state, or too comfortable a Jewish role in society, poses a threat to the gentile world. Contemporary images in the news confirm this picture: Israel forced to allow Iraqi Scud missiles to fall in its midst rather than take the offensive; the rise of anti-Semitism following the fall of Communism in Eastern Europe; Pope John Paul II bestowing a papal knighthood on former Austrian Chancellor Kurt Waldheim, who is accused of assisting in the destruction of groups of Jews during the Holocaust. *Schindler's List*, certainly by virtue of its historical subject, but also because it is a modern tale, has absorbed much of the ambivalence inherent in society relating to the Jews and Israel.

Schindler's List informs us, like many of the films that preceded it, that the Jew is at the mercy of Christian/gentile society. David Flusser, professor of comparative religion at the Hebrew University in Jerusalem, told the following story:

> It was some days after the Six Day War that a team of the Dutch Church Television came to make a film here (in Jerusalem) about the Jews. Now they could make the pictures in the original sites in the Old City of Jerusalem. Then I met a new reaction to the Jewish reality. These professing Christians disliked Jewish soldiers—the conquerors—and said openly how much more beautiful were the eyes of the Jews saved from Auschwitz than the proud looks of the soldiers.[21]

This tale serves to corroborate a truth: The weakness during World War II that found European Jewry in a situation of dependence for its survival might still be preferred, in the post-Holocaust climate, by the Christian/gentile world. The image embodied in the model of the weak, feminine Jew in need of the protection of the strong, masculine Christian weaves its pattern through films dealing with the Final Solution, the most recent example being the truly commanding *Schindler's List*. We recall Sander Gilman's insight that stereotypes may ebb only to resurface when needed. In an article on *Schindler's List* in a Jewish newspaper, the editor of the paper ruminated: "We Jews can never tell who will be our next Cyrus the Great, Emperor Napoleon or Harry Truman who will serve as our rescuer."[22] While the lingering stereotype of the feminized Jew exists here only on celluloid, its duration suggests an ongoing condition that promises no cure.

Notes

1. Gertrude Grace Sill, *A Handbook of Symbols in Christian Art* (New York: Collier, 1975), pp. 102–103.
2. See Judith E. Doneson, "The Jew as a Female Figure in Holocaust Film," *Shoah:*

A Review of Holocaust Studies and Commemorations 1, no. 1 (1978), pp. 11–13, 18. Also, Judith E. Doneson, "Feminine Stereotypes of Jews in Holocaust Films: Focus on the Diary of Anne Frank," in G. Jan Colijn and Marcia S. Littell, eds., *The Netherlands and Nazi Genocide: Papers of the 21st Annual Scholars' Conference* (Lewiston, N.Y.: Mellen, 1992), pp. 139–53.

    3. Sander Gilman, *Seeing the Insane* (New York: Wiley, 1982), pp. xii and 224.

    4. George L. Mosse, *Nationalism and Sexuality* (New York: Howard Fertig, 1985), pp. 133, 150.

    5. Mosse, pp. 144–45.

    6. Mosse, p. 17.

    7. Ibid.

    8. Otto Weininger, *Sex and Character* (rpt. of 1906 edition; London: W. Heinemann, 1975), p. 302.

    9. Ibid., p. 308, and Mosse, pp. 142–43.

    10. See the entry for Otto Weininger, *Encyclopedia Judaica* (Jerusalem: Keter, 1974), vol. 16, p. 403, and Weininger, pp. 324–28.

    11. Weininger, pp. 303, 309.

    12. Sill, p. 96.

    13. Doneson, *Shoah*, p. 12.

    14. Bruno Bettelheim, *Freud's Vienna and Other Essays* (New York: Knopf, 1990). Many of us are familiar with the accusations of Jewish passivity espoused by Bettelheim in "Freedom from Ghetto Thinking," *Midstream* (Spring 1962), pp. 16–25; "The Ignored Lesson of Anne Frank," *Harper's Magazine* (November 1960), pp. 45–50; and *The Informed Heart* (Great Britain: Paladin, 1970). Other important figures in the Bettelheim camp include Raul Hilberg, *The Destruction of the European Jews* (Chicago: Quadrangle, 1961), and Hannah Arendt, *Eichmann in Jerusalem* (New York: Viking, 1968).

    15. Bettelheim, *Freud's Vienna*, p. 260.

    16. See Isaiah Trunk, *Judenrat* (New York: Macmillan, 1972).

    17. See, for example, the edition of Thomas Keneally, *Schindler's List* (New York: Touchstone, 1993), p. 131. Here, Keneally refers to Tadeus Pankiewciz's pharmacy, the only Polish establishment located in the ghetto, as a link for mail, information, and messages between the Jewish combat organization (ZOB) and the partisans of the Polish People's Army.

    18. See, for example, Malvina Graf, *The Krakow Ghetto and the Plaszow Camp Remembered* (Tallahassee: Florida State University Press, 1989); Yisrael Gutman, ed., *The Encyclopedia of the Holocaust* (New York: Macmillan, 1990), vol. 2, pp. 829–33; Isaac Kowalski, ed., *Anthology of Armed Jewish Resistance, 1939–1945* (Brooklyn: Jewish Combatants Publishing House, 1984), vol. 1, pp. 45–46; Roman Mogilanski, ed., *The Ghetto Anthology* (Los Angeles: American Congress of Jews from Poland and Survivors of Concentration Camps, 1985), pp. 145–46; Tadeusz Pankiewicz, *The Cracow Ghetto Pharmacy* (New York: Waldon Press, 1987). With reference to Keneally's novel (see n. 17), and regarding the ZOB and their use of Pankiewicz's pharmacy, Pankiewicz writes: "It was important not to implicate Tadeus Pankiewicz by their projects, which—unlike the cooperative policies of the *Judenrat*—involved furious and unequivocal resistance" (p. 131).

    19. In a telephone conversation on 14 September 1994 with Leo Page a.k.a. Leopold Pfefferberg, the man who convinced Thomas Keneally to write his novel on Schindler, Page informed me that indeed, Stern was married and his wife was with him in Kraków and Plaszów. He did not recall if Stern had any children. According to Page, Mrs. Stern was on the set of *Schindler's List* as an adviser. We do see her in the final scenes as she lays a stone on Schindler's grave in Jerusalem. She is accompanied by Ben Kingsley, who plays Stern in the film.

20. There has been much written about historical recreations in fiction films. As a basic introduction to the subject, see Pierre Sorlin, *The Film in History: Restaging the Past* (Totowa, N.J.: Barnes and Noble, 1980), who continually reminds us that a film about history is also a film about the present.

21. Joel Fishman, "The Anneke Beckman Affair and the Dutch News Media," *Jewish Social Studies* 15 no. 1 (Winter 1978), p. 24.

22. Robert A. Cohn, "Spielberg Triumphs with *Schindler's List*," *St. Louis Jewish Light* 8 (December 1993), p. 7.

8 | Schindler's Discourse

America Discusses the Holocaust and Its Mediation, from NBC's Miniseries to Spielberg's Film

Jeffrey Shandler

S*CHINDLER'S LIST* HAS generated an extensive public discussion on the nature of the Holocaust and its mediation—in print, on radio, television, and e-mail bulletin boards,[1] at symposia, and in classrooms, among other venues—the likes of which hasn't been seen in the United States since the premiere broadcast of NBC's *Holocaust* miniseries in April 1978. A comparison of the two works—and, moreover, of the discourses they have engendered—offers an opportunity to reflect on the dynamics of the Holocaust as a presence in the American consciousness over the past two decades and to consider the role that popular dramatic mediations of this subject play in shaping Holocaust memory culture.

Since its first broadcast, the NBC miniseries has been widely regarded as a landmark work. Some critics hail the drama as "the climax of the process of the Americanization of the Final Solution" as well as being "among the first popular films to focus on the Final Solution as a specifically Jewish event,"[2] or "the prototype for all succeeding—and successful—television projects on the era."[3] Even its many detractors recognize *Holocaust* as a watershed. For example, Ilan Avisar writes that, despite "Hollywood's inherent incapacity when it comes to dealing with a subject of the magnitude of the Holocaust," the miniseries demonstrated that "the formidable power of Hollywood's universal appeal . . . can be instrumental in enlightening ignorant people about the course and nature of the Nazi evil."[4]

Scholars frequently cite the premiere broadcast of *Holocaust* as a threshold event in the dynamics of Holocaust consciousness in America: "the Holocaust had fully 'arrived' on the American scene, with tens of millions of Americans watching Gerald Green's soap opera,"[5] or, the miniseries "brought the word Holocaust . . . into virtual 'household' use."[6] Such acknowledgments generally focus on the role of the miniseries in familiarizing mass audiences with the Holocaust as a discrete episode of modern history in which Jews figure significantly and centrally. Yet the miniseries also marks a watershed in the discourse of Holocaust memory culture, both in America and abroad. The extensive critical response to NBC's *Holocaust* constitutes the first major public discussion of "Holocaust television" as a genre. The consensus emerging from this response was that the medium—generally thought of as small-scale, vulgar, venal, frivolous, quotidian—is by nature incapable of properly mediating the subject—widely understood as vast, profound, incomprehensible, disturbing, unique. This notion has problematized much of subsequent criticism of popular mediations of the Holocaust, not only television dramas, but other media and genres. In this light, it is worth considering the extent to which the discourse surrounding *Schindler's List*, as well as the film itself, are a continuation of the response to NBC's miniseries.

NBC first aired *Holocaust* on four consecutive evenings (April 16–19, 1978) as a presentation of *The Big Event*, the network's regularly scheduled series of movies, concerts, and other special broadcasts. The telecast followed weeks of advance publicity unusual in scope and variety for a television drama: this included the distribution of educational viewing guides,[7] the publication of a paperback novelization of Gerald Green's teleplay,[8] and the promotion of the Holocaust as "topic of the week" in church and synagogue sermons.[9] NBC scheduled the concluding night of the broadcast to coincide with the thirty-fifth anniversary of the beginning of the Warsaw ghetto uprising, the primary annual event in public Holocaust commemoration. For many American Jews the anticipated broadcast took on a special meaning independent of the network's appeals to a general national audience. A feature on the miniseries in the April 1978 issue of *Moment*, a popular Jewish monthly magazine, states that "for Jews, the watching [of *Holocaust*] has about it the quality of a religious obligation."[10]

The telecast of *Holocaust* also initiated a period of extensive public response. Reactions to the first American broadcast of the miniseries—seen at least in part by an estimated 120 million viewers nationwide[11]—were voluminous, prolonged, conspicuous, and contentious, constituting a "big event" in American culture above and beyond the miniseries itself. In the days following the broadcast, *Holocaust* generated an exceptional quantity and variety of print coverage, including reviews by media critics, news articles on the program's audience size, viewer reactions, and reports on such related topics as Holocaust education programs. Newspapers also served as public forums for the exchange of views on the miniseries and its merits. Letters to the editor and editorial essays linked the broadcast of *Holocaust* to various contemporary political issues: For example, in the *New York Times* Wisconsin Senator William Proxmire used the opportunity to advocate the United States' long-delayed ratification of the United Nation's Genocide Convention; and columnist William Safire spoke out against contemporary persecutions in Soviet slave labor camps, Uganda, Iraq, and Cambodia.[12] For several months following the broadcast, reviews and commentaries continued to appear in periodicals ranging from *Nation* to the *National Review*.[13] The American Jewish Committee and the Jewish Anti-Defamation League published the results of studies of the program's impact on American audiences.[14] Plans to broadcast the miniseries abroad, especially in West Germany and Israel, extended public interest in NBC's *Holocaust* into the following year, when the network reaired the miniseries, this time marking the fortieth anniversary of the beginning of World War II.[15]

While most public responses to the miniseries appeared in print, television offered its own assessment of the impact of *Holocaust*. On September 13, 1970, NBC aired a one-hour news special, *Holocaust: A Postscript*, which presented a range of opinions on the quality of the drama and its effect on viewers. The program also offered as examples of the consequences of *Holocaust* events ranging from Pope John Paul II's visit to Auschwitz and West Germany's extension of laws providing for the pursuit of Nazi war criminals to the Carter administration's establishment of the President's Commission on the Holocaust.

Since 1978 a number of examples of Holocaust memory culture—including films, such as Markus Imhoof's *Das Boot Ist Voll* (1981) and Edgar Reitz's *Heimat* (1984),[16] and educational and memorial projects, such as the Fortunoff Video Archive for Holocaust Testimonies at Yale University—have been described by their creators as efforts undertaken as a reaction against the miniseries. For example, according to journalist Judith Miller *Holocaust* figured as the "spark" that, in 1979, ignited the grass-roots effort that eventually developed into the Fortunoff Archive: "Though the program scored record ratings and was widely credited with having prompted interest in the Holocaust among young Americans and Europeans, survivors in Connecticut and elsewhere were angered by what they saw as the program's trivialization of the searing experiences. 'Everything had been taken from them. Now television was trying to take away their stories too,' said [archive project manager Joanne] Rudof."[17]

To what extent might *Schindler's List* also be part of this ongoing, often negative, response to the NBC miniseries? Consider, for example, the most distinctive aesthetic feature of *Schindler's List*—the use of black-and-white throughout the film (with the exception of selected colorizing in the body of the work—notably, the girl in the red coat—and its epilogue, which was filmed in color). Both producer/director Steven Spielberg and cinematographer Janusz Kaminski explain the decision as having been motivated by a desire "to remain true to the spirit of documentaries and stills from the period" of World War II. Indeed, by filming *Schindler's List* in black-and-white stock (as opposed to using color stock and then printing the film in black-and-white, as Universal Studios had suggested),[18] Spielberg created a document formally analogous to vintage photographic records. (Leon Wieseltier comments in the *New Republic* that "the film is designed to look like a restored print of itself.")[19]

Moreover, Spielberg has described the use of black-and-white in *Schindler's List* as constituting a more "realistic" approach to the subject, making the film "closer to [a] documentary":

> I think black and white stands for reality. . . . I don't think color is real. I think certainly color is real to the people who survived the Holocaust, but to people who are going to watch the story for the first time, I think black and white is going to be the real experience for them. My only experience with the Holocaust has been through black-and-white documentaries. I've never seen the Holocaust in color. I don't know what Auschwitz looks like in color. Even though I was there, it's still black and white in my eyes. I think color would have added a veneer of almost farce.[20]

Spielberg's remarks not only contradict conventional notions of color photography as being more "realistic" (i.e., more verisimilitudinous) than black-and-white. His comments also evince the distinctively privileged stature that documentary images recorded during World War II have had for Americans as points of contact with the Holocaust. This differs from the relationship with the Holocaust of most Europeans—whose physical landscape is strewn with various landmarks of the Nazi era and of the Holocaust—as it differs from the situation of Israelis, for whom the Holocaust has figured as a central, galvanizing event in their national mythos.

For the overwhelming majority of Americans, however, primary encounters with the Holocaust have always been mediated ones, beginning with reports on the Allies' liberation of concentration camps in the spring of 1945 as featured in newspapers, on radio, and, even more significantly, in commercially distributed newsreels. According to Spielberg, this creates a fundamental distinction between Holocaust survivors and everyone else—only the former, by virtue of their status as eyewitnesses to the actual events that have come to be known as the Holocaust, can honestly "see" this chapter of history in color. To "colorize" what is, for the rest of the population, inherently a black-and-white experience thus constitutes an aesthetic—and, indeed, historiographical—heresy tantamount to adding color to *Casablanca* or *Citizen Kane*.[21]

Significantly, Universal was reported to be interested in having a color version of *Schindler's List* so that the film could eventually be sold to television. (Whereas black-and-white can connote "art film" or "Hollywood classic" in the realm of cinematic features, it apparently lacks such a cachet on the smaller screen.) Yet in 1978 several critics faulted the producers of the *Holocaust* miniseries for their use of color. For example, the largely favorable review in *Variety* concludes with the suggestion that "the cinematographer Brian West should have photographed the miniseries in black-and-white. The hard-edged color gives a picture-postcard prettiness to scenes that cry out for the murky and somber tones of [Alain Resnais's 1955 documentary] 'Night and Fog.' "[22] Lance Morrow writes in *Time* magazine that "the sometimes garish colors seemed to produce a falsification." Morrow suggests that not merely the documentary record of the Holocaust but the events themselves took place in black and white: "If any world needed to be filmed in black and white, it was what French writer David Rousset called l'univers concentrationnaire. All that obscenity transpired in an absence of color: ashes and smoke were gray, the SS uniforms black, the skin ash white, the bones white. Franz Stangl, the commandant of Sobibor, used to greet the trains wearing a white riding costume."[23]

These discussions of the significance of color vs. black-and-white resonate with other, larger issues concerning the Holocaust and its mediation. Televising the Holocaust is distinguished from virtually all other mediations due to television's advent as a mass medium soon after the end of World War II. Thus, television, when creating its own representations of the subject, always depends to some degree on other mediations of the Holocaust—be they vintage stills and footage, the recollections of Holocaust survivors, or the dramatic conventions of theater and film. Because it remains just on the other side of television's boundary with its own past, the Holocaust stands beyond the grasp of the medium's special ability to create a sense of "immediate" contact between viewer and subject that is widely considered key to its power as a medium. A color television drama about the Holocaust—indeed, any televised presentation of the Holocaust—is fundamentally removed by one more dimension of "mediacy" from a subject already distanced from American audiences by the measures of geography, culture, and time.

This issue of distance has been especially critical in the discourse of the Holocaust, as its conceptualization is so intimately bound up with questions of credibility, authenticity, and representability (consider, for example, historian Saul Friedlander's positioning of the Holocaust at the "limits of representation").[24] Here again, television appears to be inherently problematic. The medium, which by its nature pulls everything it presents into the ongoing flow of a continuous present, violates notions of the Holocaust as a singular event that is somehow removed from the normal flow of time and situated on a separate ontological plateau.

Thus, much of the negative reaction directed at NBC's miniseries is, in essence, criticism of it as a work of "Holocaust television," which critics often regard, albeit implicitly, as an impossible genre. Many describe the effort of presenting the Holocaust on television as an ill-fated effort to reconcile the lofty with the low (in his seminal attack on the miniseries, Elie Wiesel denounces *Holocaust* as "transform[ing] an ontological event into soap-opera"),[25] the epic with the domestic (media critic Molly Haskell writes that "the Holocaust is simply too vast, the elimination of 6 million people from the earth too incomprehensible, to fit into . . . the reductive context of the small screen").[26]

Significantly, the most common complaint about *Holocaust* did not concern any aspect of the drama itself but rather that it was punctuated by 130 advertisements during the course of the broadcast. Numerous critics carped about the idea of commodifying the Holocaust "much like toothpaste,"[27] or about unfelicitous juxtapositions of commercials and programming (*New York Times* television critic John O'Connor, for example, notes that a "story that includes victims being told that the gas chambers are only disinfecting areas is interrupted by a message about Lysol and its usefulness in 'killing germs' ").[28] Indeed, some critics suggest that the miniseries was so misguided an effort to present its subject in an incompatible medium that the program only succeeded in perpetuating the Holocaust. Jean Baudrillard, for example, describes the ostensibly worthy goal of the miniseries to recall the Holocaust and to impart a moral lesson from its history as having been subverted by the nature of television, "a medium which is itself cold, radiating oblivion, dissuasion and extermination in an ever more systematic manner, if this is possible, than the [concentration] camps themselves. TV, the veritable final solution to the historicity of every event."[29]

In light of prevailing sentiments that a proper mediation of the Holocaust cannot take place in a commercial, popular venue, the distinctive presentation of *Schindler's List* in American cinemas might also be seen as part of the ongoing reactions against the NBC miniseries. Although made by a major Hollywood studio and shown in mainstream movie theaters, *Schindler's List* has been screened like an art film, without the usual prefeature promotions that tout refreshments available in the lobby or present trailers for coming attractions, and with credits that most discreetly acknowledge Spielberg's production company, Amblin Entertainment.[30] While before the film's premiere Spielberg claimed he had "no illusions" that he would "recoup his investment" in *Schindler's List*,[31] the producer has since announced that any profits he makes on the film will be donated to a Holocaust-related charity. (Shortly thereafter, Spielberg established the Survivors of the Shoah Visual History Foundation to videotape and archive the testimonies of thousands of Holocaust survivors.) These decisions, echoing Spielberg's descriptions of *Schindler's List* as "a document, not an entertainment,"[32] strive to situate the film beyond the realm of mass-produced, commercial art or popular diversion.

Nevertheless, NBC's *Holocaust* and Spielberg's film have much in common: Both are epic in scale, making unusual demands on the viewing habits of mainstream television or movie audiences. Both works aspire to test the boundaries of their popular genres in other ways as well, especially with regard to the limits of verisimilitude; both *Schindler's List* and the miniseries have generated considerable critical discussion of their graphic violence and nudity. The two works also make similar efforts to articulate the seriousness of a common mission to edify mass audiences by both transcending and exploiting the devices of entertainment. On the one hand, the miniseries and the film employ a selective use of documentary film conventions (for example, the incorporation of vintage images in expository sections of *Holocaust*; the analogous use of narrative titles in *Schindler's List*). On the other hand, their respective promotions manipulate the tension between being compelling drama and lesson in history. Promotion for the miniseries described it as "only a story" that "really happened";[33] Spielberg, who in 1993 also produced the enormously popular *Jurassic Park*, states in an interview that "if it takes my name to get people to [see *Schindler's List*], so be it."[34]

Despite these distinctions, both *Schindler's List* and *Holocaust* honor many of their respective genres' conventions, especially with regard to narrative. While the stories that they relate are quite different from each other, both plots trace the chronology of the Holocaust as a discrete event—beginning with the enactment of Nazi anti-Jewish legislation, climaxing with the gas chambers of Auschwitz, and ending with liberation—thereby paralleling the established master narrative of the Holocaust found in one-volume histories and documentaries on the subject, as well as the exhibitions in the Holocaust museums in Los Angeles and Washington, D.C. Also, the two works each use sympathetic individual characters as a point of entry into the large canvas of momentous historical events. Consequently, both feature dialogue in which characters speak portentiously about history being made.

Just as there are formal features and contextual concerns that link the two works, the discourses surrounding *Schindler's List* and the NBC miniseries often address similar, larger issues. Several critics faulted the *Holocaust* miniseries—subtitled the *Story of the Family Weiss*—for trying to use a family saga to address the master narrative of the Holocaust ("Too much appears to have been done by [the protagonists] to be credible," writes Menachem Rosensaft in *Midstream*, for example).[35] Indeed, Green's teleplay manages to situate members of the Jewish Weiss and German Dorf families at many major events and sites of the Holocaust's master narrative: *Kristallnacht*, Wannsee, the Warsaw ghetto, Babi Yar, Auschwitz. Similarly, screenwriter Steven Zaillian describes a "balancing act" between his and Spielberg's ideas of the scope of the film: "I felt very strongly that by telling Schindler's story, we would tell the story of the Holocaust. I felt that that was enough. Steven felt that he wanted an even larger picture."[36] While Spielberg has said that *Schindler's List* "must never be looked upon as *the* Holocaust story; it is only *a* Holocaust story,"[37] he has also embraced promotion of the film as a "cinematic shout to remember" the Holocaust as a whole. Indeed, Spielberg states his hope that, as a result of seeing the film, "people will say, 'I now feel a need to tell my children about the Holocaust and someday show them not only this movie, but other films and documentaries about it.' "[38] Moreover, he touts *Schindler's List* as having even greater significance; it is not only about the Nazi persecution of European Jewry, "but it's [also] about AIDS, the Armenians, the Bosnians. It's a part of all of us."[39]

A number of critics have commented on the troubling consequences of aggrandizing the agenda of *Schindler's List*. Much of the attention, both positive and negative, focuses on Spielberg (for example, "Spielberg takes on the Holocaust," the subtitle of a *Newsweek* cover feature on the film).[40] This contrasts with discussions of the miniseries, in which, as a rule, critics directed their comments at its medium rather than its producer, director, or scenarist. Echoing an oft-repeated trope in negative reviews of the miniseries, some have derided *Schindler's List* as a Hollywood trivialization of the subject. But whereas the most common epithet hurled at *Holocaust* was that it was a "soap opera," critics of *Schindler's List* assail its *auteur*: J. Hoberman wisecracks that the Holocaust has been "Spielbergized";[41] Tom Segev dubs the film "Spielberg's Holocaust Park."[42] Even in more nuanced critiques, Spielberg is held primarily responsible for the consequences of the film's much vaunted status. Jason Epstein, for example, writes in the *New York Review of Books* that the "aesthetic and moral failure" of the film is a matter of "misplaced emphasis." By celebrating the deeds of "an exotic exception" to the pattern of pervasive acquiescence in or complicity with the Nazis throughout occupied Europe, Spielberg's film fails to address the "terrible questions about the quality of our species" raised by the Holocaust—"questions that Stephen [sic] Spielberg, for all his good intentions and craftsmanship, did not ask, perhaps because they did not occur to him." Moreover, by misleadlingly suggesting that Schindler "made a huge difference" in the course of this chapter of history, Epstein wonders if "the film means to suggest that if only there had been enough Schindlers, the problem of evil which the Holocaust raises would have been solved."[43]

Both *Schindler's List* and *Holocaust* have also raised questions regarding the representation of various parties who figure in the narrative of the Holocaust. Jewish responses have been central in both cases, many finding fault with the portrayal of individual Jewish characters or of Jews as a whole. Ruth Wisse, for example, was one of several detractors of the miniseries to find the nominal Jewishness of the Weiss family to have unsettling implications, creating what she describes as a "deracinated" Holocaust drama that is typical of the "Hollywood image of accidental particularism."[44] Similarly, several critics have variously complained that *Schindler's List* shows Jews as "victims . . . interchangeable in their misery";[45] as figures "who have the generic feel of composites, . . . as forgettable as the chorus in a touring company of 'Fiddler on the Roof' ";[46] or as "caricatures [that] . . . seem lifted less from the self-mockery of Catskill *tummlers* than from the pages of *Der Stuermer*."[47]

Other groups have also faulted both the NBC miniseries and Spielberg's film for misrepresenting them or their role in the Holocaust. The Ukrainian Anti-Defamation League, as well as Polish and Czech groups, decried the miniseries's portrayal of their involvement in the persecution of Jews during World War II.[48] As was also the case with the miniseries, the American media has reported on the responses to *Schindler's List* as it makes its debut in other countries, especially those whose populations have a special connection to the Holocaust. While Israeli responses to the film are generally contextualized within the Holocaust's pervasive presence in their national culture ("We can't escape the Holocaust; it sits on our shoulders," one Israeli told a *Time* magazine journalist covering the film's premiere in Tel Aviv),[49] reports on the reception of *Schindler's List* in Europe have focused on concerns about the portrayals of non-Jews. Noting the paucity of Polish characters in the film, columnist Agnieszka Wroblewska comments that "it's not an anti-Polish film: Poland basically does not exist in it." Nonetheless, she argues, the film "requires a touch of balance," as it fails to allude to Polish victims of Nazis or to those Poles who, like Schindler, helped save Jewish lives.[50]

While much of the discussion of *Schindler's List* appears to be a continuation of issues raised by the miniseries, there are several distinctions that indicate changes in American Holocaust memory culture from the late 1970s to the mid-1990s. The first of these distinctions centers on the issue of geography. Although the miniseries was also shot on location in Europe, including at Mauthausen, much more has been made of filming *Schindler's List* in Poland (Hoberman describes the country as comprising a "special effect" in the film), especially at Auschwitz. Here Spielberg encountered protests from the World Jewish Congress, which objected to his plans to construct a "fake gas chamber" on the premises and otherwise "disturb the dignity of a site that . . . requires solemnity."[51] Eventually yielding to these objections (and filming the Auschwitz scenes just outside the camp's main gate), Spielberg has described the encounter with the geography as profoundly moving: "All of us were very aware . . . that we were making a movie . . . not about fiction, but about events that actually took place underneath our feet 50 years before. . . . We became painfully close to the ground underneath our feet."[52] This resonates with a growing attention among Americans to the physical landscape of the Holocaust during the past two decades, as manifest in a burgeoning of visits, both private and institutional, to the sites of the Holocaust; in an increased interest in the politics of marking and preserving these sites; and in the creation of virtual Holocaust sites in American Holocaust memorials and museums.[53] Indeed, the sites of Kraków and its environs, where *Schindler's List* was filmed, have become important attractions for Jewish tourists now visiting Poland.[54]

The advent of these phenomena, in turn, reflects the considerable extent to which the dynamics of Holocaust memory culture follow the aging of Holocaust survivors. In the mid- to late 1970s survivors—who are, to a considerable extent, a cohort group—emerged as respected elders within the Jewish community and, moreover, as authoritative embodiments of the Holocaust. Since then, concern that these living cultural resources (whom Spielberg described, in his acceptance speech at the 1993 Academy Awards, as "350,000 experts") would soon pass away has heightened the urgency of Holocaust documentation, education, and commemoration with increasing intensity.

The second of these distinctions concerns the conceptualization of the Holocaust as a subject not only centered on European Jewry but also one over which Jews have special provenance. Early presentations of the Holocaust to general American audiences—epitomized for many critics by Frances Goodrich and Albert Hackett's 1956 play *The Diary of Anne Frank*—tend to stress the universality of the subject. Since the mid-1970s the cultural specificity of what historian Lucy Dawidowicz calls "the war against the Jews"[55] has figured more prominently in films, plays, television programs, and other American mediations of the Holocaust. Moreover, some have come to regard the Holocaust as specifically, even exclusively, Jewish cultural property (literary scholar Edward Alexander describes it as the Jews' "moral capital"[56]) that requires vigilant protection against misuse or misappropriation.

Within this context—which is, to a considerable extent, responsive to a concurrent rise in concern over Holocaust revisionist histories and Holocaust denials—much has been made of *Schindler's List* as an affirmation of Spielberg's Jewish identity. In several interviews he has described the Holocaust as an ongoing presence in his life, and he has characterized the decision to make the film as addressing his desire to create "something that would confirm my Judaism to my family and myself."[57] Moreover, some profiles of the filmmaker hail him as "the one true heir to the great Jewish moguls who created Hollywood,"[58] who, by making *Schindler's List*, has somehow redeemed the "film capital['s] . . . long-held aversion to depicting the Holocaust."[59] In contrast, the publicity surrounding NBC's *Holocaust* offered no such public affirmations of their Jewishness by executive producer Herbert Brodkin, producer Robert Berger, director Marvin Chomsky, or scenarist Green. Something akin to this did occur, however, several years later, when Brodkin produced *Skokie* (CBS, 1981). This made-for-television movie is based on the clash between the National Socialist Party of America and the village of Skokie, Illinois, in

1977–1978 over the rights of the neo-Nazi group to stage a public demonstration in the Chicago suburb—half of whose residents were Jews, several thousand of them Holocaust survivors. Throughout *Skokie* characters proudly affirm their Jewishness; this virtual performance is echoed off-camera in press releases, issued by CBS in advance of the broadcast, featuring interviews with Danny Kaye, Carl Reiner, John Rubinstein and Eli Wallach (all of whom appear in *Skokie*), who proclaim the importance of the program and its subject and voice their pride in taking part in its realization.[60]

The third set of distinctions concerns the emergence, since the late 1970s, of the Holocaust as a master moral paradigm in American culture. Much of the discussion of *Schindler's List* demonstrates how Americans repeatedly invoke the Holocaust as a model not only for other genocides—most recently in Bosnia and Rwanda—but also for an expanding range of cultural issues. As Peter Novick observes, "in recent decades . . . the Holocaust . . . is evoked as reference point in discussions of everything from AIDS to abortion."[61] Indeed, on World AIDS Day in 1993 (December 1) President Clinton responded to a heckler from the activist organization ACT UP, who had interrupted the President at a public meeting on AIDS, by bringing up *Schindler's List*. Clinton talked about the film, which he had seen at a special screening the previous evening, and urged everyone to see it. Describing it as "an astonishing thing," he explained how *Schindler's List* had helped him understand the nature of human suffering and its appropriate response: "The reason I ask you to go see the movie is you will see portrait after portrait after portrait of the painful difference between people who have no hope and have no rage left and people who still have hope and still have rage. I'd rather that man [i.e., the heckler] be in here screaming at me than having given up altogether, much rather."[62]

At the same time, the response to *Schindler's List* both in America and abroad also illustrates the problematic nature of using the Holocaust as a moral paradigm. Reactions to an incident that took place at a screening of the film in Oakland, California, on Martin Luther King Day (January 17) in 1994—during which African American teenagers in the audience were expeled from the theater after laughing at a scene of a Nazi shooting a Jew—became a national "Rorschach" test, as Amy Schwartz wrote in an editorial for the *Washington Post*. The Oakland incident began with a teacher's apparently well-intentioned, if poorly thought-out, plan to expose students to the Holocaust as a paradigmatic lesson on the evils of racism on a national holiday honoring one of America's champions of civil rights and interracial harmony; the ensuing event provoked an array of charges of Jewish racism and black anti-Semitism, comprising "a morality tale on the dangers of the current hair-trigger mind-set toward anything that might qualify as cultural insensitivity."[63]

Shortly thereafter *Schindler's List* was the subject of contention in several

Islamic nations, where the film was banned for reasons ranging from concerns about its "nudity, sexual content and violence" to sentiments that the film is a form of "propaganda with the purpose of asking for sympathy" for Jews. Spielberg not only refused to allow scenes deemed offensive to be cut from *Schindler's List*, he also expressed surprise at this response: "It shocks me because I thought the Islamic countries would feel this film could be an instrument of their own issues in what was happening in Bosnia. . . . This movie speaks not only on the Jewish Holocaust, but of every Holocaust, by anyone's definition."[64]

These two incidents are reminiscent of controversies surrounding two television programs dealing with the Holocaust that were aired since the first broadcast of the NBC miniseries: *Playing for Time* (CBS, 1980), Arthur Miller's dramatization of Fania Fénelon's eponymous Auschwitz memoir, created a considerable stir when it was announced that Vanessa Redgrave, an ardent anti-Zionist and supporter of the Palestine Liberation Organization, was engaged to portray Fénelon. Many Jews—including Fénelon herself—found the casting of Redgrave offensive ("Wagner was an artistic genius with an evil mind and so is Vanessa Redgrave," begins a notice in the *Near East Report*),[65] while others argued that to refuse Redgrave the part because of her political views was "anathema," recalling the intolerance of "blacklisting and the McCarthy era."[66] *Liberators: Fighting on Two Fronts in World War II* (PBS, 1992), a documentary on African American servicemen whose wartime actions included the liberation of Nazi concentration camps, was at the center of a prolonged controversy, both over questions about its accuracy[67] and regarding its agenda to promote an image of liberation as constituting a bond between African American soldiers and Jewish Holocaust survivors that would serve as an edifying symbol for contemporary audiences. As a result of the filmmakers' "honest desire" to ameliorate black-Jewish relations, journalist Jeffrey Goldberg argues, "they left the track a bit. . . . It was all too pretty a package. History doesn't come packaged so neatly."[68]

Late in 1993 ABC's *Nightline* cited a number of sources that proclaimed it to be "the year of the Holocaust."[69] Together with the opening of Holocaust museums in Washington and Los Angeles, *Schindler's List* played a leading role in marking this as a watershed year in American Holocaust memory culture. Moreover, the emergence of the Holocaust as a master paradigm in American consciousness is a remarkable phenomenon, for unlike other events of modern history that have become powerful symbols in this nation's culture, such as the assassination of President Kennedy or the war in Vietnam, the Holocaust did not take place in the United States, nor did it directly involve the great majority of Americans. *Schindler's List* and the discussions it has engendered do not merely constitute a cultural milestone; along with NBC's *Holocaust* and its subsequent discourse, they are bound up in this nation's complex, ongoing response—now over a half-century old—to one of the most disturbing chapters of modern history and to the equally daunting question of what its place in our lives might be.

Notes

Some of the discussion of the *Holocaust* miniseries herein appears in the author's doctoral dissertation on the presentation of the Holocaust on American television. The author wishes to thank Stuart Schear for his assistance in the preparation of this essay.

1. There was an extensive exchange of views on *Schindler's List* on HOLOCAUS, an electronic mail discussion group (or "list") that is part of H-Net, a project run by the University of Illinois, Chicago. HOLOCAUS is sponsored by the University's History Department and its Jewish Studies Program. The list address is HOLO-CAUS@uicvm.bitnet; for more information, contact list owner, jimmott@spss.com

2. Judith E. Doneson, *The Holocaust in American Film* (Philadelphia: Jewish Publication Society, 1987), pp. 143, 149.

3. Michael Elkin, "Holocaust as a Media Event," *Jewish Exponent* (Philadelphia), March 14, 1986, p. 31.

4. Ilan Avisar, *Screening the Holocaust: Cinema's Images of the Unimaginable* (Bloomington: Indiana University Press, 1988), p. 129.

5. Peter Novick, "Holocaust Memory in America," in *The Art of Memory: Holocaust Memorials in History*, ed. James E. Young (New York: Jewish Museum/Munich: Prestel, 1994), p. 162.

6. Owen S. Rachleff, "Assessing *Holocaust*," *Midstream* 24, no. 6 (June/July 1978), p. 51.

7. See Sander A. Diamond, " 'Holocaust' Film's Impact on Americans," *Patterns of Prejudice* 12, no. 4 (July/August 1978), p. 4.

8. Bantam Books stocked bookstores with over one million copies of *Holocaust* during the week of the telecast. See Ray Walters, "Paperback Talk," *New York Times*, April 16, 1978, sec. 7, pp. 44–45.

9. The day on which the first episode of the miniseries was broadcast "was unofficially proclaimed 'Holocaust Sunday' " throughout the country. (" 'Khurbn-Zuntik' iz opgerikht gevorn vi an oysdruk fun solidaritet mit yidn in Nyu-york un in land," ["Holocaust Sunday" is observed as an expression of solidarity with Jews in New York and throughout the country], *Jewish Daily Forward*, April 18, 1978, p. 8.)

10. "Watching Holocaust," *Moment* 3, no. 5 (April 1978), p. 34.

11. Doneson, *The Holocaust in American Film*, p. 189.

12. [Proxmire letter], *New York Times*, April 25, 1978, p. 36; William Safire, " Silence is Guilt," *New York Times*, April 24, 1978, p. A23.

13. For a bibliographic overview of the American media response to the premiere of *Holocaust*, see Diamond, " 'Holocaust Film's Impact on Americans," pp. 1–9, 17.

14. American Jewish Committee, *Americans Confront the Holocaust: A Study of Reactions to NBC-TV's Four-part Drama on the Nazi Era* (New York: Institute of Human Relations, 1978); "Impact: Four days in April saw greater awareness of the Holocaust, and its significance, than in three decades preceding," *Anti-Defamation League Bulletin* 35

(June 1978). For a sampling of studies of reactions to the *Holocaust* miniseries in the United States and abroad, see the special issue of *International Journal of Political Education* 4, no. 1/2 (May 1981).

15. *Holocaust* has since been released on video cassette and was reaired as recently as April 1994 on the CBN Family Cable Network. The miniseries was also rebroadcast in 1993 in Germany, "in a bid to expose the horrors of racism" to the citizens of the recently reunited nation, faced with the rise of neo-Nazi groups and racist attacks ("Hollywood Holocaust Film Revived in Germany," March 2, 1993, Reuters).

16. See Anton Kaes, "History and Film: Public Memory in the Age of Electronic Dissemination," *History and Memory* 2, no. 1 (Fall 1990), p. 116; Doneson, *The Holocaust in American Film*, p. 208.

17. Judith Miller, *One, by One, by One: The Landmark Exploration of the Holocaust and the Uses of Memory* (New York: Simon & Schuster, 1990), p. 273.

18. Andrew Nagorski, "Spielberg's Risk," *Newsweek* 121, no. 21 (May 24, 1993), pp. 60–61. In an interview on *ABC News: Nightline* aired on March 21, 1994, Kaminski also credits the photography of Roman Vishniac as "the guiding force for visual interpretation" of *Schindler's List*. ("The Film Makers," show #3346, transcript, p. 2.) Vishniac's pictures of Polish Jewry taken during the late 1930s have become among the most widely familiar images of "pre-Holocaust" European Jews. They have been published in several books since the end of the war (*Polish Jews: A Pictorial Record* [New York: Schocken, 1947]; *A Vanished World* [New York: Farrar Straus Giroux, 1983]; *To Give Them Light: The Legacy of Roman Vishniac* [New York: Simon & Schuster, 1993]) and are prominently displayed in the United States Holocaust Memorial Museum in Washington, D.C.

19. Leon Wieseltier, "Washington Diarist: Close Encounters of the Nazi Kind," *New Republic* 210, no. 4 (January 24, 1994), p. 42.

20. Curt Schleier, "Steven Spielberg's New Direction," *Jewish Monthly* 108, no. 4 (January/February 1994), p. 12.

21. The association of the Holocaust with the aesthetics of black-and-white photography can also be seen in other forms of its memory culture. The somber, colorless design of the interior of the United States Holocaust Memorial Museum in Washington, D.C., for example, resembles that of the vintage images that dominate its main installation. Similarly, in the Beit Hashoah/Museum of Tolerance in Los Angeles, visitors walk through dioramas depicting life in pre–World War II Germany rendered in black, white, and grey—in effect, museum-goers travel back to the past by entering a black-and-white world.

22. "Television Reviews: Holocaust—Part One," *Variety*, April 19, 1978, p. 48.

23. Lance Morrow, "Television and the Holocaust," *Time* 111, no. 18 (May 1, 1987), p. 53.

24. Saul Friedlander, ed., *Probing the Limits of Representation: Nazism and the "Final Solution"* (Cambridge: Harvard University Press, 1992).

25. Elie Wiesel, "Trivializing the Holocaust: Semi-Fact and Semi-Fiction," *New York Times*, April 16, 1978, sec. 2, p. 1.

26. Molly Haskell, "A Failure to Connect," *New York* 11, no. 20 (May 15, 1978), p. 79.

27. Henry Feingold, "Four Days in April: A Review of NBC's Dramatization of The Holocaust," *Shoah: A Journal of Resources on the Holocaust* 1, no. 1 (1978), p. 15.

28. John J. O'Connor, "TV: NBC 'Holocaust,' Art Versus Mammon," *New York Times*, April 20, 1978, p. C22.

29. Jean Baudrillard, *The Evil Demon of Images* (Sydney, Australia: Power Institute Publications, University of Sydney, 1987), p. 23.

30. I am indebted to Barbara Kirshenblatt-Gimblett for this observation.

31. Nagorski, "Spielberg's Risk," p. 60.

32. Andrew Nagorski, " 'Schindler's List' Hits Home," *Newsweek* 123, no. 11 (March 14, 1994), p. 77.

33. Owen S. Rachleff, "Assessing *Holocaust*," *Midstream* 24, no. 6 (June/July 1978), p. 50.

34. Schleier, "Steven Spielberg's New Direction," p. 13.

35. Menachem Z. Rosensaft, "Distorting the Holocaust," *Midstream* 24, no. 6 (June/July 1978), p. 54.

36. "The Film Makers," *ABC News Nightline*, March 21, 1994, transcript, p. 3.

37. Nagorski, " 'Schindler's List' Hits Home," p. 77.

38. Arthur J. Magida, "Spielberg's Triumph: 'Schindler's List' Comes to the Screen," *Baltimore Jewish Times* 214, no. 7 (December 17, 1993), pp. 50, 53.

39. Dotson Rader, "We Can't Just Sit Back and Hope," *Parade Magazine* [*Washington Post* edition], March 27, 1994, p. 7.

40. *Newsweek* 122, no. 25 (December 20, 1993), front cover.

41. J. Hoberman, "Spielberg's Oskar," *Village Voice*, December 21, 1993, p. 63.

42. See Richard Corliss, "Schindler Comes Home," *Time* 143, no. 11 (March 14, 1994), p. 110.

43. Jacob Epstein, "A Dissent on 'Schindler's List,' " *New York Review of Books* 41, no. 8 (April 21, 1994), p. 65.

44. Ruth R. Wisse, "The Anxious American Jew," *Commentary* 66, no. 3 (September 1978), p. 47.

45. Sheli Teitelbaum, "A Game with No Rules," *Jerusalem Report* 4, no. 17 (December 30, 1993), p. 43.

46. Frank Rich, "Extras in the Shadows," *New York Times*, January 2, 1994, sec. 4, p. 9.

47. Philip Gourevitch, "A Dissent on 'Schindler's List,' " *Commentary* 97, no. 2 (February 1994), p. 51.

48. See Diamond, " 'Holocaust' Film's Impact on Americans," p. 8.

49. Corliss, "Schindler Comes Home," p. 110.

50. As cited in Nagorski, " 'Schindler's List' Hits Home," p. 77.

51. "Jews Try to Halt Auschwitz Filming," *New York Times*, January 17, 1993, sec. 1, p. 25.

52. Schleier, "Steven Spielberg's New Direction," p. 12.

53. On American Jewish visits to Holocaust sites in Europe, see Jack Kugelmass. "The Rites of the Tribe: The Meaning of Poland for American Jewish Tourists," *YIVO Annual* 21 (1992), pp. 395–453; on Holocaust monuments, see James E. Young, *The Texture of Memory: Holocaust Memorials and Meaning* (New Haven: Yale University Press, 1993), and James E. Young, *The Art of Memory*. On Holocaust museums see Edward T. Linenthal, "Contested Memories, Contested Space: The Holocaust Museum Gets Pushed Back," *Moment* 18, no. 3 (June 1993), pp. 46–53; Edward T. Linenthal, *Preserving Memory: The Struggle to Create America's Museum* (New York: Viking, 1995).

54. Dierdre Berger on Jewish culture in Poland, *National Public Radio: All Things Considered* [radio broadcast], July 7, 1994.

55. Lucy S. Dawidowicz, *The War Against the Jews, 1933–1945* (New York: Holt, Rinehart and Winston, 1975).

56. Edward Alexander, "Stealing the Holocaust," *Midstream* 26, no. 9 (November 1980), p. 48.

57. Rader, "We Can't Just Sit Back and Hope," p. 7.

58. Calev Ben-David and Sheli Teitelbaum, "Spielberg's Close Encounter," *Jerusalem Report* 4, no. 17 (December 30, 1993), p. 40.

59. Magida, "Spielberg's Triumph," p. 49.

60. Similarly, press releases invoke the filming of the program on location in Skokie, using actual landmarks and residents, not merely as a sign of the program's authenticity, but as a tacit endorsement by participants in the actual events reenacted. See "Danny Kaye, John Rubinstein, Carl Reiner, Kim Hunter and Eli Wallach Star in 'Skokie' Drama Special. . . . " CBS Television Network Press Information, September 18, 1981. National Jewish Archive of Broadcasting, Jewish Museum of New York.

61. Novick, "Holocaust Memory in America," p. 159.

62. "Excerpts from President's Speech on AIDS Research Efforts," *New York Times*, December 2, 1993, p. B10.

63. Amy E. Schwartz, "Laughter in the Movie House," *Washington Post*, March 16, 1994, p. A19.

64. Bernard Weinraub, "Islamic Nations Move to Keep Out 'Schindler's List,' " *New York Times*, April 7, 1994, p. C15.

65. "The Redgrave Controversy," *Near East Report* 24, no. 40 (October 3, 1980), p. 183.

66. Tony Schwartz, "Names of Redgrave Film's Sponsors Guarded by CBS-TV and Ad Agencies," *New York Times*, September 25, 1980, p. C26.

67. In February 1993, public television station WNET, which helped produce *Liberators*, withdrew the documentary from circulation and convened a review board to scrutinize the accuracy of the documentary's claims about the role of all-black units as liberators of Buchenwald and Dachau. Later that year the review board found the film's portrayal of these events to be inaccurate. See Joseph B. Treatser, "WNET Inquiry Finds No Proof Black Unit Freed 2 Nazi Camps," *New York Times*, September 8, 1993, p. B3.

68. John Carmody, "The TV Column: Report on a Controversy," *Washington Post* September 8, 1993, p. D6.

69. "America Remembers the Holocaust," *ABC News Nightline*, December 28, 1993.

Fig. 9.1: *Der Spiegel* 8 (February 21, 1994), cover

9 | The Tale of a Good German

Reflections on the German
Reception of *Schindler's List*

Liliane Weissberg

Act(ing) of State

S*CHINDLER'S LISTE*, the German-language version of Steven Spielberg's film about Oskar Schindler and his rescue of Jews during the Holocaust, opened in Germany on March 1, 1994, as a gala event. Michael Graeter's account of this festive occasion was published in the society pages of the popular journal *Bunte*; it was placed between a report on the American Grammy Awards celebration and a description of an elegant *Schützenfest* (riflemen's meeting), organized by a Munich delicatessen firm.[1] In his article, Graeter revealed that Spielberg, who had come to Frankfurt to attend the movie's opening, had already been to Germany before. He had made two previous visits to this country to promote his earlier films *Jaws* and *Close Encounters of the Third Kind*.

Not many people seem to have remembered Spielberg's earlier visits, but Graeter is able to document the more recent event. His article presents the gala's exciting guest list and the guests' new evening fashions. Photographs feature Spielberg and his wife, the actress Kate Capshaw, as well as Senta Berger and Iris Berben, German movie actresses who acquired fame in the early postwar German cinema. Also pictured are the literary critic Marcel Reich-Ranicki and his wife, Teofila. Several months earlier, the German news weekly *Der Spiegel* had dedicated a lead article to this Jewish *Literaturpapst*;[2] he was featured on the journal's cover as a bulldog, eager to devour a (German?) book— a subversive and bespectacled *Jaws* himself.[3] At the film premiere, however, Reich-Ranicki appeared as a member of the German cultural as well as Jewish establishment, providing a link between invited Holocaust survivors and former and current media stars. At the gala opening of *Schindlers Liste*, these Jewish guests generated a new interest in the actors, and the actors present provoked, in turn, media attention for the Jewish guests.

Movies do not tend to open in Frankfurt, a city mostly known as a center of banking and high finance; Frankfurt lacks the film studios or big movie houses of Munich or Berlin. Indeed, the first screening of *Schindlers Liste* took place in the city's main dramatic theater, the Schauspielhaus. Spielberg's attendance transformed the event into one of international importance. His presence had an unexpected flair, moreover; he seemed to resemble a character from his own movies, offering perhaps an encounter of a third kind. A reporter for the *Frankfurter Allgemeine Zeitung* described Spielberg as a younger and tamer *Literaturpapst*, namely, as a shy man with the beard and glasses of a modest American college professor.[4] Other journalists were well aware of the arrival of someone equally exotic: a Hollywood star. After all, Spielberg jetted to Frankfurt in his private Gulfstream III and booked the entire first floor of the Frankfurter Hof, one of the city's luxury hotels.[5] Graeter, for one, reveled in this fact with a mixture of wonder and cynicism that resembles the reaction of many Germans to those wealthy Americans who arrived in Frankfurt after the war and made claims, as members of the allied forces or as tourists, to this city in the former "American zone." The Frankfurter Hof, however, has a long tradition that is hardly ever mentioned. Before housing postwar Americans, it had served as a favored abode for politicians and party officials during the Third Reich, among them Adolf Hitler himself.

But was Spielberg's visit and the film's opening merely a social event? Graeter reports the extraordinary security measures taken to protect Spielberg and his entourage—a level one security alert that involved sixty policemen and forty employees from a private security firm, mobilized to supplement Spielberg's own two body guards. In addition, a large number of police cars surrounded the theater. Never before had so many police officers arrived at the scene of a movie opening. The movie centered, of course, around a "Jewish" issue, and all Jewish institutions and events are guarded in Germany by (albeit fewer) police. Famous stars, too, deserve (somewhat lower levels) of special protection. Clearly, however, the opening of *Schindlers Liste* was to be viewed as a political affair as well and Spielberg's presence as a state visit of sorts.

This did not seem extraordinary. Spielberg's twenty-four-hour stay was sandwiched between brief sojourns in Paris and Kraków, where he was also scheduled to introduce his film. Shortly before his arrival in Frankfurt, Spielberg had met with French president François Mitterrand. In Frankfurt, German president Richard von Weizsäcker attended the first screening of the film, as did several local politicians. Indeed, to many journalists, it was not Weizsäcker's presence, but chancellor Helmut Kohl's absence that caused surprise. In Germany, the president is given a largely ceremonial function, while the political power rests in the chancellor's hands. Many papers criticized the chancellor's choice of engagements, if only by drawing attention to this fact.[6] Did not Kohl include a visit to the German soldier's cemetery at Bitburg in an American state visit in 1985? Why had he decided not to attend the funerals of Turkish guest workers who were murdered by members of a right-wing organization in the summer of 1993? And was not the opening of the movie

Schindlers Liste an event of similar importance? The chancellor's office released Kohl's schedule of that day in an attempt to defuse any possible claim concerning Kohl's insensitivity in regard to Jewish issues.[7] At the same time, journalists insisted on asking Spielberg how he felt about the chancellor's absence at the movie's opening. During his brief remarks before the screening of his film, Spielberg excused Kohl's absence publicly, stating that he was sure that Kohl would see his film in the near future: "No bad feelings."[8]

The gala opening of *Schindlers Liste* was preceded by an official luncheon in the Römer, the reconstructed old town hall that has become Frankfurt's symbol. Members of the city council and "highly placed personalities" gathered for a festive meal to celebrate the director, his film, and the actions of its hero, Oskar Schindler.[9] Spielberg was asked to enter his name in the *Goldenes Buch*, the city's official guest book for visiting dignitaries, and the city council presented him with a model of the Paulskirche, a Frankfurt church that has come to stand for a German liberal political tradition. The luncheon's proceeds benefited the organization "Wider dem Vergessen" (Against Forgetting). The organization, which had already sponsored a series of popular music events in the previous months, collects money for the rebuilding of the Auschwitz concentration camp from which Schindler once had rescued some of his Jewish employees. Spielberg's film thus spoke not only for the destruction of these camps, but for their reconstruction, too, as a monument similar to that which the film itself had already become.[10]

Frankfurt was chosen as the site of the movie's German opening, as Spielberg stated, because Schindler had lived in this city during the last years of his life.[11] But the choice of city and theater had another resonance as well. In 1985, the year of Kohl's and Ronald Reagan's visit to Bitburg, Günther Rühle, then head of Frankfurt's Schauspielhaus, decided to stage the premiere of a play by the recently deceased German film director Rainer Werner Fassbinder. The drama, *Der Müll, die Stadt und der Tod* (The garbage, the city, and death), centered on Frankfurt's postwar building boom, and it pictured ruthless and money-hungry Jewish investors. Its main character was a Jew whom one had "forgotten to have gassed," one who feels safe in his despicable dealings: "The city protects me, because it has to."[12] He was said to be modeled after Ignatz Bubis, a businessman and Frankfurt Jew.

Der Müll, die Stadt und der Tod could easily be placed within an anti-Semitic tradition, and there ensued a public debate on whether or not this drama should be staged at all. Rühle's justification for the inclusion of Fassbinder's drama in his theater's program caused further stir, however, as he claimed that the *Schonzeit* (closed season) for Jews had ended.[13] At the time of the play's opening, members of Frankfurt's Jewish community stormed the stage. Following this protest, the play was removed from the theater's schedule. The discussion about the play's importance, the freedom of artistic expression, and political sensitivity toward German Jews continued for several months.[14]

At the time of the opening of *Schindlers Liste* in Frankfurt's city theater, this local scandal seemed forgotten. Bubis, who had meanwhile become the leader of Germany's Jewish community, attended the event. Rühle, now a critic for the Berlin *Tagesspiegel*, was asked to write a review of the film; there he commented on the movie's tremendous commercial success and speculated about the money it would generate.[15] Graeter, finally, did not mention any *Schonzeit* but placed his report next to an account of a *Schützenfest*. This time, as Germany's past became the center of a gala event, no noise of protest was heard in the theater; instead, journalists remarked on the moviegoers' tears and a silence that provided an incongruous close to the gala festivities and the initially "relaxed and almost merry atmosphere."[16] As the movie ended, "human vanities collapsed" (11); critic Reich-Ranicki refused to comment, and even Weizsäcker, famed for eloquent speeches in which he often tried to face Germany's (and his own family's) Nazi past, was described, again and again, as having been "speechless": "I cannot, I don't want to say anything right now."[17]

Celebrating Mourning

Silence can be a way of mourning. Spielberg had referred to his own mourning in many of the interviews in which he offered comments about his own historical research, his personal history, the filming in Poland, or his decision not to direct another film in the coming year.[18] Headlines such as the following examples from *Die Welt* and the *Frankfurter Neue Presse* merge his personal with the expected public experience and move the site of mourning firmly into German lands: "Guests at the Opening Night Struggle with Their Tears: *Schindlers Liste* in Germany for the First Time—'It Was Like Making a Film in a Cemetery,' " "Steven Spielberg on Cinema, Holocaust and Germany: 'Making the Film Was a Nightmare: Four Long Months in a Cemetery.' "[19] The silence which was to greet the film marked its impact and success—"*Schindlers Liste* works,"[20] and terms were coined to signify this particular impact. If Spielberg claimed to present "authentic" events, this authenticity resulted in the sincere affections of *Beklemmung* and *Betroffenheit*. While *beklemmend* refers to an effect that may come close to being paralyzed,[21] *betroffen* has its origin in the viewer, who may be provoked to further thought. The word *Betroffenheit*, which recurs in many of the articles and reviews that deal with Spielberg's film,[22] derives from *treffen* (to meet, to hit, to aim), a general term used also for hunting and wartime shooting. It is related to *Betroffene*, i.e., people who have been afflicted by a particular event. Linguistically, the *Betroffene* who had suffered in the concentration camps,[23] and the movie audience struck by what they saw, were therefore made to bond.

Silence, as a reaction to a film's emotional impact, differs from a silence as a repression of experience or knowledge. In 1967, the Frankfurt psychoanalysts Alexander and Margarete Mitscherlich summed up the political and mental climate of the postwar Federal Republic with a phrase that became the title of their best-selling book: "The Inability to Mourn."[24] As the authors pointed out, remaining silent about the past prevents a working through. A silence of this kind has marked the often cursory treatment of the Holocaust in German high schools since the war, or the exclusion of any discussion of the Holocaust within the private space of one's family. This was a silence against which West Germany's younger generation had protested in the late sixties.

During the war, there was a "knowing" silence as well, staged as a protective mantle for those who had decided, more or less, to become fellow travelers (*Mitläufer*) of the Nazi regime. It seemed safe not to argue. Sometimes, this silence did not differ much from an "inner emigration," yet another, self-enforced silence assumed by writers and cultural critics as a form of resistance or passive protest. Despite the Third Reich's propaganda machine, and the constant references to the Nazi past in postwar German media, silence about, and silence inspired by the past plays an important, if not crucial, part in the country's postwar politics and self-perception.

Since the fall of the Berlin wall in 1989, moreover, and the reunion of East and West, other kinds of silences have been defined. The German Democratic Republic had regarded itself as an antifascist state, and this had given its citizens the license to view the western Federal Republic as the only "successor" to the Nazi state. But many West German political scientists, as well as a large segment of the general public, have likened the communist to the Nazi government as a totalitarian regime, thus treating the GDR period as "Germany's second past."[25] After 1989, many former GDR citizens chose not to mention their previous political involvement in the Communist Party. As GDR secret service files have been declassified, investigations of former agents and political informers have turned into political witch-hunts that produce constant headlines.[26]

Since the end of the war, and especially since the founding of the Federal Republic in 1948, reunification had been stated as the West German government's prime agenda. The notion of reunification did not imply that Germany was divided into two different states; indeed, the GDR was not officially recognized by West Germany for many years after its formation. Instead, Germany was viewed by the West as a national body whose members were separated but yearned to grow together. In 1989, Leipzig's citizens followed this cue by changing their banners of protest from "We are the people" to "We are one people," thus questioning the legitimacy of the GDR regime as well.

Since 1989, however, the metaphor of an integral national body has been recognized as little more than mere fiction. Not only do many citizens in the West resent carrying the economic burden of supporting their previously severed Eastern limbs but the cultural, ideological, and political differences between East and West seem more articulated than ever. Germany (East and West) has become a state desiring nationhood, despite its selves. While the nationalism of the past is deemed undesirable, a positive concept of nationhood has not yet been fully constructed. Paradoxically, however, West and East have to look back to the thirties and forties to find the recent "common" history and past from which to proceed and to find a sense of continuity. Turning toward the Nazi past has assumed a new significance.

In March 1994, when *Schindlers Liste* opened in Germany, the preparations for the D-day celebrations marking the fiftieth anniversary of the landing of allied troops in Normandy were well under way; so was a public discussion of whether or not German officials should participate in the events that would commemorate the beginning of the country's defeat in World War II.[27] Germany had not been invited to the ceremonies, and Kohl insisted that he never sought an invitation in the first place.[28] When François Mitterrand asked German troops to participate with other European forces in a parade on Bastille Day the following month, this could be interpreted as a trade-off as well as a gesture of reconciliation marking the difference between past and present German governments. Despite some public protest, Mitterrand did not rescind his invitation and, for the first time since the Hitler regime, German troops, displaying their arms discreetly, drove down the Champs Elysées in their tanks. For many Germans, the discussions surrounding these events became a test of whether or not the state had achieved a desired "normalcy" that would define Germany as just another—though economically leading—European country. "For 45 years," Theo Sommer writes, "the Federal Republic has been on the way to find itself. Now, it has arrived: it is reunited; no longer threatened in its national, yes: physical existence; rid of the legal shackles (*Souveränitätsfesseln*) of its occupying forces. . . . The united Germany is, from now on, one state among others."[29]

This newly (re)constituted European country should, however, not only be a state but a nation as well that would reunite East and West. In the effort to gain independence from any allied forces, a new nationalism has even been espoused by (formerly) left-leaning authors such as Martin Walser, Botho Strauss, and Hans Magnus Enzensberger who write for journals such as *Der Spiegel*. And Kohl's government, which censures violent outbreaks against foreigners by right-wing groups, has at the same time limited foreign immigration. The general argument given is simple. While political refugees may have been victims in their own country, Germany itself has become a "victim" of its former, more liberal immigration policies. In an article commenting on the discussions surrounding the D-day event, the German writer Peter Schneider describes "the unconscious attempt to efface the difference between assailant and assaulted that characterizes the Germans' view of themselves and the stance they take on issues."[30] The rhetoric of Germany's official immigration policy may be a further case in point—as is the linguistic leveling of the *Betroffene* who watch, and become victim to, the effects of Spielberg's film.

Against this background, can the silence with which the German audience responds to *Schindlers Liste* be compared to the silence that follows a screening in the United States? Does this silence acknowledge past guilt or indicate redemption? Is it related to the tragedy of the extermination of Jews, or the surprise of an individual's action of rescue against all odds? And what, precisely, were the odds?

A Good German Is Hard to Find

Germany's new nationalism tries to distinguish itself from the undesirable ideology of the past by its moral dimension. In the Federal Republic of 1994, not the proper citizen but, above all, the good German is in demand. Within the context of reviving and redefining nationhood, *Schindlers Liste* has come to play an important part.

In general, Spielberg's film was received enthusiastically in Germany, and the tremendous number of reviews published seem to counter the audience's silent response. Early reviews in *Die Zeit* and *Der Spiegel* appeared even before the film's German distribution,[31] and once the German version was released, the film received more attention than any other movie in recent German history. *Schindlers Liste*, wrote Wolfgang Hübner for the East German *Neues Deutschland*, "conquers Germany."[32] Newspapers, journals, and talk shows concentrated on the persecution of the Jews, on Spielberg and his actors, and on Schindler and his actions. Schindler's widow Emma was flown to Germany from Argentina to be interviewed in journals and on television specials.[33] Numerous newspaper articles dealt with "Schindler Jews" and other Holocaust victims and survivors. A Bavarian politician advised schools to view the film,[34] although school outings to movie houses were previously discouraged as being too reminiscent of the required visits to view propaganda films—both during the Third Reich and in the GDR.[35] The Bundeszentrale für politische Bildung, a government institution affiliated with the Bundestag, distributed, upon request, instructional material as aids for teachers.[36] In the first few weeks, *Schindlers Liste* grossed more than any other film in recent German history and was taken as an example for the revitalization of the movie indus-try.[37] For many, to see this film has become a moral obligation, nearly 100,000 viewers saw the film in the first four days, although only 45 copies were avail-able at that time.[38] "One has to see this film," urges Dana Horáková in the popular *Bild Zeitung* immediately changing her voice into the more intimate address, the "Du," that urges her reader-as-friend to follow her advice, espe-cially now that neo-Nazism seems to be on the rise.[39] Michael Knopf in the *Süddeutsche Zeitung* bemoans the fact that some young people refuse to see the movie and seem uninterested in it.[40] As Marion Gräfin Dönhoff, editor of *Die Zeit*, points out, the film is not only educational but has redefined education as a matter of predisposition or a "political litmus test." Right-wing youth, as she gratefully acknowledges, do not show much interest in the film.[41] Educa-tion is a privilege these youths did not earn and one that should be reserved for those who do deserve it. For Dönhoff, the film's advantageous effect is not a unification of all Germans but a separation of the good from the undesirable elements of the population; it thus constructs a respectable Germany against its negative image.

When the American television miniseries *Holocaust* was aired on German television fifteen years earlier, it attracted similar attention. References to the German past have been a constant presence on German television, but *Holo-caust* seemed to have touched the emotions of many of its German viewers in a way that previous discussions did not. Although the series instigated a dis-cussion about the Holocaust, it was generally recognized as a fictional tale commenting on historical events. *Schindlers Liste*, on the other hand, has been billed as an "authentic" story, a claim enforced by Spielberg's statements about his own research as well as his technical devices, such as the use of black-and-white film or a hand-held camera.[42] In contrast to *Holocaust*, *Schindlers Liste* was praised by many as a masterwork—either as a historical rendering that tri-umphs over film, or as art that triumphs over documentary imprecision.[43] But the most important difference may lie elsewhere. *Holocaust* offered a negative image of Germans, unmasking even silence as a form of compliance. Spiel-berg's film not only offers a reflection on the *Holocaust* but also the story of a problematic person who loved women, liquor, and gambling alike. Well-dressed and compassionate, Spielberg's hero is an antiskinhead who, at the same time, works against the system. Spielberg does not show what "Ger-mans" did but what *individual* Germans did, offering hope that one of them—Schindler—would become one of many. Unlike *Holocaust*, but also unlike Fass-binder's fiction of the bad Jew, Spielberg can tell a "true tale" that must seem doubly strange. While the events in *Schindlers Liste* may contradict the idea of the Nazi state as the perfect machine, the state's and Schindler's deficiencies provide a paradox of choice—"the other Nazi,"[44] the German who did good.

Goodness is not a commodity in constant high demand. Oskar Schindler's rescue of his Jewish factory employees was not always viewed as an act of particular distinction by German government officials. After the war, Schindler settled on a farm in Argentina; he returned to Germany in the fifties, impoverished and without promise of any further financial support. He had spent an early reparation payment that compensated him for the loss of his factory, and he had applied for a pension, a process that did not result in immediate success.

On February 17, 1965, Karl Carstens, a former member of the NSDAP and then a politician with the conservative CDU party, wrote a confidential letter to Georg August Zinn, the head of the state of Hesse in which Frankfurt is located. As West Germany's consul general in Los Angeles, Carstens saw it as his duty to inform Zinn of the rumor that the MGM film studios were planning a movie with well-known actors about Schindler, "a German citizen resident in Frankfurt/M."[45] Schindler, a man who had rescued the lives of more than 1000 Jews, was supposed to visit America soon. Carstens made Zinn aware that Schindler had not yet received any German medal or citation, and he wondered whether any reparation had been paid. In light of the expected international attention, the matter of Schindler's pension should be looked into and some recognition considered. Ten years earlier, Chancellor Konrad Adenauer had used diplomatic channels to ban Alain Resnais's film *Night and Fog* from the Cannes Film Festival; Adenauer had feared that such a well-publicized screening would damage the image of the Federal Republic abroad.[46] In the case of the MGM project, such censorship across borders was less advisable, but preventive measures were called for. In January 1966, Schindler received a medal, the Bundesverdienstkreuz (Carstens became president of West Germany in 1979).

It took another year for Schindler to receive a modest pension of DM 500 per month. His case had not been helped by questions concerning Schindler's private conduct, which was observed and dutifully recorded in his pension file. In April 1965, for example, Schindler was convicted of drunk driving and his driver's license was temporarily withdrawn. In 1958, he had been sentenced to pay a sum of money because he had beaten a man who called him *Judenknecht*—a servant of the Jews.[47] All of this did not speak for respectable citizenship. There was a lingering suspicion, moreover, that Schindler lived in more luxurious surroundings than he actually did. In fact, Schindler lived in a small furnished studio apartment near the Frankfurt railroad station; he was visited on weekends by his girlfriend, a doctor from Cologne, and supported at times by members of the Jewish community.[48] In October 1974, Schindler died in a hospital in Hildesheim and was buried at the Catholic cemetery in Jerusalem. Perhaps it is the final irony that the body of this man who liked to gamble would be transferred to Israel with the help of proceeds from the German lottery, the Deutsche Klassenlotterie. A dead-end street was named after him in Frankfurt's modern high-rise suburb of Bonames, where many Eastern immigrants settled.[49]

At the gala opening of Spielberg's movie, city officials spoke of Schindler's post-war fate with some embarrassment, and noted that most Germans still remained ignorant of Schindler's wartime actions. Not only the times had changed, however. The city officials belonged to a new generation which did not have much experience of its own of the war; praising Schindler did not involve questioning their own political past. One representative of the conservative CDU party in the current city council is Michel Friedman, a member of the Jewish community as well as the son of "Schindler Jews." Friedman was often interviewed and asked to comment on Spielberg's movie, and the *Journal Frankfurt* dedicated its lead article to him in time for the film's gala opening.[50]

In recent years, the notion of heroism has undergone some changes, too. While Hesse's officials focused on Schindler's conduct, Schindler's weaknesses and brushes with the law have turned into a positive asset. In a response to a negative review of Spielberg's film published in the *New York Review of Books*, Dönhoff praises the director's treatment of the Holocaust and eagerly points to the distinction between "inhuman" and "ahuman" beings, counting the war criminals in the latter category because they behaved like machines.[51] Despite his party affiliation, Schindler's weaknesses establish him as particularly human. Where humaneness and heroism are able to merge and become one, goodness can be made accessible again as faults can be forgiven.

While larger than life, Schindler appears also to be like life, or rather, to be like film. In the German press, Spielberg's movie has been used most strikingly to comment on Schindler's life, often in unexpected ways. Some early reviewers of *Schindlers Liste* have commented on Spielberg's choice of beautiful female victims.[52] But photos of naked actresses playing victims were also used in one article to strengthen his widow's claim about her former husband's affairs.[53] In the reception of *Schindlers Liste*, the Holocaust could thus be transformed into a stage for Schindler, whose weaknesses were positively enhanced by the victims' attractiveness. In refusing to become a good Nazi, Schindler became a good man who happened to be a Nazi but could be heroic as well.

This move was helped, of course, by Spielberg's film. The director who viewed the Nazi government as a "casting studio" transformed Schindler's heroism into various movie genres.[54] If Jews were treated like cattle, Schindler was their Western cowboy; if Jewish women were beautiful, Schindler could act as a sex symbol. He could be the Paul Newman of the gambling table or, if excess was part of his private and professional life, become a Richard Burton who had stumbled upon a mission. In short, Spielberg's Schindler became a "typical American hero," an "action man."[55] But was this true for the "real" Schindler as well? Did not Schindler trick Nazi officers into deals by mere acting?

With the movie's German reception, the images of Schindler and of Liam Neeson—the actor who played Schindler and who accompanied Spielberg to Germany—seemed to merge as well. As the *Bunte* points out, Neeson wanted to become a butcher before deciding upon acting and was a former womanizer as well; in short, he was a "man just like Schindler."[56] The East German newspaper *Neues Deutschland* praised Neeson's "captivating presence" and attributes that define Neeson as well as Schindler and that could best be expressed in English as: "charisma, sex appeal," or the "flair" of a "gentleman."[57] *Der Spiegel*, finally, put Neeson's picture on its cover. While the headline on this cover refers to a current German scandal involving politics and sex, the photograph's caption reads: "The Good German, Spielberg's Holocaust Drama: Jew-Rescuer Schindler."[58] As Neeson-Schindler, Spielberg's hero was a rescuer, not a savior; a human, not a holy man; an actor par excellence.

Moving Pictures

Germans who had rescued Jews were more often recognized for their actions in Israel or the United States than in Germany. Schneider suggests that the reason may be obvious: any German who saved a Jew points up at those who did not.[59] *Schindlers Liste* confirms, however, a quite different recent tendency. Schindler's figure may not only be able to counter this German "original sin" by his humaneness, he may be able to reconcile past and present. "A good German" can act against the state and for his people, he can represent them as an exception that may prove the rule. An officer such as Amon Goeth may not turn into a German Goethe, and in the dubbed German version, the actor Ralph Fiennes was provided with a strong Austrian accent, which subtly proves this point. Schindler, in turn, could offer a paradox: a Nazi who did good. He could not only rescue Jews, but redeem Germans as well. And perhaps he would not have to do this single-handedly. Articles about other German heroes flooded the German press and included accounts of prominent businessmen as well as ordinary citizens.[60] Count Claus Schenk von Stauffenberg, a conservative officer and member of the Nazi party who attempted to assassinate Hitler toward the end of World War II, was celebrated more than ever as a symbol of resistance.[61] If the participants in the recent German *Historikerstreit* tried to come to terms with the question of whether the Holocaust constituted a unique historical event, reviewers of *Schindlers Liste* insisted on Schindler's uniqueness by creating competition for his heroic deeds. The person Schindler had to be multiplied, as his individual story became subject to the laws of technological reproduction. Both multiplication and reproduction would serve the dissemination of a new national image.

The concept of nationhood is, as Benedict Anderson insists, created in the imaginary. To create a common, if mythical, bond for people, the idea of "nationhood" has not only to be constructed but circulated as well. As Anderson points out, news and book print have been the earliest means of such dissemination.[62] It should not come as a surprise that Hitler also utilized the persuasive power of a new medium, film, to forge an image of an Aryan nation, as can be witnessed, for example, in the work by Leni Riefenstahl. In 1994, a non-German speaking Irish actor would create the new German symbol Oskar Schindler, as filmed by a director identifying himself as an American Jew. There is, however, an astonishing similarity between Riefenstahl's and Spielberg's perception of a German's physical presence, one to which Schindler has easily been made to conform. One of the problems he had with Neeson, Spielberg claimed, was that he stooped too much; the director had to teach him to stand straight and live up to his proper size.[63]

The question of why *Schindlers Liste* had not been produced and directed by a German became the most prevailing question asked by the German press. In a lead article in *Die Zeit*, Andreas Kilb greeted the movie with this question even before its German opening;[64] and it was posed to Spielberg himself at the opening of his film.[65] The conservative historian Michael Wolffsohn and the left-leaning journalist Henryk Broder repeated the question several months later.[66] Broder, a Jewish writer now living in Israel, has become a critical voice on German affairs, and his query was embedded in an argument that tried to trace the latent anti-Semitism of those film critics who wrote negatively of *Schindlers Liste*.[67] In a statement for *Der Spiegel*, the film producer Artur Brauner, who had issued *Europa, Europa* just a few years earlier, posed this question as well and recounted his own attempts to find financial backing for a project on Schindler's story that failed because of insufficient government support and the public film office's lack of interest.[68] Not only Schindler, but also the book by Thomas Keneally that served as the main material for Spielberg's movie seem to have gone unnoticed, even though a German translation had been published.[69] The question of why *Schindlers Liste* was not directed by a German must be posed against a background of German government's film production policies as well as "the Germans' " inability to deal with the Holocaust. But it implied more than this. If history is the story of people in power, the Holocaust was not only Jewish, but first of all German history.

Schindler's story is not simply a story about murdered Jews but about rescued ones. In America, too, Holocaust studies have begun to concentrate on rescuers rather than on victims.[70] Schindler's life offers a positive tale par excellence, and if Schindler was a German, his story should be viewed as a national treasure. As a national treasure, it can be likened to a fairy tale; to parables and stories that were collected in the nineteenth-century as a *Schatz-kästlein* or treasure trove, to serve an emerging national identity.[71] Moreover, while Spielberg tried to create a film that would come close to history, the reviewers readily equated story and film. This may, indeed, explain another paradox. While reviewers stressed Spielberg's masterful handling of scenes or pointed at some flawed direction, his film—like Schindler's life—is not personal but public property. The film does not need an individual creative mind to imagine it, other persons could have done the same. The question of why no German director made *Schindlers Liste* (and not just any comparable film) insists, therefore, on Spielberg's authorship by making his person exchangeable; it presupposes a loose bond between story and directorial skills that could have resulted, if the circumstances were more favorable, in a German movie as a "world event."[72] What was, however, the significance of Spielberg doing this film "first"?

Spielberg is, of course, an American. This was pointed out even in many details that may seem fairly incidental. For the introduction of his movie at the gala opening, Spielberg arrived, for example, in a Cadillac, while Mercedes were offered to other guests (they were, however, not as nice as the luxury models shown in Spielberg's film itself, as the *Bunte* reported).[73] And while this American may have directed *Schindlers Liste*, he is not the first American filmmaker to concern himself with the Holocaust. Indeed, he is part of a "tradition" that reaches far beyond the successful television melodrama.

American forces (as well as British and Russian troops) liberated the concentration camps with cameras in hand, documenting both the evidence of the atrocities and their soldiers' shocked reactions. While Spielberg relied on newly discovered period photographs to create "authenticity,"[74] the director George Stevens, then an American army officer, filmed a camp's liberation in the newer medium, color; he would later proceed to direct *The Diary of Anne Frank* (1959). Billy Wilder, enlisted as a film specialist by the American forces after the war, remembers that some of these films were screened to a German public as part of reeducation efforts and that food stamps could only be acquired after having seen these films.[75] Years later, after viewing Spielberg's film, Wilder would tell *Die Zeit* about another, more personal military victory: He had "escaped Hitler" as a Jew and had "conquered Hollywood."[76] Wilder, too, thought about filming Schindler's story and wondered how Spielberg's film would be received in present-day Germany, a "land of the skinheads" (43).

But *Schindlers Liste* does not only come from a country that had been victorious in the war and that engaged previously in moral instruction for Germans. As journalists stressed again and again, *Schindlers Liste* was directed by a Jew. This may not have been a task entirely without risk. "Did you fear that you would be reproached as a Jew to have depicted a Nazi who was a good man?" the *Schädelspalter*'s interviewer asked.[77] Spielberg's Jewishness may be yet another answer to the question of why a movie such as this had not been made in Germany before, and one that Kilb implies.[78] There are not many film directors among the small number of Jews now living in Germany. The responsibility for producing a film such as *Schindlers Liste* was first given to and accepted by a German Jew, however. Artur Brauner, ready to elaborate on his own attempts to produce *Schindlers Liste*, is a prominent member of Berlin's Jewish community.

The Lesson of the Jew

It is curious that German redemption and the confirmation of a new national image cannot be brought about by anyone other than a Jew. Steven Spielberg's Jewishness is a factor every article that deals with *Schindlers Liste* insists upon, and a fact that may have been more easy to overlook in regard to any one of his previous films. Spielberg's Jewishness, moreover, is not just a simple given, but has been acquired—not least because, or as a result of, the Holocaust and the making of this film.

In their interviews with Spielberg, German journalists insist on asking him about his Jewish sensibility; they are eager to elicit personal comments that turn his movie on the Holocaust into an autobiographical statement as well. While growing up in America, Spielberg explains, he had encountered anti-Semitism in his school and in the suburbs. For years, he had tried to deny or forget about his Jewishness, but a few years ago, he "reconverted" to Judaism and took religious instruction together with his wife.[79] Although raised as an Episcopalian, Capshaw acquired victimhood in her own right, as the *Frankfurter Rundschau* simply changed her name to Capture.[80] For German interviewers, *Schindlers Liste* is a document of Spielberg's return to his Jewish "roots," a strengthening of family values, and a testimony to a newly found faith. He had found new peace in his "Jewish pride."[81]

Spielberg's acceptance of Judaism is the story of a homecoming and a *Bildungsroman* that bears striking resemblance to Schindler's own story as pictured on the screen. If Amon Goeth is Schindler's alter ego in the movie, Spielberg can also be viewed as Schindler's double; he, too, is a "Mensch."[82] Spielberg's *Bildungsroman*, moreover, leads from childhood to adulthood, to a sense of responsibility toward himself, his audience, and history.[83] *Schindlers Liste* becomes his school diploma, a document of maturity, a *Reifezeugnis*.[84] While Spielberg may have styled himself an adolescent genius, Schindler's early attraction toward power seems both glamorous and childish. Is Schindler, in turn, a new Citizen Kane for whom a Nazi affiliation has become simply a matter of immaturity?

While Judaism may be a religion, it is a mark of ethnicity as well. For German readers, Spielberg's early denial of his ethnic background and his return to it would be a familiar reaction. It recalls the German Jews' prewar striving for assimilation, but also the postwar Germans' silent rejection of their own national identity, which should now be recovered. While Schindler could be transformed from a negative *Judenknecht* to a German who positively acts on the Jews' behalf, Spielberg, as a Jew, could be thus more than a (negative?) American—he could be German as well.

Since Johann Gottfried Herder, Jews have been described in Germany as a nation without land, as "parasitical" (at their worst), or "highly adaptable" (at their best).[85] Viewed as a representative of a nomadic people, the Jew emerged as his own peculiar "moving picture." Perhaps it is no accident, therefore, that at least one member of Spielberg's entourage arrived in Germany without a passport—a fact generously overlooked by government officials but not by the press.[86]

Spielberg's Jewishness could thus be used to transform this American millionaire and Hollywood star par excellence into a person whose truly American background could be questioned. Indeed, while many Jews today may be Americans, being Jewish speaks against Spielberg's American ancestry. He can be viewed as part of an extended emigration, as somebody Germany had lost—and a German at heart. In interviews with Spielberg, questions often concentrate on Spielberg's family history and on his personal interest in exploring the events of the Holocaust. But could one find a particular relationship to Germany in his past as well? Spielberg seemed ready to answer this demand. He refers to relatives in Germany and Austria, and while most of his answers to the interviews are nearly identical rephrasings of a set of statements, the death toll reported varies like a personal, peculiar stock in authenticity: eight, more than eight, ten, or seventeen of these relatives had died during the war.[87] Spielberg thus acts with double authority. The figures of death provide legitimacy to his role as a Jew; he is a victim only once removed. His film produces its energy from an experience that may not have been his own but has still been a personal one. His family history, moreover, refers him back to Germany.

In Germany, which does not offer passports to persons born there but to persons of German ancestry, Spielberg may, indeed, not only qualify as a Jew but as a German as well. There is an odd mechanism at work. While the film tells the story of a "good German," its director has to be turned into a good German himself to be able to tell the tale. And did he not have to turn into a Nazi of sorts while directing his film, calling out "action!" before each scene like a German Sonderkommando rounding up Jews?[88] And Spielberg's film may provide further evidence for Spielberg's "Germanification" in its very attempt to be accessible to a wide audience by keeping its emotions in check[89]—indeed, at the end of the gala opening, Spielberg is the only one able to smile.[90] *Schindlers Liste* seems to adopt, moreover, rites of purification that readily confirm German clichés: even the victims are well-scrubbed, Jewesses are beautiful, the streets are clean—and showers, after all, work just as they should, as showers. While Spielberg the American dazzles and annoys his viewers with a Hollywood budget and Hollywood effects, Spielberg the German delivers the "miracle" of a "European" movie.[91] Can this movie, or Spielberg, subsume all these identities at once?

As a German, Spielberg can reconcile any feelings of envy or competition. As a Jew, Spielberg is given particular license. Fassbinder was not allowed to picture a bad Jew, but Spielberg is able to imagine a good German—and make him believable as well. And a slightly different educational task has extended to other members of the German Jewish community. Viewers, identified as Jewish, were turned into film critics to comment on their reactions to the movie, as well as on the movie's intrinsic qualities.[92] They had to decide as well whether Schindler "was really good."[93] They symbolized both moral conscience and the ability to witness German crimes, as well as Schindler's actions. This is not limited to the World War II generation. As the case of Friedman shows, witnessing extends to the next generation as well and becomes a Jewish inheritance. For postwar Germans, these surviving Jews recapture the proper *Ordnung* of judgments and emotion; they have thus become not just a chosen people but a people of chosen parents. Parents are needed for those who may be not only unable to learn about the good but about the bad, about those Nazis who have become the "others" as members of a different generation and, hopefully, a different species as well:

> Many of these brutal beasts are still among us, but one cannot recognize them. The friendly old man at the newspaper stand at the corner . . . the lovely grandma who walks with her grandchild through the park, perhaps she had been a supervisor in a concentration camp, killing little children. Because it did not happen that long ago. . . . [94]

While journalists did not wait for Weizsäcker's muteness to end, Bubis was established as a moral guide, aiding the public as an analyst-turned-Ms. Manners. Placed next to a series of film stills that advise the reader when to cry or close his or her eyes in the movie theater, an article entitled "Herr Bubis, What Do My Tears Signify?" gives answers to the following questions: "Which facts do I have to know, before I view this film?"; "I am a young German and feel guilty. Which arguments would help me?"; "Am I allowed to avert my gaze if some scenes seem particularly gruesome?"; "What can I tell my 15-year-old daughter, when she asks me why her grandfather did not aid the Jews as well?"; "Does this film hurt the German image abroad?"; "My neighbor eats popcorn during the film. Should I do something about it?"[95]

Where popcorn can become a moral issue, negative criticism of Spielberg's film has to come from the proper source as well, just to avoid any misunderstanding—both of the reviewer's stance and the film's political status. It is best supplied by Jewish critics, and German journalists refer at times to their American colleagues. Monika Gierig's article in the *Frankfurter Rundschau* is thus entitled "Abyss of Memory: What American-Jewish Critics Minded about Spielberg's New Film 'Schindler's List.'"[96] Here, the criticism of a forced happy ending, sensational imagery, or technical overkill that is often voiced by German critics in regard to American films is reduced to a mere quotation by the "other."

While the Jew has thus turned into the German's moral conscience, the German, even when quoting the American voice, knows better—and can, indeed, become a teacher for Americans. Reporting from Oakland, California, where black students had interrupted a screening of *Schindler's List* with repeated laughter, Rolf Paasch describes the event as further evidence of a racism common within American society.[97] Americans, moreover, seem to know little about the Holocaust, if they believe at all in its existence. Only every fourth or fifth American, Ruprecht Skasa-Weiß writes in the *Stuttgarter Zeitung*, takes the Final Solution as a fact.[98] For Paasch, whose article was published on the day of the movie's opening in Germany, freedom of speech encourages Americans in a "freedom to hate" (3). Indeed, it is America, not Germany, in which racism currently thrives. Germans may view themselves as a nation after the Fall—but Americans, innocent of the Holocaust, are not necessarily in a more advantageous position. Deprived of Schindler as well as of the Final Solution, America simply did not have the proper lesson from which it could learn.

Notes

1. Michael Graeter, "Das Whitney-Houston-Märchen. Graeter bei der Grammy-Verleihung. Triumphe und Tränen," *Bunte* 11 (March 10, 1994), pp. 210–25; on Spielberg's visit to Frankfurt, see pp. 214–15.

2. For the term *Literaturpapst* (pope of literature), see for example, Welt-Nachrichtendienst, "Premierengäste kämpften mit den Tränen: 'Schindlers Liste' erstmals in Deutschland—'Es war wie das Drehen auf einem Friedhof,'" *Die Welt* (March 3, 1994), p. 11.

3. "Der Verreißer: Kritiker Marcel Reich-Ranicki," cover, *Der Spiegel* 40 (October 4, 1993). The article (anon., "Marcel Reich-Ranicki—vom Kritiker zum Fernsehstar") appeared on pp. 268–79.

4. [Hans Riebsamen], "Premiere in der Heimatstadt des Filmhelden," *Frankfurter Allgemeine Zeitung* (March 2, 1994), pp. 41–42; here p. 41.

5. Graeter, "Das Whitney-Houston-Märchen," p. 215.

6. Welt-Nachrichtendienst, "Premierengäste kämpften mit den Tränen," p. 11. See also Craig R. Whitney, "The German Premiere of 'Schindler's List' Brings Tears and Praise," *New York Times* (March 2, 1994), p. C15.

7. Kohl was reported to have visited Frankfurt on the previous day to honor the Rothschild family; see Whitney, "The German Premiere of 'Schindler's List,' " p. C15.

8. Welt-Nachrichtendienst, "Premierengäste kämpften mit den Tränen," p. 11. Whitney quotes Spielberg somewhat differently for the *New York Times*: "I would have loved to have bent Mr. Kohl's ear" ("The German Premiere of 'Schindler's List,' " p. C15).

9. Peter Körte, "Sterns Liste oder: Die vergebliche Erinnerung. Über Steven Spielbergs neuen Film 'Schindlers Liste' und dessen beredte Aufnahme in der deutschen Öffentlichkeit," *Frankfurter Rundschau* (March 1, 1994), p. 8. For a description of the events, see abi/ing, "Prominenz und ein Regisseur: Empfang für Spielberg," *Frankfurter Rundschau* (March 2, 1994), p. 19.

10. For a discussion of German reactions and attitudes toward Holocaust memorials, see my essay, "Memory Confined," *documents* 4/5 (1994), pp. 81–98.

11. [Riebsamen] "Premiere in der Heimatstadt des Filmhelden," p. 41.

12. Helmut Schmitz, "Müllkutscher Fassbinder," *Frankfurter Rundschau* (March 12, 1976), reprinted in Heiner Lichtenstein, ed., *Die Fassbinder-Kontroverse oder Das Ende der Schonzeit* (Frankfurt/M: Athenäum, 1986), pp. 25–28; here p. 26. The review appeared after the publication of the play by the Frankfurt Suhrkamp Verlag in 1976.

13. See the documentation by Lichtenstein, ed., *Die Fassbinder Kontroverse*. The book contains articles and reviews relating to Fassbinder's play and the ensuing scandal of its staging. The book was banned for a brief period by the German government at the instigation of Günther Rühle, who suspected slander.

14. See Lichtenstein, ed., *Die Fassbinder Kontroverse*.

15. See Henryk M. Broder, "Kritik der dummen Kerls: Spielbergs Widersacher," *Frankfurter Allgemeine Zeitung* (March 15, 1994); reprinted in *Arbeitshilfen zum Film Schindlers Liste* (Bonn: Bundeszentrale für politische Bildung, 1994), pp. 57–58. Broder cites Rühle and points at Rühle's involvement in the staging of Fassbinder's play.

16. Welt-Nachrichtendienst, "Premierengäste kämpften mit den Tränen," p. 11; see also dpa/AP, "Als ob es gestern war: Premiere von 'Schindlers Liste,' " *Süddeutsche Zeitung* (March 3, 1994), p. 13.

17. See, for example, Welt-Nachrichtendienst, "Premierengäste kämpften mit den Tränen," p. 11, and Steffen Ball, "Premiere im Schauspielhaus: Ein Mann weint, viele schluchzen," *Bild Zeitung Frankfurt* (March 3, 1994), p. 6; and Laszlo Trankovits, "Dem Bundespräsidenten fehlten die Worte," *Frankfurter Neue Presse* (March 3, 1994), title page.

18. See, for example, Helmuth Karasek, interview with Spielberg, "Spiegel-Gespräch: Die ganze Wahrheit schwarz auf weiß. Regisseur Steven Spielberg über seinen Film 'Schindlers Liste,' " *Der Spiegel* 8 (February 21, 1994), pp. 183–86; anon., interview with Spielberg, "Hollywoods Holocaust," *Schädelspalter* 3 (1994), pp. 44–45; interview, " 'Ich mußte heulen,' " *Die Woche* (March 3, 1994), reprinted in *Arbeitshilfen*, p. 12; Patrick Roth, interview with Spielberg, "Grauenhafte Wahrheit," *Journal Frankfurt* 5 (February 25–March 10, 1994), pp. 38–39.

19. Titles of the articles in German: Welt-Nachrichtendienst, "Premierengäste kämpften mit den Tränen"; anon., interview with Spielberg, "Steven Spielberg zu Kino,

Holocaust und Deutschland: 'Die Dreharbeiten waren ein Alptraum: Vier lange Monate auf einem Friedhof,' " *Frankfurter Neue Presse* (March 3, 1994), p. 13.

20. Ball, "Premiere im Schauspielhaus," p. 6.

21. "How can one separate any aesthetic judgment from the *Beklemmung* that one feels as a person who knows, who has been a witness of that time and, above all, is a German?" asks Ruprecht Skasa-Weiß, "Lebemann, Lebensretter: 'Schindlers Liste', Steven Spielbergs großer Holocaust Film," *Stuttgarter Zeitung* (March 3, 1994), p. 35. See also Karasek, interview, "Die ganze Wahrheit schwarz auf weiß," p. 183.

22. See, for example, the caption "Betroffene Kinobesucher in München," placed under a photograph of moviegoers in *Bunte* 11 (March 10, 1994), p. 16.

23. See, for example, the collection of statements in "KZ-Überlebende fordern: 'Alle sollen den Film sehen,' " *cinema* 3 (1994), p. 54.

24. Alexander und Margarete Mitscherlich, *Die Unfähigkeit zu trauern. Grundlagen kollektiven Verhaltens* (Munich: Piper, 1967); the book appeared in English translation in 1975 as *The Inability to Mourn: Principles of Collective Behavior*, trans. Beverley R. Placzek (New York: Grove).

25. See Peter Schneider, "Invasion and Evasions," *New York Times* (June 7, 1994), p. A23.

26. One of the latest subjects of investigation is, indeed, Marcel Reich-Ranicki, who worked for the Polish secret service after the war and whose period of membership in the Polish Communist Party has been under scrutiny. See, for example, Janusz Tycner, "Die Akte Ranicki," *Die Zeit* 49 (July 22, 1994), pp. 13–14.

27. See Craig R. Whitney, "Mixture of Feelings," *New York Times* (June 9, 1994), p. A8, and Schneider, "Invasion and Evasions," p. A23.

28. Whitney, "Mixture of Feelings," p. A8.

29. See, for example, Theo Sommer, "Nicht jede Macht muß alles müssen," *Die Zeit* 49 (July 22, 1994), title page.

30. Schneider, "Invasion and Evasions," p. A23.

31. See Andreas Kilb, "Warten, bis Spielberg kommt. Von 'Holocaust' bis 'Schindlers Liste': Hollywood bewältigt die deutsche Vergangenheit. Und wir?" *Die Zeit* (January 28, 1994), title page; anon., " 'Schindlers Liste'—Spielbergs Film-Monument über den Holocaust," *Der Spiegel* 8 (February 21, 1994), pp. 168–83.

32. Wolfgang Hübner, "Schindlers Qual: Ein einst Verfemter wird zum Helden," *Neues Deutschland* (March 4, 1994), reprinted in *Arbeitshilfen*, p. 64.

33. See, for example, Christoph Stopka, interview with Emma Schindler, "Ich bin Frau Schindler: Mein Mann war ein Held, aber ich hasse ihn," *Bunte* 8 (February 17, 1994), pp. 22–25; and the early comments by Peter Körte, "Sterns Liste oder: Die vergebliche Erinnerung. Über Steven Spielbergs neuen Film 'Schindlers Liste' und dessen beredte Aufnahme in der deutschen Öffentlichkeit," *Frankfurter Rundschau* (March 1, 1994), p. 8.

34. This early recommendation was given by Hans Zehetmair, a member of the conservative CSU and head of the Bavarian *Kultusministerkonferenz*; see AP, "Schindlers Liste: Hunderttausend Besucher, eine Empfehlung," *Frankfurter Allgemeine Zeitung* (March 9, 1994), p. 33.

35. See m.h., "Kino als Schulpensum," *Neue Zeit* (February 11, 1994), reprinted in *Arbeitshilfen*, p. 88.

36. *Arbeitshilfen* offers a selection of newspaper clippings and a guide to questions about the film that can be used to initiate class discussion. While the newspaper clippings concentrate on German and German language publications, the question and discussion part is adapted from a previously published English teacher's aid.

37. See Volker Mazassek, "Opas Kino war nur scheintot. Lichtspielhäuser boomen," *Frankfurter Rundschau* (March 3, 1994), p. 29.

38. AP, " 'Schindlers Liste,' " p. 33; see also Wolf Schön, " 'Schindlers Liste'—ein Pflichtfilm," *Rheinischer Merkur* (March 11, 1994), reprinted in *Arbeitshilfen*, p. 69.

39. Dana Horáková, "Film der Woche: Der andere Nazi: 'Schindlers Liste,' " *Bild Zeitung Frankfurt* (March 3, 1994), p. 6.

40. Michael Knopf, " 'Viele wollen nichts wissen': Ratlosigkeit nach dem Entsetzen: Wie Jugendliche auf Spielbergs 'Schindlers Liste' reagieren," *Süddeutsche Zeitung* (March 9, 1994), reprinted in *Arbeitshilfen*, p. 87.

41. Marion Gräfin Dönhoff, Letter to the Editor, *New York Review of Books* (June 9, 1994), p. 60. See also Knopf, " 'Viele wollen nichts wissen,' " p. 87. The *Bild Zeitung Frankfurt*, on the other hand, censures teachers who were invited to see the film with their classes but rejected this opportunity: "With such 'pedagogues,' one does not have to be surpised if a section of our youth turn into rioting skinheads" ("Bild-Info 2" [March 3, 1994], p. 6).

42. See, for example, anon., interview with Spielberg, "Steven Spielberg: 'Haß auf Hitler,' " *cinema* 3 (March 1994), pp. 56–57, here p. 56; Sabine Horst, "Schwarz fließt das Blut: Lektion aus Hollywood: Steven Spielbergs Holocaust-Film 'Schindlers Liste,' " *Kultur!News* 3 (1994), pp. 18–19; Peter Buchka, "Der Schwarzmarkt des Todes: Das Unfilmbare filmen: Steven Spielbergs 'Schindlers Liste,' " *Süddeutsche Zeitung* (March 3, 1994), p. 13.

43. See Wolfgang Benz, "Bilder statt Fußnoten. Wie authentisch muß der Bericht über ein geschichtliches Ereignis sein? Anmerkungen eines Historikers zu 'Schindlers List,' " *Die Zeit* 49 (March 4, 1994), p. 59.

44. See Horáková, "Film der Woche," p. 6.

45. For an account of this incident and Schindler's reparation and pension payments, see Helmut Schmitz, "Wie ein großzügiger Habenichts zur Ehrenrente kam: Ein Blick in die Akte Oskar Schindler der hessischen Staatskanzlei deckt die Wege der deutschen Bürokratie auf," *Frankfurter Rundschau* (March 1, 1994), p. 3. Unless otherwise noted, I follow Schmitz's report here.

46. Sabine Horst, " 'We couldn't show that,' " *Konkret* 3 (1994), pp. 40–42, here p. 42.

47. Hübner, "Schindlers Qual," p. 64; Hella Kaiser, "Im Nachkriegsdeutschland war der 'Judenfreund' nicht gern gesehen. Manci und Henry Rosner erinnern sich an Oskar Schindler, den Mann, dem sie ihr Leben verdanken," *Tagesspiegel* (March 3, 1994), p. 2.

48. I am supplementing here the account of Schmitz, "Wie ein großzügiger Habenichts zur Ehrenrente kam," p. 3, with my personal recollections.

49. Ball, "Premiere im Schauspielhaus," p. 6; see also Hans Riebsamen, "Vergessner Held," *Frankfurter Allgemeine Zeitung* (March 2, 1994), p. 41.

50. Edith Kohn, "Michel Friedman: Der Paradiesvogel," *Journal Frankfurt* (February 2–March 10, 1994), pp. 28–30; the journal also published an interview with Steven Spielberg in the same issue. For comments on and by Friedman, see, for example, Ball, "Premiere im Schauspielhaus," p. 6.

51. Dönhoff, Letter to the Editor, p. 60.

52. See, for example, Sigrid Löffler, "Kino als Ablaß: Spielbergs mißlungener Holocaust-Film," *Wochenpost* (February 24, 1994), reprinted in *Arbeitshilfen*, p. 49.

53. Stopka, interview, "Ich bin Frau Schindler," p. 24.

54. Karasek, interview, "Die ganze Wahrheit schwarz auf weiß," p. 186.

55. Horst, "Schwarz fließt das Blut," p. 18, and Skasa-Weiß, "Lebemann, Lebensret-

ter: 'Schindlers Liste,' " p. 35; see also Will Tremper, "Indiana Jones im Ghetto von Krakau," *Die Welt* (February 26, 1994), reprinted in *Arbeitshilfen*, pp. 50–51.

56. Anon., "Ein Mann wie Schindler," *Bunte* 11 (March 10, 1994), p. 5.

57. J. D., "*Starkasten*: Liam Neeson," *Neues Deutschland* (March 3, 1994), p. 13.

58. *Der Spiegel* 8 (February 2, 1994), cover. See also the caption, "The industrialist Oskar Schindler" used for a picture of Liam Neeson in *Bunte* 11 (March 10, 1994), p. 18.

59. Schneider, "Invasion and Evasions," p. A23.

60. See anon., " 'Sie schrien nach ihren Männern': Wie Juden mit List und Zivilcourage vor dem Holocaust gerettet wurden," *Der Spiegel* 8 (February 21, 1994), p. 178; but also the article in the Swiss *Neue Zürcher Zeitung*, kü, "Oskar Schindler war nicht der einzige" (March 3, 1994), p. 8.

61. See Donald Koblitz, "A Plot. A Bomb. A Pariah. A Hero. Germans Need Their Martyrs," *New York Times* (July 19, 1994), p. A19.

62. Benedict Anderson, *Imagined Communities: Reflections on the Origin and Spread of Nationalism*, rev. ed. (London: Verso, 1991), pp. 37–38.

63. Anon., interview, " 'Haß auf Hitler,' " p. 57.

64. Kilb, "Warten, bis Spielberg kommt," title page.

65. Anon., interview, "Steven Spielberg zu Kino, Holocaust und Deutschland," p. 13.

66. Michael Wolffsohn, "Wo bleibt der Mut zum Widerstand?" *Rheinischer Merkur* (March 4, 1994), p. 17; Henryk M. Broder, "Deutsche Ausreden," *Die Woche* (March 3, 1994), reprinted in *Arbeitshilfen*, p. 68.

67. Broder, "Kritik der dummen Kerls," pp. 57–58.

68. Anon., " 'Engel in der Hölle': Die Filmförderung boykottierte ein deutsches Schindler-Projekt," *Der Spiegel* 8 (February 21, 1994), p. 174.

69. Thomas Keneally, *Schindlers Liste: Roman*, trans. Günther Danehl (Munich: Bertelsmann, 1983; the American edition appeared in 1982).

70. See Diana Jean Schemo, "Good Germans: Honoring the Heroes. And Hiding the Holocaust," *New York Times* (June 12, 1994), Week in Review 1, p. 6.

71. See Johann Peter Hebel's collection of tales and anecdotes, *Schatzkästlein des rheinischen Hausfreundes* (1811), and especially the numerous *Hausbücher* of fairy tales collected by the brothers Grimm.

72. Anon., " 'Grenze für Greuel,' " *Der Spiegel* 11 (March 14, 1994), pp. 192–96, here p. 192.

73. See Graeter, "Das Whitney-Houston-Märchen," p. 215, and abi/ing, "Prominenz und ein Regisseur," p. 19.

74. See Janet Maslin, "Imagining the Holocaust to Remember It," *New York Times* (December 15, 1993), p. C19.

75. Quoted in Andreas Kilb, "Des Teufels Saboteur: Steven Spielbergs Film-Epos über den Völkermord an den europäischen Juden—'Schindlers Liste,' " *Die Zeit* 49 (March 4, 1994), pp. 57–58; here p. 58. A selection of these films is being shown at the United States Holocaust Memorial Museum in Washington.

76. Billy Wilder, "Man sah überall nur Taschentücher," *Die Zeit*, magazine supplement (February 18, 1994), reprinted in *Arbeitschilfen*, p. 41.

77. Anon., interview, "Hollywoods Holocaust," p. 44.

78. Kilb, "Warten bis Spielberg kommt," title page.

79. See anon., interview, "Steven Spielberg: 'Haß auf Hitler,' " p. 56; and Roth, interview, "Grauenhafte Wahrheit," p. 39.

80. abi/ing, "Prominenz und ein Regisseur," p. 19.

81. Heiko Rosner, " 'Schindlers Liste': Der definitive Film über das Grauen des Naziterrors," *cinema* 3 (March 1994), pp. 50–56; here p. 54.

82. Billy Wilder, quoted in "Hausmitteilung: Betr.: Schindler-Film," *Der Spiegel* 8 (February 21, 1994), p. 3; compare Spielberg's remarks about Schindler, in pek, " 'He was a mensch': Spielberg und die Presse," *Frankfurter Rundschau* (March 2, 1994), p. 19.

83. See, for example, such statements "Director Steven Spielberg is growing up," in anon., "Ci im März," *cinema* 2 (1994), p. 156.

84. Buchka, "Der Schwarzmarkt des Todes," p. 13.

85. See my essay, "Hebräer oder Juden? Religiöse und politische Bekehrung bei Herder," in: *Johann Gottfried Herder: Geschichte und Kultur*, ed. Martin Bollacher (Würzburg: Königshausen und Neumann, 1994), pp. 191–211.

86. Graeter, "Das Whitney-Houston-Märchen," p. 215.

87. Anon., interview, "Steven Spielberg: 'Haß auf Hitler,' " p. 57; Roth, interview, "Grauenhafte Wahrheit," p. 39; anon., interview, "Steven Spielberg zu Kino, Holocaust und Deutschland," p. 13; anon., interview, "Hollywoods Holocaust," p. 44.

88. See Roth, interview, "Grauenhafte Wahrheit," p. 38.

89. See, for example, Frank Schirmacher, " 'Schindlers Liste,' " *Frankfurter Allgemeine Zeitung* (March 2, 1994), title page.

90. Ball, "Premiere im Schauspielhaus," p. 6.

91. Karasek, interview, "Die ganze Wahrheit," 186; see also Horst "Schwarz fließt das Blut," p. 19.

92. See, for example, the anonymous collection of statements, "Das meinen Premierengäste," *Bild Zeitung Frankfurt* (March 3, 1994), p. 6; anon., collection of statements, "KZ-Überlebende fordern," p. 54.

93. Christa Piotrowski, "War Schindler wirklich gut? Steven Spielbergs Film setzt Oskar Schindler ein Denkmal. Sechs überlebende 'Schindlerjuden' erzählen ihre Geschichte—und die ihres Retters," *Die Woche* (March 3, 1994), reprinted in *Arbeitshilfen*, pp. 22–23; here p. 22.

94. Rosner, " 'Schindlers Liste': Der definitive Film über das Grauen des Naziterrors," p. 50.

95. Anon., interview with Bubis, "Herr Bubis, was bedeuten meine Tränen?" *Bunte* 11 (March 10, 1994), pp. 19–21. Compare as well Annette Kögel, " 'Auch wenn ich was auf die Nase kriege: Dafür lohnt es sich. 'Schindlers Liste'—eine fesselnde Schulstunde mit Ignatz Bubis," *Der Tagesspiegel* (March 17, 1994), reprinted in *Arbeitshilfen*, p. 86.

96. Monika Gierig, "Abgrund der Erinnerung: Was amerikanisch-jüdische Kritiker an Spielbergs neuen Film 'Schindler's List' bemängeln," *Frankfurter Rundschau* (January 15, 1994), reprinted in *Arbeitshilfen*, p. 76.

97. Rolf Paasch, "Wo die Gewalt vor der eigenen Haustür beginnt: Spielbergs Film 'Schindlers Liste' stößt bei den Jugendlichen der Schwarzen-Gettos in USA auf Unverständnis," *Frankfurter Rundschau* (March 1, 1994), p. 3. See also anon., " 'Grenze für Greuel,' " p. 192.

98. Skasa-Weiß, "Lebemann, Lebensretter," p. 35.

10 | The Great Taboo Broken

Reflections on the Israeli Reception of *Schindler's List*

Haim Bresheeth

T‍HE RECEPTION OF *Schindler's List* in Israel was always going to be "different"; in some respects, the only valid comparison is to its reception in Germany—both audiences were viewing the film from very different points of departure, but both audiences were coming to it highly charged. The ferocity of the re-action was closely matched by its range—more was written in a short time about *Schindler's List* than about any other film shown in Israel. Thus, the reac-tion is more revealing about contemporary Israeli public discourse than about this individual film.

By all accounts, the Israeli reaction to *Schindler's List* has been quite a trau-matic affair. Both supporters of the film and its detractors have used strong and emotive language and argumentation of a kind not heard before in film reviews in Israel; the debate was still flaring months after the first showing. It is my contention that the film constitutes a further disturbance of an outdated status quo on Holocaust issues, a status quo undermined by a decade of recent change. Hence, both the formative period and the recent changes in position-ing need to be examined. It is that process of positioning, of reworking the collective memory of the Diaspora and the Holocaust, which necessarily con-ditions Israeli reactions to this film.

The Prewar Years

The creation of Israel, the final goal of the Zionist project, was, after all, a negation of the Diaspora, the antithesis of two thousand years of Jewish exis-tence and survival. While Diaspora Jews were important for Zionism as the future settlers of Palestine, the concept itself was anathema. Many of Zion-ism's leaders, themselves immigrants to Palestine, treated the Diaspora with disdain, if not hostility.[1] Ben Gurion "regarded the Holocaust as the ultimate fruit of Jewish life in Exile. As such, it represented a Diaspora that deserved not only to be destroyed, but also forgotten".[2] This attitude was not surprising. The Zionist project was not just a project of physical revival; it was even more crucial as a cultural and ideological revival, concentrating on the creation and perfection of the identity of the "new Jew" in Palestine.[3] By definition, the new Jew was measured by the distance from the old Jew, the ghetto Jew. The old Jew in Zionist iconography was not dissimilar to the standard anti-Semitic portrait—the "inversion of what is productive," the rootless, cosmopolitan, unproductive, and passive entity, inevitably attracting the hatred of its social environment, as it were. Zionism was to eradicate this type of Jewishness and replace it with the new Jew.

It is important to understand the complexity and contradictory nature of some of the sources and inspiration for the new Jew stereotype. Both the cultural and historical materials used in this synthesizing project, and the discourse, argument, and ideological positioning used in this effort of identity-construction, have a bearing on the later, contradictory role played by the Holocaust in Israeli popular memory and official history. Because of the nature and function of the new Jew stereotype before 1948, the ghetto Jew was one of the main "others" the Israeli "self" came to define itself against. While the European Diaspora Jew was seen as the Yiddish-speaking, spineless ghetto trader, eking out an existence by cunning and wit but lacking self-respect, and getting little respect from the society around him, the new Jew is a combination of all the values and qualities missing from the ghetto Jew. While the ghetto Jew depends for existence on the producing classes, the new Jew is self-sufficient, exploits no one, and controls an empty land there for the taking. The ghetto Jew was doomed from the Zionist perspective—human dust, as Weizmann named him, a historical type with a despicable past and no future. Thus, the ghetto Jew became the antithesis of the Israeli Jew, even before the creation of the Israeli state.

This is very different from how every other Jewish community, notably the buoyant American Jewish community, has perceived the European Jews. For most other Jews, European Jewry was the font of their history, culture, and religion—the direct ancestor, a representative of the Patriarchs.[4] The *shtetl* may well have represented a provincial and archaic past they had partly separated from, but there was no direct denial of that past. This difference was also evident during the war years, with the community in Palestine taking a much more detached line on the plight of Jews in Europe, lest it may come at the cost of the support of their own plight. The silencing of critical voices, and also the lack of public concern with the destruction process as it became gradually known during the war,[5] will also be the key attitude after the war, with one important exception.

The 1930s—the "Cruel Zionism" debate

One should mention here the two main tendencies within Zionism toward Europe's Jews during the 1930s in order to contextualize later developments.

Immediately after the coming to power of the Nazi Party, fascism became a central issue in Palestine, dividing left and right, or more accurately, Labor Zionism, led by Ben Gurion, from the Revisionist camp, led by Jabotinsky. Both sides labeled the opposition protofascist, and there was limited substance to both their claims. The Revisionists, a typical European rightist force, were greatly influenced by Mussolini, adopting some of the trappings of fascism: motorcades of blackshirts, a party publication was renamed "Diary of a Fascist," and some training camps were held in fascist Italy. Jabotinsky himself was quick to deny fascist tendencies, and he spent most of the period after Hitler's ascension to power traveling through Eastern Europe campaigning for his evacuation plan, which was based on his realistic fears for the future of Europe's Jews under Nazism. His plan was not favored by Labor Zionism which, for its part, was developing a limited dialogue with the Nazi regime through official means such as the Ha'avara (Transfer) Agreement. The agreement was hotly debated in Zionist circles, as the majority of Jews elsewhere were behind the anti-Nazi boycott and hence opposed any agreement which would neutralize the boycott. The Labor Zionist view, even if not widely publicized, was that European Jewry was doomed and that those who qualified as "good settlement material" should be brought to Palestine. So the priorities were quite different—while Jabotinsky talked about evacuating Jews to anywhere at all, Labor Zionists were concentrating on the Palestine project and its priorities. This position was dubbed "Cruel Zionism" by its opponents, who described it, with some justification, as being deaf and blind to the plight of the Jewish refugees displaced by fascism. This blunt approach to the victims will become the basis for the official and ideological positioning in post-1948 Israel and will play an important role in Israeli politics in the 1950s, re-emerging during the 1980's with Menachem Begin's rise to power.

The Period after 1948

Almost immediately after the war, with many survivors settling in Israel, it was no longer possible for Israeli civil society to avoid this topic. The new Israeli state and society had just experienced a severe bloodletting—over six thousand Israelis died during the 1948 war of independence, many of them survivors of the camps. This may have been only a thousandth of the number of Jews who perished in the Holocaust, but the effect it had on the young Israeli community was far-reaching—the perspective on survivors has been greatly influenced by this traumatic experience. The attitude that most typified the new positioning is probably embodied in the words of one of the most important historians of the destruction of the Warsaw ghetto, Emanuel Ringelblum. Writing about the Warsaw ghetto *Judenrat*, he criticized the co-opted leadership with the seminal words: "We are going like lambs to the slaughter. . . . " The words of the sanguine historian, intimately living the pain and agony of the common Warsaw Jew, became the key to the Israeli interpretation of the conditions, attitudes, and choices facing the Jews during the Holocaust. Behind the question: "Why did they not fight?" which every Israeli child was taught to pose not as a query but as an historical judgment, was the corollary of that query: "We, the new Jews, will NOT go like lambs to the slaughter." This simplified picture of the Jewish dilemma during the war, for which Ringelblum bears no responsibility whatsoever, has been relaxed only in one area, which then became the rule—the few substantial acts of Jewish resistance were canonized; and to some extent, the heroic acts of the few displaced the suffering of the many in the Israeli psyche. Center stage was occupied (and quite literally so) by school plays about the Warsaw uprising or the heroic mission of Hannah Senesh. "For us, *Yom HaShoah Vehagvurah* (Day of Holocaust and Heroism) was not 'Martyrs' Day' as my *current* Israeli calendar translates it, but rather a celebration of resistance and national pride, a prolegomenon to the Israeli Day of Independence."[6] Thus, even in their extraordinary death agony, the millions of European Jews had not attracted sympathy— a minimum expectation from an important Jewish community. The Holocaust thus affirmed what Zionist education claimed: that the future belonged to the national revival in the Land of Israel: "Jewish life in Exile could only lead to death and destruction."[7] Sympathy and understanding were reserved for those who were the closest to the new Jew in their behavior—the Jewish underground fighters. "In this way, Holocaust remembrance fosters a unity of identity between martyrs and a new generation of Israelis. The martyrs are not forgotten but are recollected heroically as the first to fall in defense of the state."[8] It was crucial to join irrevocably the creation of a Jewish state with the last stand of the European Jews so as to provide a cataclysmic rationale and validation for the existence of Israel: " . . . the victims are memorable primarily for the ways they demonstrate the need for fighters, who, in turn, are remembered for their part in the state's founding."[9]

This position contrasted with another tendency, which presented the Holocaust not just as "belonging" to the Jewish people but even more exclusively, to the Israeli state, which took upon itself representation of the dead and their worldly possessions and past sufferings and which has, by virtue of the Reparations Agreement with West Germany, collected funds in lieu of both the dead Jews and the survivors living in Israel. Thus, Israel has become the speaker for (and inheritor of) the Jewish dead, the very dead which its ideological positioning denied proper empathy and reduced to lambs going to the slaughter. As a result of this appropriation, referred to later in this essay, any attempt by non-Israelis to represent the Holocaust may well attract suspicion and will rarely be celebrated in Israel. This is one argument repeatedly used against *Schindler's List.*

This appropriation of the Holocaust also meant that it was perceived as taking place between the Jews of Europe and the Nazis, more or less excluding the nations of Europe from the formulation. This has also led to a descriptive model of the Holocaust which is very stark—victim versus executioner. This grand simplification dehistoricized the Holocaust in Israeli public discourse, making it part of the metahistoric, anti-Semitic reaction to Judaism. The very specific nature and characteristics of the "final solution" have almost disappeared through this ideological filtration. The very European nature of the Holocaust, the linkage to the modern European state, had to wait for a later period.

The Reparations Agreement Debate

While the Holocaust as a subject was not actively discussed during the first few years following the 1948 war, it took center stage during the public debate fired by the Reparations Agreement; that debate was both furious and painful. The opposition, led by Menachem Begin, claimed treason and sell-out and attacked the Labor (Mapai)-led coalition as whitewashing the worst crime against humanity and the Jewish people. The arguments used by Ben Gurion, based on the fact that the reparations were actually a very small part of the possessions lost by the dead millions, stolen and robbed by the SS, were much less moving than the emotive arguments of his detractors. In this debate, the coalition and its leader were seen to be somewhat "too practical" in their attitude to the enormity of the crime committed by the German nation and its representatives. The urgency behind this agreement stemmed from the need to house and feed the many Jewish refugees and immigrants who had flooded the gates of the new state; reparations were seen as the solution. The ashes of this old debate seem to have been rekindled into a lively bonfire in the wake of *Schindler's List*'s introduction to the Israeli public.

But the typifying factor of the early years after 1948 was indeed the silencing of the Holocaust as an autonomous system of memory and experience, and its cooption and inclusion as a painful (sometimes, almost necessary) stage in achieving the goal of state building. The context of the Holocaust debate became the very different, post-factum Israeli realities of the struggle for political autonomy in Palestine. "During those years Israeli society showed a clear tendency to own the 'heroic' behaviour of European Jewry and suppress their 'nonheroic' past during World War II."[10] The daily evidence of such a development was the debate between those who, in the majority, demanded a "normalization" in the wake of the Reparations Agreement, and a minority of "dissidents" who would not forget and would not forgive, especially not in the shadow of a financial settlement. Some of the policies recommended were a continued boycott of German goods, such as Volkswagen cars. This was never a successful or popular boycott and was limited to survivors, with the rest of Israel taking no part in it. One feature was a certain cultural "ban" on German music, especially the total ban on Wagner's work, still almost unchanged today; but this is the exception that proves the rule. The needs of the state won out over the pain, anger, and frustrations of the survivors. As described by scholar Yael Feldman, the presentation of the Holocaust period, typically to school children on Holocaust Day, was not only from the vantage point of a backward-rationalizing Zionism but also "totally Hebraic. Everyone in this story spoke Hebrew: the ghetto mother singing a lullaby in the shadow of Ponar, the leaders of the Jewish resistance, and even the Polish underground."[11]

The turning point in the relationship of most Israelis to the events of the Holocaust was the Eichmann trial of 1960, as most commentators have pointed out. The trial, every minute of which was broadcast, at once lifted the veil of convenient silence over the Holocaust and drove difficult realities into the average Israeli home, a place well-protected from those horrors since the creation of the state. This change is mirrored in a gradual openness in areas which were not seen as important before. A range of literary and dramatic representations gradually opened up vistas which were unknown to the first generation of Israelis, who typically had no first-hand experience of existence in the Diaspora. The change was rather slow, but it was profound; it would take two decades for the personal involvement of youngsters with the Holocaust to become possible through the educational system. One of the most striking examples of this new tendency is the March of the Living, for which Israeli and Jewish school children are flown to Poland every year for Holocaust Day and are marched to the death camps, notably Birkenau/Auschwitz, as an act affirming the continuity of Jewish life but also as a way of giving many Israeli children an immediate experience of the camps and the museums they contain. These trips usually include visits to the historical centers of Jewish life in Poland and so are not limited to the destruction of European Jewry but also cover community life before the Holocaust. While in some cases the Israeli guides were intially still inculcating the old lessons of Zionism (this time on the grounds of the great killing fields), the experience itself could not fail to impress upon the children the complexity of the Holocaust, and the long-denied empathy with the victims, the hopelessness and enormity of their plight. A new sense of humility, and a growing interest in Jewish communal life before the war, has led to a new mood. The Yad Vashem museum and archives now face a range of types of personal involvement—from the numerous high school students researching the period for their projects, to young Israelis searching for information about family members destroyed by the Nazis and their lives before and during the war. The wheel has turned full circle—from the denial and disdain of the 1940s and 1950s toward many Israelis seeking their roots and existential reasoning in the period so berated previously. Of the cinematic contributions toward this change, Claude Lanzmann's *Shoah* takes center stage; but some Israeli films have been extremely successful in placing before the public some taboos and dark areas. One such film is Orna Ben-Dor Niv's *Because of That War* (1988); it is a notable example that dramatizes the problematic of silence and suppression, and also of the reworking of personal experience into a coherent and moving artistic expression. This validation of survivors and second generation experience in Israel, a difficult and traumatic experience in itself, forms the shift in public visibility and positioning. The publication of David Grossman's novel *Ayen Erech Ahava* (1989) (published in English as *See under Love*), and the theatrical production *Arbeit Macht Frei* (1991) by the Acre Theatre, are further dramatic examples of this development and of the intense social pain involved. The picture in this area is far from simple, though. The fact that the literary expressions of the period were, in many cases, not written by survivors, and that those survivors who have written about their experiences remained outside the main body of Israeli literature and were rarely canonized, is part of Felman's argument about the appropriation of the Holocaust narrative by Israeli and Hebrew traditions.[12] The exception which proves the rule is the novelist Aharon Appelfeld who, Feldman argues, was only canonized after a complex change in his orientation. "My claim is that in these narratives Appelfeld gave up his initially bewildered, uncomprehending 'take' on his experiences in the Shoah and its aftermath, and imperceptibly entered the old/new paradigm of the Jewish tradition."[13] Elsewhere this act of repositioning is termed "cooption" by Feldman. Old tendencies die hard.

The Film's Reception in Israel

Schindler's List has breached an important taboo, central to Israeli cultural discourse. The original one is the old taboo against "graven images," important enough to be included in the Ten Commandments. This taboo has been kept intact throughout Jewish history—though it was originally intended as a taboo against images of God, it was interpreted harshly, like many Jewish religious taboos and imperatives. It meant that, as in Islamic cultures, the development of Jewish visual art was somewhat stunted—it did not include graven images, not just of God but of nature as a whole. This ruled out realism of any kind and left the Word as the main artistic and expressive domain. It seems to me that after the Holocaust, another reading of this taboo has taken hold in Israel—a taboo over pictorial representation of the Holocaust. Some of the writers who survived the horrors have refused to detail any part of it; Aharon Appelfeld is a prime example: "His famous avoidance of direct representation of the Holocaust itself may be attributable not only to ethical inhibitions, as Howe would have it. It may be his way to avoid the structural difficulty that such a representation of necessity entails."[14] The connection made, in extending the taboo, between God and the Holocaust is an interesting one and is not merely one concerning order-of-magnitude.

While textual research of the facts, events, and systems behind the destruction process began almost immediately after 1945—with the long-standing Jewish proclivity for history taking over, ranging from document-based to oral history—the pictorial aspect of this research remained archived for longer than any other. This is hardly surprising—the ability of pictures to shock is much stronger. Pictures relate to Nora's *lieux de mémoire* in a more direct fashion.[15] This attitude did not die away. A strong proponent of it is Claude Lanzmann who, when asked about *Schindler's List*, talked about what one can, or should, show on film:

> there is a certain ultimate degree of horror that cannot be transmitted. To claim it is possible to do so, is to be guilty of the most serious transgression. Fiction is a transgression. I deeply believe that there are things that cannot and should not be represented.[16]

While Lanzmann makes many other important points against *Schindler's List*, it is probably the crucial reference to the great taboo, coming from an authority on the subject, which has made its mark on the Israeli debate. Lanzmann's argument was taken on by a variety of Israeli writers who were mostly, like Lanzmann himself, nonpracticing Jews. Interestingly, some of the defenders of the film are indeed Holocaust historians such as Yehuda Bauer, while some of its detractors have no personal background or professional relationship with the subject. Not all those attacking *Schindler's List* share the clarity and authority of Lanzmann. Much of the press coverage and reaction is especially vitriolic and full of argumentation totally unrelated to the film itself (some of the most aggressive pieces were even written in advance of viewing it!).[17] It is important to try and decipher the subtext behind such attitudes. Lanzmann's argument that the film fabricates by using documentary techniques was used in some quarters immediately after the publication of his interview in Hebrew. Idan Lando, an Israeli film critic, says: "Spielberg's film, after all, is not a documentary: it is an artefact using historical materials in order to construct a narrative with its own internal logic (hence the uselessness of the populist claim that this film is valuable as an instrument against revisionist historians and their followers; the opposite is true: who if not the revisionists will leap on this film enthusiastically, arguing that it proves their old claim—it is not difficult to fabricate documentary proof for the realities of the destruction process. They would be right, obviously . . . ").[18]

It may be useful to divide the arguments made against the film into a number of broad conceptual groupings:

The taboo argument. An ethical objection to pictorial/realistic representations of the Holocaust, this objection sometimes has a more localized description ("Realism is the wrong generic mode for relating to this subject"). This model, originally presented by Lanzmann, attracted many followers, including historians such as Tom Segev, author of *The Seventh Million*; it is also the original position taken by Appelfeld in his prose. Tom Segev's reaction is an interesting example. The tone of his piece, entitled "Spielberg's Holocaust Park,"[19] is quite aggressive: "Every few years someone discovers the Holocaust, pretending it is his own invention . . . In a TV interview, Spielberg came up with the following: 'This movie is my second Bar Mitzvah!' Happy birthday to you, Spielberg; you did not invest 24 million dollars in your Bar Mitzvah. You invested this money in order to make a profit, as in *E.T.* and *Jurassic Park*, and that's legitimate. Just spare us the bullshit!"[20]

This argument and its tone were not universally accepted; many survivors have written articles and letters to editors, expressing their gratitude to Spielberg for giving a "realistic expression" to their plight, which otherwise was difficult to visualize. The critic Uri Schin writes: "For many years it was claimed that it is not possible to use the catastrophe of the Holocaust in narrative cinema, only in documentary film, and even that with difficulty. Claude Lanzmann's documentary film, *Shoah*, became the prime example. According to Lanzmann, the Holocaust did not end, cannot ever end, and another Holocaust is a question of time. . . . Spielberg, in comparison, is a humanist, and that is his starting point in the film. He talks about mercy and sanity in a mad, chaotic, and cruel universe. Spielberg finds in the film a partial but complex way of dealing with the painful subject of the Holocaust, without slipping into the pornography of horror. Spielberg succeeds where the many and good have failed."[21] Schin also raises the question, posed by Saul Friedlander, about kitsch and death, and though he does not say so clearly, one gets the impression that he does not find *Schindler's List* lacking in this respect. Nissim Dayan, an Israeli filmmaker and critic, writes in a similar vein: "Even Claude Lanzmann himself attacked Spielberg and his film. . . . Lanzmann is angry that Spielberg did in his film everything which he did not in his film; that is Spielberg's great achievement."[22]

The "good Nazi" argument. In a film about the Holocaust (a line repeated in many articles, though it is clear this is not a film *about* the Holocaust) it is incorrect to have as the main hero a successful Nazi who is presented positively. Such a presentation whitewashes the many Nazis still alive. Diana J. Schemo has called it "embracing the anomaly and calling it history." This view is supported by Raul Hilberg, interviewed for the same article: "The need for heroes is so strong that we'll manufacture them."[23] This is an argument repeated in many of the responses in Israel. Shlomo Zand, an Israeli historian: "Spielberg's film is almost insignificant. This time, the Germans need not worry. The story does not take place in Berlin and the hero is a good German and even somewhat of a Nazi. You see, not all Nazis were murderers, only the crazy ones . . . in all the political salons and the congratulatory galas, the film will achieve a safe consensus; it is a non-tragic tearjerker, it evokes empathy without casting any blame. . . . "[24] Another critic, Alisa Wollach, quotes M. Stern, the nephew of the Jewish hero of *Schindler's List*, Itzhak Stern: "Forty, and even thirty years ago, the world was not ready to accept the concept of the good German, even if he shares some negative human traits."[25]

Another aspect of this tension is the sudden flaring up of an old debate: Is it right and proper still to hate the Germans, after all the years that have passed since the war? In a poignant exchange between Irit Linor, one of Israel's youngest and most outspoken novelists and journalists, and the two historians Moshe Zukermann and Moshe Zimmermann, this subject was broached again. The two scholars had been busy researching patterns of racism in contemporary Germany. Their research, financed in part by German funds, seems to have led them to believe that the widespread hatred of Germany in Israeli society is unjustified as racism in Germany is, according to them, on the decline. "When the claim is made that all Germans are anti-Semitic, it is my duty to point out that this is incorrect, that research proves otherwise."[26] They also claim that expressions of hatred toward Germans as Germans are essentially racist. Linor disagrees: "Today the Germans can argue they were all Schindlers, apart from some psychopaths that nobody ever met, and a German judge can annul the punishment of a Holocaust denier and call him an intelligent man, and Reagan can honor the grave of SS soldiers. . . . Why do we hate Germans? Why indeed. Because of the Holocaust."[27] This debate, echoing a similar one in the early 1950s reported above, is clear evidence of the unresolved issues that surround the memory of the Holocaust and forgiveness of the current generation of Germans, the direct descendants of those who carried out the destruction so efficiently.

The impersonal Jews argument. In a film about the Holocaust, the Jews cannot be represented as a mass, without individualized portraits. Some film critics claimed that the Jews end up as extras in their own tragedy. This was an argument repeated by most detractors of the film. It is obviously related to the good Nazi argument discussed above, but is much more specific—by concentrating on the good Nazi, it became impossible to give center stage to any of the Jews featured in the story. In a piece called "*Schindler's List*—Lost in the Forest of Numbers," critic Idan Lando argues that, true to his background, Spielberg chose to dramatize by making everything as large as possible: " . . . more Jews, more shoes, more trains, more Holocaust. The memories get mixed into a large impersonal dough of the universal Jew with a million faces and names but not a single biography . . . a single diary of one Anne Frank is more shocking as a human document than 1,100 names without embodiment. The many zeroes carefully collected throughout the film turn—with no one intending this—into human zeroes, faceless entities."[28] Leaving aside the validity of this claim when discussing the Holocaust, it is clear that the disagreement is not with the numbers themselves—these are objectively justified—but with the impersonal view we receive of the Jews, as opposed to the two characters who are psychologically developed—Schindler and Goeth. Referring to a number of scenes in the film, Lando claims: "Such scenes and others reinforce this impression: the victims are anonymous. Even when they have names or faces, the film does not allow the viewer to build around these mere details any persuasive kernel of individual identity."[29] Lando questions the validity of representation by large numbers which, to him, leads to the dehumanization of the victims. "The film does not succeed in moving people in the way that Lanzmann succeeded in *Shoah*. . . . Spielberg made a film about the Holocaust, Lanzmann made a film about people in the Holocaust."[30]

The flip side of both arguments against the film is the fact that by describing a Nazi who helped save Jews, Spielberg may be supplying an argument against all those who acquiesced in the destruction, claiming total impotence against the Nazi machine. "This film, without saying it, is proof of my argument: Even during the Holocaust period, it was possible to save and help if there were those who were prepared to risk themselves in order to assist,"[31] says Moshe Beisky, one of the survivors saved by Schindler and a former Supreme Court judge. In this sense, the importance of representing the dilemma facing the non-Jew during the Holocaust is not in doubt and is pointed out by Thomas Keneally in an article defending the film: "But the Holocaust remains for me not a Jewish problem but a European one . . . and that is not the Jews' fault. It is the fault of Europe, which has pursued anti-Semitism consistently since the Middle Ages and has still not yet repented of it."[32]

The mismatch argument. The film combines elements of kitsch and melodrama, inappropriate to a subject of such gravity. An interesting twist in this direction is a claim in Segev's piece: "Spielberg filmed in black-and-white to create the feel of a documentary. As this is not documentary material, and as nowadays no one films in black-and-white[33] anymore, one is quite correct in identifying this as a trick, fooling the viewer . . . all this is in order to create an illusion that this is real material. This story is real, true; it needs no tricks. Trying to hoodwink the viewer can only undermine the story's credibility." And after calling the scene of the Plaszów women in the supposed gas chamber pornography, Segev concludes: "The Holocaust does not need dramatic injections or emotional manipulation. Spielberg needs the Holocaust, but the Holocaust does not need Spielberg. It is quite enough the way it happened."[34] Segev's article predated the film's premiere by a few weeks, as did another important intervention, that of Leon Wieseltier in the *New Republic*, which started the debate proper. Wieseltier's piece, translated into Hebrew from the English original, is better argued than Segev's, though the sentiment is quite similar; the piece starts by demolishing Spielberg, presenting him as the great purveyor of lies: "For no figure in American culture has worked harder to stupefy it, to stuff it with illusion, to deny the reality of evil, to blur the distinction between fantasy and fact, and to preach the child's view of the world than Steven Spielberg."[35] The article then proceeds to its main argument: "The power of realism in art is owed to the continuity between the world which it makes and the world in which, and for which, it is made. For this reason, the realistic depiction of radical evil must end, if it is to stay honest, where the continuity ends. . . . No discontinuity has been observed. No limit has been met. No rupture has reared itself."[36] This serious questioning of Spielberg's mechanism of audience positioning may well have been missed by most Israeli readers, but the point is taken up again and again by other writers. A few days after the premiere, the Israeli film critic Uri Kleine wrote about Spielberg, the "man without doubts,"[37] the director who creates illusions so realistic that he is unable to doubt his own creations. By using the example of Alain Resnais's *Night and Fog*, Kleine argues that the only possible film about the Holocaust is one that questions the possibility of making such a film in the first place. This argument for a self-reflexive production, based on Resnais's memorable film, is contrasted with *Schindler's List*: "It seems that Spielberg's film is innocently clear of the questions and issues which engaged artists examining the representation of the Holocaust in culture generally, and in the cinema in particular, issues of documentation and historical consciousness, memory and reconstruction, silence and evidence, presentation and hiding. He [Spielberg] knows those problems exist but believes in repressing them in the name of therapy and some historic mission."[38] Kleine points out the excessive clarity of the situations presented and the lack of one of the qualities most essential when dealing with this subject—the enigmatic and equivocal, the less than penetrable; that quality is missing in this film, which to him seems to be fired by the positivist drive and mission that typifies Spielberg's work. Ilan Avisar, a film scholar, agrees: "One can find here a special problematic, one the film fails in— a text dealing with the Holocaust must include inner dissonances, stuttering, hesitations, silences. All this reminds one that what you are showing is not the Holocaust. This does not exist in Spielberg's film. He does not hesitate to recreate scenes. His lack of humility as a director is problematic. In *Night and Fog* Resnais uses 'fogging' tactics, and in Primo Levi's novels one reads many times the line: 'But these are not the same words.' "[39]

Someone who questions the points made by Segev is the Holocaust scholar, Yehuda Bauer. He claims, as a historian, that the film is extremely close to the events it portrays, "as close as a film can be to the reality of the Holocaust." Bauer points out that Spielberg has chosen to use a binary opposition in narrative terms—Schindler on the one side, as a main character, and the combined character of the Kraków Jews as a main character on the other; in the circumstances, he argues, this is a valid strategy: "Segev does not like this because he has an ideological platform: The Holocaust should not be represented, it should be left alone. This platform is total nonsense."[40] In the debate with Segev, and through him with Lanzmann and Appelfeld, Bauer argues that the "codes" selected by Spielberg to deal with the Holocaust are appropriate "for dealing with evil."[41]

Historical accuracy argument. The film is inaccurate in its details; there are many subheadings under this point, but the main thrust of the argument attacks a narrative fiction based on historical fact for being exactly that. This argument harbors a deep misunderstanding of the workings of narrative genre conventions. In Lando's piece, for example, an argument against aerial and crane views of the victims is made, on the grounds that "in fact, this vantage point is totally fictional: in reality, no historical witness could have viewed it thus."[42] The use of black-and-white is also considered an inaccuracy, as it is seen—by Segev, for example—as a trick by which the film purports to be a documentary. Many commentators point out the main historical incongruity—the use of "Jerusalem of Gold" on the soundtrack, a crude decision which Spielberg seems to have regretted in hindsight; the inclusion of this song, which originated after the 1967 war as the unofficial victory hymn, troubled most Israelis at the previews; as a result, Spielberg exchanged it for "To Caesarea" by Hannah Senesh, a Palestine Zionist-Communist originally from Budapest who was parachuted by the British into Hungary in 1944 in order to organize Jewish resistance. Many other details are pointed out, such as a variety of accents, including a totally inappropriate Israeli accent. When talking about the film to my own parents, both Auschwitz survivors, my mother criticized the Auschwitz shower scene: "This is not how it happened; when we went in, we waited for the gas to come out of the pipes and kill us; but after some minutes a little water came out of the pipes, it was dripping, really, not flowing like in the film." While to the rest of us this is a mere detail, a variant of the great mystery called Auschwitz, for my mother it was an unforgivable error—after all, that is when her life was not taken; there is no way it can be differently shown. The words used here are an echo of Primo Levi's hesitation—somehow, it is felt, representation fails in the task of describing the horror due to the simplification and construction involved.

All in all, this is one of the weakest arguments against the film. Anyone who has checked the details behind the Plaszów camp, for example, would come to the conclusion that the film tries to stick to all the available evidence, pictorial and verbal. But the criticism implied by this argument is important for another reason; some of the commentators argue that after this film, the pictures which most people will remember of the Holocaust are Spielberg's images. The film, particularly because of its style, is seen as displacing the evidence and documentation on which it is based, acting in people's minds as a metatext of historical evidence. This seems to me a valid point.

It seems that the film is trapped between two essentializing claims: One argues that it is not close enough to history, the other that it is too close. Because the film offers a text closely balanced between narrative and document, it cannot by definition satisfy either of these camps. What in other circumstances may have been an unquestionable achievement has become a conceptual and ethical trap.

Some of the arguments made in support of the film are also not directly related to it. The political commentator Dan Margalit criticized the decision to ban the film in Egypt. "The banning of the film is a blunt expression, in this sensitive area, of the Arab world's relationship to the Holocaust and their two-sided links with the Nazi regime."[43] Discussing the complexities of the linkage between the Holocaust and the creation of Israel, he says: "The Arabs know well that in its ceaseless struggle for a Jewish state, Zionism did not base itself on the destruction of Jewry during the Holocaust. There were good reasons for it despite the Holocaust, and before it. The murder of the six million only dramatized, at a terrible cost, the urgent need for Jewish self-determination. . . . Spielberg's film does nothing to detract from the rights of the Palestinians, but a thorough viewing with Arabic subtitles would reinforce the understanding that Jews have the same right, and maybe more than the same right."[44] The decision to ban the film from cinemas is interesting—the film would be shown in clubs and cinematheques in Cairo, but nowhere else. The limitation of viewing *Schindler's List* to the Egyptian elite is quite extraordinary in itself. The film was totally banned in the rest of the Arab world.

The "Americanization" of the Holocaust. After a long period in which dealing with the Holocaust was assumed in Israel to "belong" to Israeli society in some vague sense, the last decade has seen the "Americanization" of the Holocaust, a process assumed to "cheapen" it. Spielberg, with his particular background in Hollywood, is a natural suspect. "Changes such as the launching of the Holocaust Museum in Washington, and the great public interest created by it, introduced a new context, without a doubt providing a fertile ground for the production of a Holocaust film" writes Alisa Wollach.[45]

In my opinion, arguments made against Spielberg as an American Jew out to make money from the Holocaust are not just facile, but relate to that deep chasm in Israeli history—the debate on the Reparations Agreement. Spielberg is seen as someone prepared to make money out of the gravest episode in Jewish history, like Ben Gurion—according to Begin. And like Ben Gurion, Spielberg's film "cleanses" the image of Germany. In a piece headed "Spielberg Sells the Holocaust," journalist Yael Yisrael describes Spielberg as a child waiting for a prize toy: "At the age of 48, Spielberg, who decided he was ready to deal with the greatest subject, the Holocaust, put aside $42 million out of the $800 million that his latest hit, *Jurassic Park*, had grossed, and invested in a film that according to his calculations would move him to the next grade, from the level of a childish filmmaker dealing in trivia to the league of 'serious' directors. . . . It is difficult to know what is served by this film and how; but it is quite clear—Spielberg's pocket will be well served. . . . "[46] Yisrael claims that the film is never moving, not for a single moment: "Though Spielberg tries hard to avoid cheap melodramatic emotionalism, he thinks Hollywood, makes Hollywood, and nothing can help him out here. Especially when he tries to sell the Holocaust to the whole world. . . . "[47] The same claim is made by a range of critics, all of whom seem to occupy a higher level of existence, looking down upon Hollywood, American culture, and commercialism, none of whose values they share. After a short "psychoanalytical" examination of Spielberg ("a victim of megalomania"),[48] Yael Yisrael concludes, enticingly, with the same sentiments toward the Diaspora Jew that were described in my introduction: "The great Spielberg fell victim to the Jewish Diaspora complex, the same complex which has trapped every single Jew in Hollywood, from the great Mayer, through the monstrous Cohn, and up to Irving Thalberg . . . the same complex which forced the Jewish community in Hollywood to act with humiliating self-denial toward goyish American culture, trying desperately to identify with it and embrace its values: power and cultural imperialism."[49] A full circle indeed, from the European ghetto Jew, to the Hollywood ghetto Jew, a shriveled, frightened individual, trying hard to be accepted, not to be noticed, not to be different. The mere attribution of those values to the Jewish community in Hollywood, and to Spielberg in particular, is not just ridiculous; it is also an example of the difficulties involved in facing certain realities within Israeli society. One writer who has noted this attitude is journalist Sever Plotzker: "When Spielberg's film *Schindler's List* was screened in the USA, many of the main papers hailed it with ecstatic reviews. . . . Not so in Israel. *Schindler's List* is being screened for the second week, and most of the reviews are cold, hostile, and snide. . . . Hollywood kitsch on the Holocaust . . . a film made by a rich and spoiled Jewish director, master of the fictional hit, who tries with this fabricated document to express his pained Diaspora Jewishness. . . . They mean, 'the American Spielberg will not teach us, the Israelis, how to honor the Holocaust on film.' But he will!"[50] And after talking about all the special qualities of the film, invoking Dante and Bosch, Plotzker claims that *Schindler's List* is above all a Jewish creation, part of Jewish culture, and a Zionist film. "None of this was noticed in Israel. The arrogance and monopolization of the Holocaust which we took upon ourselves has blinded our eyes, has blocked our senses, has disabled our sensibilities. Our pettiness has been fully exposed. I am searching for the flowers which they denied Spielberg."[51]

Fragments of a Conclusion

This limited examination of the reception of *Schindler's List* in Israel seems to suggest some interesting patterns in the public reaction to the film. The first one is the intensity of the debate which the film has aroused, its close relationship to some of the most established taboos of the Israeli psyche, and hence the level of disturbance caused. To deal in one piece with the Holocaust, with diasporic existence, with good and bad Nazis, with dilemmas without solution, all this is heady stuff at the best of times. But to do this through the use of a format which in itself negates both the taboos and the ideological weight behind their enforcement, that is indeed a major transgression.

But one should not see this film in isolation. The pattern of change and deep emotional transformation in the Israeli and Jewish understanding and remembrance of the Holocaust is too strong now to be eluded or mistaken. The reasons for the many examples of this metamorphosis in Israel (some much more far-reaching than *Schindler's List*) are complex. Some of the most important explanations will no doubt be found in the unusual historical juncture, enabled by the peace with Egypt, and leading to the current exciting and risky developments, still unfolding but moving unmistakably toward a new era of Israeli existence, and hence, Israeli identity. It is my contention that the sense of helplessness and humiliation suffered by most Israelis during the 1991 Gulf War has not only enabled a new attitude in the peace process but has also brought many Israelis closer to a better understanding of the dilemmas facing the ghetto Jews during the Holocaust. The all-powerful might of Israel has been exposed as a conditional strength, a mixed blessing; methods other than brute force were to be the key to the future; hence, a set of options based on less-than-perfect security guarantees became more interesting to evaluate.

This also meant that the military option became somewhat normalized: it is now increasingly seen as the last option in a complicated option tree; the knee-jerk reaction as a panacea is under severe strain.

This is an exciting set of developments—the sense of political realism emerging from a relative weakness, rather than the total supremacy of the past, which may have disabled real progress in the region. This is also true when examining the reactions to *Schindler's List*. Not only did the Israelis change their priorities as a society but the other large Jewish communities have become somewhat more autonomous on a number of issues, and most importantly on their understanding of the Holocaust and the importance of peace as the guarantee of the future existence of Israel. In this process, these communities no longer accept Israel's exclusive role as speaker for the Jewish dead; they have established their own set of memory mechanisms, ranging from more and more museums, shows, and publications, to the film under consideration here. This development is mirrored in Israel; the official and highly ritualized forms of remembrance and memory with their inbuilt alienation have been swept aside by a multitude of grass roots efforts and representations. As opposed to the propaganda of the past, the new expressions occupy the arenas of both popular and high culture, eliciting a level of identification hitherto unknown on this subject. The emotional sway of the music and lyrics of Yehuda Poliker, or the immense impact on the audience of shows such as *Arbeit Macht Frei*, may now be more important than the ossified remains of Holocaust rituals. Participation is paramount, memory rather than history is crucial in this phase, and contradictions can no longer be covered up—they have to be discussed, reenacted, encompassed. *Schindler's List* is part of this new and complex development; but when as powerful a film as this is made by the professional and commercial acumen of Spielberg, it seems too strong to be accepted by an Israeli society undergoing what is probably the most important, and the most painful, transformation of its short history. To my mind, the backlash tone, so typical of many of the reactions, is also evidence of the depth of the change, and of its importance.

On the specific questions raised by the various arguments for and against the film, one suspects that many will soon perish while others may well persist. The argument of historical accuracy will, in my judgment die quietly, as Spielberg has been appropriately careful about historical details, enough to force a standard on future attempts. The film has become a temporary conceptual locus for arguments about very important questions facing Israeli society—its own identity in vis-à-vis European Jewry destroyed in the Holocaust, and a relaxation of the censuring of the victim's behavior—all in relation to the peace negotiations now proceeding. The Holocaust has been used stereotypically for a long period, supplying post-factum justification not just for the existence of Israel but also for its defensive (and offensive) military stance. This is where the reevaluation of Holocaust memories leads to a resultant re-evaluation of that stance. Due to the centrality of this position for past Israeli identity, any changes would not be easily accepted. This is well evidenced in the debates about the "good Nazi," for example. Is the world now possibly more safe for Israeli Jews, or will they continue to represent every act against the state of Israel as a prelude or an echo of a new Holocaust? This dilemma was made very clear during Begin's period, when he compared Arafat in besieged Beirut to Hitler in his bunker while the rest of the world saw a possible connection with the ghetto uprising. The debate clearly represents an important stage in moving from forms of Holocaust remembrance controlled by the state and, to some extent, delaying a political solution, to a new phase where popular understanding of the Holocaust may assist in bringing about such a solution.

The crucial arguments about *Schindler's List* still to be carried out are those related to the representation of Jewish pain, misery, and suffering during the Holocaust; Spielberg has not tried his hand at this, perhaps wisely. If the anger at *Schindler's List* is as intense as it was, one can only imagine what storm would be created by a similar attempt at representing that level of human misery which he avoided touching directly. This may well be a task for the future, for another generation of filmmakers; but whoever manages to convey such depth will be indebted to Spielberg for his attempt at breaking the representational taboos.

It may also be safe to assume that the change in positions described above will affect Israel's relationship with the communities of the Jewish Diaspora, parallel with the normalization of its relationships within the region, as the country enters what may be termed its post-Zionist period. The sharp and disturbing voices echoing the old attitudes toward Diaspora Jews, disagreeable as they are, are voices of the past, of those fighting a battle already lost. The series of taboos broken in a number of the texts mentioned above as well as in *Schindler's List* makes rolling back the conceptual tide quite unlikely. These new cultural expressions are the deep utterances of a social and political change, one held back for a long time, for much too long. In opposition to many commentators who see these expressions as signs of weakness and stress, I tend to read them as some basic signs of belief in the future and in the continuity of existence, hence the preparedness to risk breaking the taboos, to cross the boundary, to commit the transgression. In that sense only I agree with Lanzmann—Schindler's List is a transgression, but a most necessary transgression, one of the acts of a society which faces its future with more confidence, with slightly less arrogance, with understanding painfully acquired.

Notes

1. Chaim Weizmann, later to become Israel's first president, wrote in 1937, when the fate awaiting the Jews of Europe was no longer unimaginable, the following lines, both prophetic and chilling in their dispassionate tone: "The old ones will pass; they will bear their fate, or they will not. They were dust, economic and moral dust in a cruel world. . . . Two millions, and perhaps less—She'erit Hapleta—only a branch will survive. They have to accept it. The rest they must leave to the future—to their youth" (Chaim Weizmann, "Dr. Weizmann's Political Address—20th Zionist Congress," quoted in *New Judea* [London, August 1937], p. 215).

2. James Young, *The Texture of Memory* (New Haven: Yale University Press, 1993), p. 211.

3. See Haim Bresheeth, "Self and Other in Zionism: Palestine and Israel in Recent Hebrew Literature," in *Palestine: A Profile of an Occupation* (London: Zed Books, 1989), pp. 120–52.

4. This is obviously a Eurocentric notion and avoids relating to the well-established and in all cases older Jewish communities in the Arab world.

5. See the description in S. B. Bet Zvi, *Ha'Zionut HaPost Ugandit Be'Mashber Hashoah* (Tel Aviv: Bronfman, 1977), and in Tom Segev, *Ha'Million Ha'Shvi'i* (Jerusalem: Keter, 1991).

6. Yael Feldman, "Whose Story Is It Anyway?" in Saul Friedlander, ed., *Probing the Limits of Representation* (Cambridge: Harvard University Press, 1992), p. 230.

7. Yael Zerubavel, "The Death of Memory and the Memory of Death: Masada and the Holocaust as Historical Metaphors," *Representations* 45 (Winter 1994), p. 79.

8. Young, *Texture of Memory*, p. 214.

9. Ibid., p. 212.

10. Zerubavel, "The Death of Memory and the Memory of Death," p. 80.

11. Feldman, "Whose Story Is It Anyway?" in Friedlander, ed., *Probing the Limits of Representation*, p. 224.

12. Ibid., pp. 226–30.

13. Ibid., p. 230.

14. Ibid., p. 231.

15. Pierre Nora, "Between Memory and History: *Les lieux de mémoire*," trans. Marc Roudebush, *Representations* 26 (1989), pp. 13–25.

16. The translation is from the English version of the interview published in the *Manchester Guardian* on April 3, 1994, under the heading "Why Spielberg Has Distorted the Truth." Israelis read the Hebrew version of the interview much earlier, in *Zman Tel Aviv* on March 4, 1994, pp. 48–50, under the interesting heading—seemingly culled from the sports pages—"Claude Lanzmann vs. Steven Spielberg," some time before they could see the film; thus this interview became quite influential in conditioning the Israeli audience, large parts of which were exposed to Lanzmann's *Shoah* in the 1980s, mainly on television.

17. For example, Haim Bar'am, "Enoshiuto Hayachasit shel HaNazi Hatov," *Kol Ha'ir*, February 25, 1994, and Eleonora Lev, "Kesheoscar Yekabel et Ha'oscar," *Shishi*, March 4, 1994, p. 25.

18. Idan Lando, "Tov'im Be'misparim," *Ha'ir*, March 18th, 1994, p. 98.

19. Much energy was expended on witty and nasty names for the reviews; some additional ones are: "Shoah Show," "A Reich of the Third Kind," and "The Ghetto of Madame d'."

20. Tom Segev, "Park HaShoah shel Spielberg," *Ha'aretz*, February 25, 1994, p. 7B.

21. Uri Schin, "Bimkom Bikoret," *Davar*, March 3, 1994, p. 12.

22. Nissim Dayan, "For Schindler's List: The most important document on the Holocaust for the coming generations," *Shishi*, March 11, 1994.

23. Diana Jean Schemo, "Good Germans: Honoring the Heroes. And Hiding the Holocaust," *New York Times*, June 12, 1994, p. 6E.

24. Shlomo Zand, "Neged Reshimat Schindler: Kitsch bachyani vedoche," *Shishi*, March 11, 1994.

25. Alisa Wollach, "Ha'yehudi ha'chacham shel ha'germani ha'tov," *Davar*, February 25, 1994, weekend supplement, p. 11.

26. Quoted in Irit Linor, "I Neimut Ktana," *Ha'aretz*, August 19, 1994, p. 110.

27. Ibid., p. 110.

28. Lando, "Tov'im Be'misparim."

29. Ibid.

30. Ibid.

31. Alisa Wollach, "Doch Beisky Al haseret," in "Ha'yehudi ha'chacham shel ha'germani ha'tov," *Davar*, February 25, 1994, weekend supplement, p. 14.

32. Thomas Keneally, "The Holocaust Is a Lesson for All," *Philadelphia Inquirer*, February 8, 1994, p. A19.

33. The issue of filming in black-and-white has exercised many commentators; Leon Wieseltier has written of *Schindler's List*: "Its renunciation of color is adduced as a sign of its stringency; but the black and white of this film is riper than most color" (Leon Wieseltier, "Close Encounters of the Nazi Kind," *New Republic*, January 24, 1994, p. 42).

34. Tom Segev, "Park Ha'Shoah shel Spielberg," *Ha'aretz*, February 25, 1994.

35. Wieseltier, "Close Encounters," p. 42. The Hebrew translation of Wieseltier's article appeared under the title, "Reshimat Schindler: Dea Acheret," in *Ha'aretz*, February 11, 1994, supplement, p. 47.

36. Wieseltier, "Close Encounters," p. 42.

37. Uri Kleine, "Ha'ish lelo sfekot," *Ha'aretz*, March 11, 1994.

38. Ibid.

39. Quoted in Nurit Loylicht and Shmulik Duvdevani, "Tazvu et Spielberg," *Ha'ir*, March 4, 1994, p. 92.

40. Yehuda Bauer, "Kod nachon laroa," *Ha'aretz*, March 9, 1994, p. 4B.

41. Ibid.

42. Lando, "Tov'im Be'misparim."

43. Dan Margalit, "Mi ha'Aravi shemefached me'Schindler?" *Ha'aretz*, June 3, 1994, p. 1B.

44. Ibid., 1B.

45. Wollach, "Ha'yehudi ha'chacham shel ha'germani ha'tov," p. 11.

46. Yael Yisrael, "Spielberg mocher Shoah," *Al Ha'mishmar*, "Chotam" supplement (March 4, 1994), p. 16.

47. Ibid., p. 16.

48. Ibid., p. 16.

49. Ibid., p. 16.

50. Sever Plotzker, "Behokarah Le'Spielberg," *Yediot Ahronot*, "24 Hours" supplement (March 16, 1994), p. 5.

51. Ibid.

11 | Between Obsession and Amnesia
Reflections on the French Reception of *Schindler's List*

Natasha Lehrer

A CURIOUSLY PARADOXICAL phenomenon has emerged over the last several years in France: the media, the apotheosis of the here and now, have become the site of strategic debate around issues related to *la mémoire*; memory has entered the domain of current affairs. It is not just that, as Umberto Eco put it in an interview in *Le Monde*, "reading the French press . . . [it is evident that] France's cupboards are still full of forgotten skeletons whose origins are unknown."[1] The press has become the arena for a polemic about the very nature of memory itself, whose constant small eruptions serve to expose the fissures and tensions in the struggle on the part of the French public to come to terms with the history of Vichy and the Occupation.

The trial of Paul Touvier for crimes against humanity began exactly a fortnight after *Schindler's List* opened in France on March 3, 1994, almost exactly twenty-three years after Marcel Ophuls's film *The Sorrow and the Pity* was released. Ophuls's film captures the dissonance between the history of what took place during the Occupation, with all its attendant ambiguities, and its memory thirty years later, as evoked by the subjects of his film. The dialectical structure of Ophuls's film, its overt distinction between two orders of truth—archival and documentary evidence set against the subjective testimony of those witnesses to the period who took part in the film—makes it the first film about the memory, as opposed to the history, of the Occupation.

The release of *The Sorrow and the Pity* in April 1971 occasioned a spectacular outburst of attention to the Occupation in the press. The film has long been considered something of a watershed in the dramatic change in public perception of the Vichy government and in the movement toward the destruction of the myth of a France united in resistance against the enemy occupiers, that began to gain momentum toward the end of the sixties and throughout the seventies. The film can also be partially credited with exposing to public view the general amnesia regarding the level of French anti-Semitism during the years of the Occupation, both official and unofficial. This anti-Semitism, though deeply rooted in French tradition and society, had been hitherto effectively effaced by a postwar historiography that unambiguously laid the blame for virulent anti-Semitic legislation on the Nazis rather than on the Vichy regime.

Film in general seems to have had a significant effect on both the formation and the transmission of memory of the war years in France and is linked to the postwar proliferation of what Pierre Nora has termed *lieux de mémoire*,[2] metonymic sites in which traces of the past are commemorated or celebrated and the collective memories of a particular group located, their meanings crystallized into a single, authoritative interpretation of history. There is increasing interest in the evolution as well as the form and content of *lieux de mémoire* and of the social practices whose purpose is the representation of the past and the perpetuation of its memory within a particular social group or society as a whole.[3] The cinema has proved to be one of the most significant as well as one of the most enduringly controversial vectors of memory, at times exerting a powerful influence on people's minds, at others acting as a significant indicator of contemporary attitudes. *The Sorrow and the Pity* was instrumental in the process of shattering the heroic Gaullist myth of France during the Occupation and in highlighting the level of French collaboration with the Nazis; yet six months after its release, in November 1971, during which time it was prevented from being aired on French television, President Pompidou saw fit quietly to pardon Paul Touvier, the former head of the Militia based in Lyons. Touvier had twice been sentenced to death in absentia, but had thus far successfully evaded capture thanks to the protection afforded him by the French Catholic Church.[4]

Memories of the past repeatedly become components of contemporary issues and crises within the "volatile memory-politics"[5] that currently dominate French public life.[6] Annette Wieviorka, a noted French historian of the genocide of the Jews and of its postwar memorialization in France, identifies a particular fixation with the *mémoire* of the Holocaust in the French media: "The last few years have been notable for the insistent presence of the genocide of the Jews in the media, an issue in France in which not only memory and history are at stake but also, significantly, in which domestic politics are at stake, giving rise to a plethora of public debates that one cannot be entirely sure are concerned solely with the preservation of memory. The brouhaha which from time to time focuses on the annihilation of the Jews actually signifies media-sited political crises."[7]

Obsession with the Holocaust in France corresponds directly with the severely traumatized memory of the Occupation and the Vichy regime. The events which befell France between 1940 and 1944—from the terrible losses of French soldiers in the war of 1939–40, to crushing military defeat, the Armistice of 1940, and the humiliation of occupation by German troops, followed swiftly by the installation of the Vichy government and its vying for control with de Gaulle's government in exile—happened so fast that, as French historian Henri Rousso puts it, "the French had no time to grasp, come to terms with, and mourn what had befallen them in one catastrophe before they found themselves caught up in yet another."[8] Rousso adopts the Freudian image of repressed memory to explain the enduring and elliptical presence of the memory of the war years in French consciousness today, as though the trauma of that time, manifested as a form of collective neurosis, is still being worked through: "The Vichy syndrome consists of a diverse set of symptoms whereby the trauma of the Occupation . . . reveals itself in political, social, and cultural life. Since the end of the war, moreover, that trauma has been perpetuated and at times exacerbated."[9]

As if to prove this thesis, when Steven Spielberg's *Schindler's List* opened in France it commanded an extraordinary amount of press interest. The film was widely welcomed as an "event," which on one level simply enabled the press to indulge in further rhetoric around the subject of the Holocaust. The enormous coverage in the popular press inevitably focused not only on the subject of the film but also on Spielberg himself, his achievement, sentimental details of his personal history and his turning toward Judaism, leading inexorably to the conflation of hero Schindler/hero Spielberg. At this level, the coverage of the film resembled that of any number of films coming out of Hollywood, backed by the economic muscle of a powerful publicity machine, the kind of hype, in fact, that we have come to expect from any Spielberg production.

But the lead feature of the middle-brow weekly *Globe Hebdo*, "Schindler—La Polémique," which coincided with the opening of the film, suggested something markedly differ ent from *Jurassic Park* and showed to what extent the arena was primed for a fight in advance of the film's opening. When in an interview Raul Hilberg was asked what he thought of Spielberg's film, he responded wryly, "Everyone in France has asked me that."[10] Even by French standards, the rhetoric which surrounded the film seemed unusually passionate. As though deciphering a palimpsest, one could trace beneath the acres of print a complex pattern of unease which, though inspired by the film, was not really about it at all.

The controversial impact of the film is indicated by the fact that it was within the pages of *Le Monde*, widely held to be the "compendium of French culture, the monitor of the intelligentsia and of French politics,"[11] that Claude Lanzmann launched the debate: "I really thought . . . that there was a pre-*Shoah* and a post-*Shoah*, and I believed that after *Shoah* there were certain things that could not be done anymore. But Spielberg has done them."[12] For Lanzmann *Schindler's List* is a breach of the sanctity of the Holocaust as history, because it dares to "reconstruct" and thus to excise its truth: "In my opinion this fictionalization is a transgression, the transgression of the forbidden, of the unrepresentability of Auschwitz." Raul Hilberg, Lanzmann's avowed mentor, was similarly unequivocal in his appraisal of Spielberg's work, acknowledging that as a historian it was difficult for him not to feel uncomfortable with Spielberg's project: "For me, it's very simple—there is only one Claude Lanzmann, only one *Shoah*. It is impossible to do better or more. To wish to treat the extermination of the Jews as a fiction is, as far as I am concerned, impossible."[13] For philosopher Alain Finkielkraut the film constitutes a "cheapening of memory."[14] Israeli writer Tom Segev, author of *The Seventh Million: The Israelis and the Holocaust*, gave a sharply negative critique, asserting: "I don't think that there is any need to dramatize the Holocaust. It is sufficiently dramatic in itself. Every artistic treatment of the Holocaust is bound to fail. Spielberg's audience is not going to learn anything about Nazism, or about Schindler."[15]

When Elisabeth Schemla wrote that it is the historians "who remain the most trustworthy guardians of the truth,"[16] she was highlighting the inevitable polarization between, on the one hand, historians and intellectuals, "the guardians of the sacred temple," and on the other, *"les bonnes gens,"*[17] in other words, the public, for whose enlightenment the integrity of the historian's endeavor is necessarily and inevitably simplified. "This debate, launched by intellectuals who can't bear the idea that a historical subject doesn't remain their exclusive domain, is completely pointless"[18]; "Why do we have to leave history to the historians?"[19] fulminated a cacophony of journalists. Pierre Billard called Lanzmann, Hilberg, and the rest "the new fundamentalists" and accused them of having "criticized Spielberg's film with a severity that was never shown toward other films made about the [Holocaust]" simply because the film was made by a Hollywood director, indeed with no regard whatsoever for the aesthetic merits of the film itself.[20] Ludi Boeken, a Dutch filmmaker and the child of two survivors, wrote that "no one has author's copyright over *la mémoire*."[21] Albert Memmi, a noted writer of North African origin, wrote in response to Lanzmann, after he threw down the gauntlet in *Le Monde*, that even if by its very nature the Holocaust is uncommunicable, it must be communicated none the less, "if one day we want to put together an adequate fresco of this terrible past, in order to draw a lesson from it for the future."[22] For filmmaker Francis Fehr, Spielberg's "aestheticizing" of the horror of the Holocaust, rather than contributing to the act of remembrance "can only contribute to the acceleration of the act of forgetting." Yet at the same time he speaks of the urgency of new attempts at aesthetic testimony, of the compulsion to reinvent means of keeping alive *la mémoire*. Fehr is unequivocal in his criticism of the "Hollywoodization" of the Holocaust in *Schindler's List*, but he implicitly acknowledges the urge to find new forms of transmission to future generations.[23] The debate became subtly polarized between those who believe in transmitting the fact of the Holocaust as widely as possible to an audience which is largely made up of people ignorant of *Shoah* and, more importantly, of the Shoah, and those for whom Adorno's (over-quoted) injunction against the aestheticizing of the Holocaust remains a fundamental imperative.

The ethics and philosophy of representation of the Holocaust is an issue that runs through the heart of this debate. Many of those writing about the film in France address this issue; the front page headline of *Libération* and the cover of *Télérama* both adopt the rhetoric of philosophical interrogation when they ask: "La Shoah de Spielberg—Peut-on filmer l'Holocauste?"[24] Many of the philosophical issues in the debate about the possibility of representing the Holocaust, though evidently applicable outside France, specifically confront issues about memory and memorialization in France itself.

Jean-François Lyotard's *Heidegger and "the jews"* is a text which is critical to this debate. Lyotard addresses the tensions inherent in a process of memorialization which, by being too definite, too representative, too narrativized, takes on the project of recovering the forgotten and in this way actually forgets it: "Whenever one represents, one inscribes in memory and this might seem a good defense against forgetting. It is, I believe, just the opposite. Only that which has been inscribed can, in the current sense of the term, be forgotten, because it could be effaced."[25] Memory in France has indeed, since the Liberation, proved to be peculiarly unstable and, it must be added, subject to a notably effective onslaught by revisionists (or negationists) who deny that the Holocaust happened.[26] With the immense proliferation of *lieux de mémoire* relating to the Occupation and the Holocaust in the last two decades, it is essential to maintain a self-conscious awareness of the ways in which the Holocaust is memorialized and the shapes which are thus imposed on the collective memory. *Libération*'s film critic, Gerard Lefort, questions whether *Schindler's List*, by encouraging the creation of a totalizing memory, will effect precisely the "closing of the gaps," of which Lyotard writes, in a memory which is inherently conflictual and lacking in homogeneity. "Will [the audience] leave the cinema with the feeling of having seen a film 'against forgetting' (*contre l'oubli*) or the opposite—the feeling of having seen yet another film about the war, in other words a film that actually encourages forgetting (*pour l'oubli*)?"[27] Alain Finkielkraut suggests that the constant positing of the binary opposition *mémoire/oubli* is a distortion of the central issue: "In fixing the debate on the opposition between forgetting and remembering, one ends up justifying everything. Face to face with Auschwitz, *la mémoire* is just not enough. . . . It is crucial to avoid any sense of reconciliation when we think about the Shoah."[28] Indeed, the heroization of Oskar Schindler effects a sort of ambiguous resolution between the antinomies of resistance and collaboration, as Bruno Frappat recognizes: "*Schindler's List* presents, in its principal character, a quasi-philosophical illustration of the fluidity of the border between good and evil."[29]

Gerard Lefort's critique of certain of the representational strategies used by Spielberg draws directly on Lyotard's notes on the politics of forgetting. "Spielberg decides to color the cape of a little girl red so that, in the eyes of Schindler, she becomes a sort of Little Red Riding Hood of horror. . . . This is nothing less than pornography. . . . It is also a well-known advertising trick: Emphasize the merchandising over and above the object itself by drawing attention to its wrapping (the miserable little cape) to the detriment of the body within (a little Jewish girl)."[30] Lefort's anxieties, seen within the context of *Heidegger and "the jews"*—whose language he exactly echoes—communicate a specific concern about the volatile nature of French memory. "If there is cause for getting all wrapped up," writes Lyotard, "it is because there is something to wrap up, something that gives rise to being wrapped up, packaged. One elevates because one must enthrall/remove. The pain brought on by shame and by doubt generates the edification of the worthy, the certain, the noble, and the just."[31] Official commemorations in France have created symbols that in each case capture only partial memories, effecting an enveloping, totalizing gesture of memorialization, whether in the service of the Gaullist version of Resistance history or in the diametric swing of the countermyth of collaboration. "Every politicisation implies this getting all wrapped up in something (*emballement*) that is also a being wrapped up, packaged (*emballage*). . . . The temporalisation implied in memorial history is itself a protective shield. . . . That is its 'political' function, its function of forgetting . . . one does not and cannot remember . . . by means of this soliciting, wrapping up gesture."[32] It is notable that French attempts to "wrap up" the memory of the war years—such as Pompidou's 1971 pardoning of Touvier—have hardly proved successful, as the constant resurfacing of polemic around it—inspired in this instance by *Schindler's List*—testifies.

Why, asked sociologist and journalist Annie Kriegel, has Spielberg's film inspired such a passionate and at times aggressive debate in the French press?[33] In part the "absurd squabble," as Kriegel calls it, stems from a very French suspicion of Hollywood, of the spirit of commercialism which is inherent in the commodity produced by the big American studios and which leads to the risk that concern with box-office figures will violate the integrity of film as an artistic medium. This suspicion is so deeply held that it found its way into the 1994 GATT talks with the French insistence on a "cultural exception" with regard to cinema. Daniel Toscan du Plantier, responding to the press furore rather than to the film itself, suggests that "it's time we stop thinking that we are the only people to believe in cinema as an art form."[34] *L'Humanité*, the organ of the French Communist Party, offers a novel twist on the French Communist tradition of refusing to focus on the Jewish specificity of the Holocaust by focusing attention on the national specificity of the French film industry rather than on the subject of the film itself: "Asked about the

GATT negotiations, Spielberg emphasized the importance of the fact that French cinema has its own tradition of making films which are truly representative of the ways in which the French think."[35] This notion of cultural specificity is a seam which runs through the extreme reactions that greeted the film in France: on one level, the specificity of the subject, on another, the film industry itself, leading to a twofold problem: "First: the subject; second: Spielberg. The Holocaust and Hollywood. We have all thrown ourselves into discussion, written articles, compiled dossiers, made television programs, around this very subject."[36]

France and the United States are the two countries which have to date produced the largest number of internationally released films based on, or with a background of, the Holocaust.[37] Annette Insdorf characterizes the essential dichotomy of films whose subject is the genocide of the Jews as being between the realism and the melodramatic conventions of Hollywood as contrasted with the density of style and dialectical complexity of European films.[38] This stylistic divergence is due not only to the very different traditions of French and American cinema but to the historical and cultural relationship of the two countries to the period itself. As Serge July, editor of *Libération*, observed in a six-page dossier devoted to the film: "There is no subject, no tragedy, no history more European than the Holocaust. The Shoah is the dark side of Europe. . . . It is by definition the most impenetrable territory of all for Hollywood." July directly links this impenetrability with Spielberg's mission as a director: "One can understand the passion Spielberg has for Schindler—commercial American fantasy cinema sees its role as nothing less than to be cinema's savior. . . . It is as though Hollywood wanted to respond to the European debate about the 'cultural exception' with its own film manifesto."[39] July clearly identifies Spielberg's mission to make an American film which stands proud amongst other significant films of the Holocaust, all of which have hitherto emerged from Europe. His examination of Spielberg's motivation suggests, albeit elliptically, another significant tension between the French and American cinematic representations of the Holocaust. For Lanzmann, the personalization of the Shoah is impossible: "*Shoah* forbids a lot of things, dispossesses people of a lot of things. *Shoah* is a pure and arid film. There is no personal story."[40] Elisabeth Schemla cautions that "individual stories must not be put in the hands of just anybody, merely on the pretext that they allow the Shoah to become more empathetic."[41] Spielberg, by daring to make the individual "exception" his subject, proclaims a specifically American "manifesto" for his Holocaust film. The individual, after all, is not just the hero of American film but the ideological lynchpin of American culture. As July says, "Spielberg tells the story which for decades has been the central theme of American cinema . . . the tale of an ordinary, selfish, indifferent person who, in the course of the film, transforms himself, becomes engaged with people and with life. It's the story of any ordinary bastard who, like all the others, transforms himself into a hero. America is, as everyone knows, the ultimate democracy of heroism." Danièle Heyman, prompted by Spielberg's choice of hero, comments acerbically: "Spielberg wants to assert his identity not only as a Jew but as a *Juste* [righteous Gentile]."[42]

July's perceptive analysis of the relationship between Spielberg's personal "mission" and the Hollywood film industry is a theme which recurs surprisingly often in the polemic around the film and which merits closer attention. July writes that "American cinema was created by the influx of a significant part of the largely Jewish, European intellectual community" exiled to the United States. Pierre Briançon, in the same issue of *Libération*, refers to "Hollywood, the capital of cinema, founded by Jewish emigrés from Europe."[43] Camille Nevers, writing in the bible of French cinema, *Cahiers du Cinéma*, suggests that "like Schindler, Hollywood gathered in and made use of those who wanted to escape the Nazi Occupation. . . . The moral is: An industry which resisted from within is an art unto itself. In *Schindler's List* Spielberg does nothing less than ask of his own art—of his own industry—a question along the lines of 'What is cinema?' "[44] The idea of "resistance" in this context is of course far more nuanced and loaded in French than it is in English. The corollary subtext to all these references to Hollywood as the "savior" of European filmmakers fleeing Nazism is the somber shadow of the memory of the French film industry under the Occupation. The French film industry of the war years was an industry whose *grands personages* enjoyed Parisian highlife to the full under the Nazis, with all the corollary ambiguities inherent in such a relationship.[45] The films of this period were frequently epic historical dramas which were themselves creating a unified, nostalgic memory in the service of Pétainist ideals of French national heritage. The irony is not, apparently, lost on some of *Schindler's List*'s more perceptive commentators.

Although Insdorf's book came out long before Spielberg's film, *Schindler's List* nonetheless follows the national and cultural rubric, which she hazards thus: "It seems that Hollywood will not risk producing a film about the Holocaust except after the material which inspired it has proved its commercial potential in another form [for example, a novel such as Thomas Keneally's *Schindler's Ark*]. . . . One could perhaps say that the cinema of a country that never experienced the Occupation is powerless to evoke the depths of experience of the Holocaust."[46] Insdorf makes an apparently uncritical elision between the Holocaust and the Occupation. Clearly there is a relationship between the Occupation and the Holocaust, but the absolute equation of the two is hardly self-evident, as tensions in official French commemorations suggest.[47] (Insdorf, incidentally, with the inclusion in her book of a film such as Louis Malle's

Lacombe Lucien, about a small-time *résistant* turned collaborator in the French countryside, very much implies that Occupation equals Holocaust, in spite of her definition of the term Holocaust in her introduction as the attempted genocide of European Jewry by the Nazis.) Perhaps it is precisely this elision which points to the pivotal if undeclared reason why *Schindler's List* roused such strong emotions in the French press, a suggestion that was underscored by the trial of Paul Touvier which began a fortnight after Spielberg's film opened.

The ramifications of the Touvier trial demonstrate the problematic issue of acknowledgment and denial of French responsibility in the Final Solution, which in turn highlights the complexity of the collective memory of the genocide of the Jews in France. Nancy Wood writes that "in recent years, the French judicial sphere has become one of the most important sites for the 'sollicitation de la mémoire nationale.' "[48] Lucette Valensi points out in the preface to the *Annales* devoted to Vichy, the Occupation, and the Jews, that in spite of the proliferation of research undertaken in recent years on Vichy itself, there has been only a limited amount of work undertaken on the participation of Vichy in the genocide of the Jews.[49] In this context, the Touvier case takes on particular importance in terms of its effect on the crystallization of a French national consciousness of the Holocaust.

In 1964 the twenty-year statute of limitations came into effect, which meant that there could be no more trials for war crimes; crimes against humanity were, however, specifically exempted from the statute.[50] Nonetheless, it was not until the 1987 trial of the Nazi Klaus Barbie that the first trial in which the defendant was accused of crimes against humanity came to court in France. As Rousso and Wood demonstrate, the legal stratification separating crimes against humanity—principally those committed against the Jews on purely racial grounds—from war crimes meant that "the nation's most vital memories—the anti-Vichy struggles of the Resistance and the death of a national martyr [the Resistance hero Jean Moulin]—were excluded from the proceedings [of the Barbie trial]."[51] The corollary of this, however, was that the legal focus now permitted the hitherto virtually ignored history of the Final Solution as it had happened in France—a history that had been relegated to the margins of national memory by the weight of official commemorations of the Resistance—to come out of the shadows.[52]

The French were only too happy to try Barbie, "the Butcher of Lyons," who was not only responsible for the deportation of Jews from the region but also for the crushing of the Resistance whose intelligence center was Lyons. The problem arose when the file against Touvier for the reprisal execution of seven Jews on June 29, 1944, was opened in 1992. There was no doubt as to the fact that Touvier had given the order for their execution. The decision to drop charges before the case came to court—on the grounds that the Vichy regime could not be held to have pursued a policy of "ideological hegemony," the key element in the definition of crimes against humanity as determined during the Barbie trial—was cynically seen as to have been "influenced by a political desire for 'civil peace' in relation to the traumatic past represented by Vichy."[53]

The uproar caused by this decision, with the implication that the courts had taken it upon themselves to rewrite history, led to the Touvier file being reopened. Two years later, on April 4, 1994, almost fifty years after the Liberation, Touvier became the first French citizen to be convicted of crimes against humanity. The conviction meant that the Vichy state had finally been juridically recognized as one whose functionaries could be judged culpable of crimes against humanity—and whose role in the Final Solution was finally recognized in the French courts.

The mirror held up to France by the Touvier *affaire* reflected the still unsettled conscience of a country that has not yet come to terms with the culpability of the Vichy regime and its thousands of collaborators during the war, collaborators who, in betraying the Jews, betrayed the ideals of the Republic and thus the very soul of modern France. Here then is located the site of the French *mémoire* of the war years and of the role of Vichy in the Final Solution— a dislocated memory shifting between the conflicting emblems of heroism and betrayal. As Bertrand Poirot-Delpech wrote in *Le Monde* on the day the trial opened, "among European countries, France has done least well in coming to terms with and managing its collective behavior during the last war. . . . Touvier's trial will not have been in vain if it at last lays the past to rest."

Whether the Touvier conviction will indeed have laid the past to rest remains to be seen. No sooner had the Touvier case come to an end than a new polemic emerged in the press in response to the details about the ambiguous war years and pre- and postwar allegiances of President Mitterrand which emerged in Pierre Péan's book, authorized by the president, *Une jeunesse française: François Mitterrand 1934–1947.*[54] The most damaging of the revelations concern Mitterrand's friendship with René Bousquet. Mitterrand disingenuously described his friend after his death (he was shot by a disturbed assassin in 1993) as "a man of exceptional standing. . . . I enjoyed our meetings. He was nothing like the things said about him."[55] These "things," as Tony Judt put it, were hardly idle gossip. Bousquet, as secretary-general of the Vichy police from April 1942 until July 1942, was directly responsible for the deportation of some 30,000 foreign Jews from both occupied France and the southern "free zone."[56]

One of the inevitable aspects of the continued polemic on the Holocaust is that it is repeatedly presented anew, without reference to previous debate. Very rarely does a journalist stand back and seek to make connections between stories and polemics that constantly emerge in the press. This might well serve as an analogy of the contemporary French memory of the war years. The Holocaust is likely to retain its currency as a topic in the French media as long as France continues working through her repressed and melancholic memory of the Second World War. There is no better shorthand symbol of the discontinuities and lacunae of French memory than the fact that, up until the late 1980s, Mitterrand laid a wreath in annual homage on the graves of both Jean Moulin and Marshal Pétain.

The debate about *Schindler's List,* like the film itself, neither came out of, nor emerged into, a vacuum. Both the film and all the discursive polemic which surrounded it are part of the process by which motifs of history and memory—collective and individual, personal and political—struggle for a place in contemporary consciousness, and in doing so themselves contribute to its redefinition. As critic James Young put it, "the memory of the past is not merely passed down *mi dor le dor*—from generation to generation—but it is necessarily regenerated in the images that transport it from one era to the next."[57] *Schindler's List,* flawed as it may be, is one such image; the polemic which it inspired, equally significant, another.

Notes

I am grateful to Mme Sara Halperyn and her colleagues at the Centre de Documentation Juive Contemporaine, Paris, for their help in collating material from the French press during the period when *Schindler's List* was released in France.

Unless otherwise specified, all translations from the French are by the author.

1. *Le Monde,* October 5, 1993.

2. Pierre Nora, *Les lieux de mémoire,* 7 vols. (Paris: Gallimard, 1984–92).

3. Ibid., vol. 1, p. xvii.

4. Claude Moniquet, *Touvier, un Milicien à l'ombre de l'Eglise* (Paris: Orban, 1989).

5. Nancy Wood, "Crimes or Misdemeanours? Memory on Trial in Contemporary France," *French Cultural Studies* 5 (1994), pp. 1–21.

6. Pompidou's official statement when he was obliged to justify the Touvier pardon makes this point abundantly clear: "Over the past thirty years or so, our country has lived through a series of dramatic events. The war, the defeat and its humiliations, the Occupation and its horrors, the Liberation, and in reaction the purge and—let us be frank—its excesses, the war in Indochina, and then the dreadful Algerian conflict and its horrors, on both sides, and the exodus of a million French citizens driven from their homes, followed immediately by the OAS and its murderous attacks and violence, and then in reaction, the repression. . . . Hasn't the time come to draw a veil over the past, to forget a time when Frenchmen disliked one another, attacked one another, and even killed one another? I say this not out of political calculation, although I see that there are some sharp minds here, but out of respect for France." Georges Pompidou, *Entretiens et Discours, 1968–1974* (Paris: Flammarion, 1984), pp. 157–58, quoted in Henry Rousso, *The Vichy Syndrome: History and Memory in France since 1944,* trans. Arthur Goldhammer (Cambridge: Harvard University Press, 1991), p. 123.

7. Annette Wieviorka *Déportation et Genocide: entre la mémoire et l'oubli* (Paris: Plon, 1992), p. 19.

8. Rousso, *The Vichy Syndrome*, p. 5.

9. Ibid., p. 10.

10. *Globe Hebdo*, March 2–8, 1994.

11. J. M. Domenach, " 'Le Monde' en question," *Esprit* (April 1976), p. 778, quoted in Henry H. Weinberg, *The Myth of the Jew in France 1967–82* (New York: Mosaic Press, 1987), p. 93.

12. Claude Lanzmann, "Holocauste, la représentation impossible," *Le Monde*, March 3, 1994, pp. 1, 7.

13. *Globe Hebdo*, March 2–8, 1994.

14. *Revue Juive*, May 6, 1994.

15. *Le Figaro*, March 4, 1994.

16. Elisabeth Schemla, "Ces héros qui ont sauvé les juifs," *Le Nouvel Observateur* (March 7–23, 1994), pp. 6–10.

17. Georges Suffert, *Le Figaro*, March 4, 1994.

18. Manek Weintraub, *Info Juive*, March 1994.

19. André Halimi, *Passages*, April 1994.

20. *Le Point*, March 12, 1994.

21. Ludi Boeken, "Shoah—pas de droits de l'auteur sur la mémoire," *Libération* (March 4, 1994).

22. Albert Memmi, "La Question de sens (suite)," *Libération* (March 14, 1994), p. 7.

23. *Le Quotidien de Paris*, February 20, 1994.

24. *Libération* (March 2, 1994); *Télérama* (March 5–11, 1994).

25. Jean-François Lyotard, *Heidegger and "the jews,"* trans. Andreas Mitchel and Mark S. Roberts, introduction by David Carroll (Minneapolis: University of Minnesota Press, 1990), p. 26.

26. See Pierre Vidal-Nacquet, *Assassins of Memory: Essays on the Denial of the Holocaust*, trans. Jeffrey Mehlman (New York: Columbia University Press, 1992), for a brilliant summation and refutation of the arguments of Robert Faurisson and his fellow negationists. Nadine Fresco has written extensively both about the history of negationism in France and the strategies which have been adopted in the campaign to deny that the Holocaust ever happened. See Nadine Fresco, "Negating the dead," in Geoffrey Hartman, ed., *Holocaust Remembrance: The Shapes of Memory* (Oxford: Blackwell, 1994), pp. 191–203.

27. Gerard Lefort, "Les armes d'Hollywood face à l'horreur," *Libération* (March 2, 1994), p. 4.

28. Pierre Hazan, "Le Plaidoyer d'Alain Finkielkraut," *Revue Juive* (May 6, 1994), p. 19.

29. Le Monde Radio-Télévision (March 13–14, 1994).

30. Lefort, "Les armes d'Hollywood face à l'horreur," p. 4.

31. Lyotard, *Heidegger and "the jews,"* p. 8.

32. Ibid., p. 8.

33. *Le Figaro*, March 30, 1994.

34. *Figaro Magazine* (March 5, 1994).

35. *L'Humanité*, March 3, 1994.

36. Camille Nevers, *Cahiers du Cinéma* 478 (April 1994).

37. See Annette Insdorf, *L'Holocauste à l'Ecran* (Paris: Cerf, 1985) [French translation of *Indelible Shadows: Film and the Holocaust*], and Ilan Avisar, *Screening the Holocaust: Cinema's Images of the Unimaginable* (Bloomington: Indiana University Press, 1988), for filmogra-

phies of works that deal, directly or indirectly, with the Holocaust, listed with release dates and countries of production.

38. Insdorf, *L'Holocauste à l'Ecran*.

39. Serge July, "La fin de l'exception culturelle," *Libération* (March 2, 1994), p. 3.

40. *Le Monde*, March 3, 1994.

41. *Nouvel Observateur*, February 17–23, 1994.

42. *Le Monde*, March 3, 1994.

43. Pierre Briançon, "Spielberg filme l'holocauste," *Libération* (March 2, 1994), pp. 2–3.

44. Camille Nevers, *Cahiers du Cinéma* 478 (April 1994).

45. See Evelyn Ehrlich, *Cinema of Paradox: French Filmmaking under the German Occupation* (New York: Columbia University Press, 1985).

46. Insdorf, *L'Holocauste à l'Ecran*, p. 33.

47. See Annette Wieviorka "1992: Réflexions sur une commémoration," *Annales ESC* 3 (May-June 1993), pp. 703–14, for an evocation of the extent to which public memorialization of the deportation of the Jews from France has changed since the end of the 1940s, demonstrating some of the tensions involved in the official commemoration of the war in France. "The contrast between the postwar commemorations and those of 1992 is striking. Those of the immediate postwar period demonstrated the desire on the part of French Jews to reintegrate themselves into the national community. . . . Those of 1992, all of which were centered on French responsibility for the destruction of the Jews, reopened an unhealed wound."

48. Wood, "Crimes or Misdemeanours?"

49. Lucette Valensi, "Présence du passé, lenteur de l'histoire," *Annales ESC* 3 (May-June 1993), pp. 491–500.

50. See Wood, "Crimes or Misdemeanours?" for a lucid discussion of the history of the concept of crimes against humanity in postwar France. Also, see Rousso, *The Vichy Syndrome*.

51. Wood, "Crimes or Misdemeanours?"

52. For a full description of the legal controversies and ramifications surrounding the Barbie trial, see Alain Finkielkraut, *La mémoire vaine du crime contre l'humanité* (Paris: Gallimard, 1989); Vidal-Nacquet, *Assassins of Memory*, pp. 131–35; Rousso, *The Vichy Syndrome*, pp. 199–216.

53. Wood, "Crimes or Misdemeanours?"

54. Mitterrand worked from the end of 1941 until January 1942 in the Légion des Combattants et des Volontaires de la Révolution Nationale, a department which was created by the notoriously anti-Semitic Xavier Vallat, Vichy's first commissioner for Jewish Questions. From May 1942 until January 1943 he worked in a government agency for the rehabilitation of ex-prisoners. Marshal Pétain was so impressed by his services that he was awarded a service medal, the Francisque, the following year. Only in the spring of 1943 did Mitterrand become involved in the Resistance.

55. Pierre Péan, *Une jeunesse française: François Mitterrand 1934–1947* (Paris: Fayard, 1994), p. 315, quoted in Tony Judt's review "Truth and Consequences," *New York Review of Books* (November 3, 1994), pp. 8–12.

56. Péan, *Une jeunesse française*, p. 315.

57. James E. Young, *Writing and Rewriting the Holocaust: Narrative and the Consequences of Interpretation* (Bloomington: Indiana University Press, 1988), p. 145.

12 | The Uncertain Certainty of *Schindler's List*[1]

Bryan Cheyette

In his preface to *Moments of Reprieve* (1981), Primo Levi characteristically apologizes for the limitations of this work, which was written to supplement his earlier memoirs, *If This Is a Man* (1958) and *The Truce* (1963): "It is possible that the distance in time has accentuated the tendency to round out the facts or heighten the colours: this tendency, or temptation, is an integral part of writing, without it one does not write stories but rather accounts." By the 1980s, Levi thought of himself primarily as a writer of stories who was fortunate enough to give a few of the "voiceless mass of the shipwrecked . . . the ambiguous perennial existence of literary characters."[2] But one should not underestimate the "ambiguity" of Levi's task. His work is dotted throughout with pained moments of hesitancy when either his memory fails him or he suddenly distrusts his ability as a wordsmith to recreate his time in Auschwitz-Birkenau. Levi needs to be a storyteller so that his words live on the page, but this task is always in agonized tension with the absolute necessity of justly accounting for those that can no longer speak for themselves.

An acute sense of the uncertainty[3] of all storytelling in relation to the Holocaust is, as I have shown elsewhere, at the heart of Levi's memoirs.[3] The ethics of this uncertainty provides the reader with a critical vocabulary in which to understand other, more contemporary, renderings of the Holocaust such as *Schindler's List*. For Levi, this uncertainty is located at precisely those points in his writing when he is not contained by any system—moral, linguistic, scientific. It is at these moments that he is able to locate his own humanity, as he puts it, outside the law, which is, by definition, ungeneralizable and unassimilable. By the time of *The Drowned and the Saved* (1986), Levi called this realm of uncertainty the "grey zone." He was, by this time, rightly suspicious of those who have, over the years, reduced the Holocaust to a Manichaean allegory that revolves around the already known aesthetic separation of good and evil:

> In anyone who today reads (or writes) the history of the Lager is evident the tendency, indeed the need, to separate evil from good, to be able to take sides, to repeat Christ's gesture on Judgment Day: here the righteous, over there the reprobates. The young above all demand clarity, a sharp cut; their experience of the world being meagre, they do not like ambiguity. In

any case, their expectation reproduces exactly that of the newcomers to the Lagers, whether young or not; all of them, with the exception of those who had already gone through an analogous experience, expected to find a terrible but decipherable world, in conformity to that simple model which we atavistically carry within us—'we' inside and the enemy outside, separated by a sharply defined geographic frontier.[4]

Levi, in this definitive chapter, talks primarily about particular groups or individuals such as the *Sonderkommandos* or the Kapos of Auschwitz-Birkenau, or Chaim Rumkowski. However, as Zygmunt Bauman has recently shown, this spurious sense of a "terrible but decipherable world" can be applied more generally to those victims trapped in the Jewish ghettos. In his chapter on "soliciting the co-operation of the victims," Bauman contends that the assumed logic of self-preservation in fact contributed to the demise of those in the ghettos who internalized this feigned rationality. That is, Jews were asked continuously to make what appeared to be perfectly rational decisions concerning their survival, which actually played into the hands of their persecutors.[5] As Levi states, what was good and what was evil in this context was deliberately blurred by those who had absolute power over their victims. The calculated dehumanization of Jewish victims in this context, which forced them to be complicit with their own destruction, will be seen to be especially relevant with regard to Spielberg's *Schindler's List*.

My contention is that the ethical uncertainty at the heart of Levi's writings is the necessary critical yardstick by which one ought to understand present-day films and novels, many of which glibly assimilate the Holocaust in a breathtakingly untroubled manner. This yardstick might at first appear unnecessarily or perversely harsh, but it seems to be more than ever appropriate when we note the Manichaean certainty of contemporary filmmakers and writers in relation to the Shoah. That Levi himself was particularly concerned with cinematic representations of the Holocaust can be seen from a brief article published toward the end of his life. In an essay included in a catalogue of photographs of the Nazi death camps, Levi reiterates his growing concern that words are of little use in describing the experience of Holocaust survivors. He goes on to claim that "their poor reception derives from the fact that we now live in a civilization of the image, registered, multiplied, televised, and that the public, particularly the young, is ever less likely to benefit from written information. . . . " The sense that televised or cinematic images have replaced written accounts of survivors is perhaps also the reason for the distrust, in *The Drowned and the Saved*, of the supposed authenticity and power of human memory. His cherished memories, Levi came to feel, had been unwittingly erased or changed over the years by many "extraneous features."[6]

The difference between extraneous images and authentic memories continues to be fraught with anxiety, in relation to the Holocaust, and this anxiety plays itself out both in the written and visual versions of *Schindler's List*. An aesthetic uncertainty in both works is usefully contrasted with the ethical uncertainty of Levi. Whereas Levi is concerned with the dangers of reducing the Holocaust to a Manichaean allegory, both Spielberg and Keneally generate a representational uncertainty with regard to the "certainty" of its supposed documentary form. I will begin with Thomas Keneally's fictionalized account of Oskar Schindler, which is most obviously split between Keneally's use of the "texture and devices of a novel" to reveal a "true story."[7] Unlike Levi's storytelling, which makes his memoirs more readable, Keneally claims the truth of history to give his fiction more authority. The omniscient and self-confident narrative voice in Keneally's novel is, however, only rarely troubled about facilely recreating the most intimate details of the past.

At the same time that he fictionalizes Schindler, Keneally refers throughout, in documentary fashion, to those who "knew Oskar" and, specifically, to the testimony of the *Schindlerjuden*. Where the facts of Schindler's exploits are unclear, such as his purported visit to Auschwitz to liberate the three hundred women destined for Brinnlitz, Keneally makes explicit such lack of knowledge. But these lapses in knowledge also indicate that his seductive narrative is, in the end, absolutely sure of itself. Thus, chapter 22 opens with the following: "We do not know in what condition of soul Oskar Schindler spent March 13th, the [Podgorze] ghetto's last and worst day" (206), as if we knew Schindler's "condition of soul" on other days. Keneally is also adept at pointing out potential fables, myths, or anecdotes with regard to Schindler. Nonetheless, this also implies that the narrative as a whole is devoid of such extraneous information. Such is the speculative ending of chapter 33: "One wonders if some of Emilie [Schindler's] kindnesses . . . may not have been absorbed into the Oskar legend" (361), which similarly hints at a documentary authority for that which is not deemed "legendary." It is significant that the interpretation of history in both the book and the film have been subsequently challenged by Emilie (whose story has not yet been told).[8] Such interventions help us realize that the events of *Schindler's List* are not always quite as straightforward as either Spielberg or Keneally would have us believe.

A comparison of the two versions of *Schindler's List* is particularly useful when highlighting the relative importance attached to specific episodes and characters in both novel and film. Steven Spielberg's film obviously had to make a large number of editorial choices with regard to those aspects of Keneally's novel which would be recreated on the screen. The full story of Amon Goeth—namely, his imprisonment and relative powerlessness by the time Schindler moved to Brinnlitz—is, most critically, not told in the film.

This means that Goeth can only ever be seen in the film (unlike the book) as the evil embodiment of absolute power. At least two other individuals, Abraham Bankier and Marcel Goldberg, are amalgamated into Spielberg's Itzhak Stern, which also makes him, in the film, a benign monodimensional figure when compared to the equivalent individuals in the book. Such simplifications apply also to the many ironies in Keneally's narrative that are often in tension with the film's sentimentality. One especially notable transformation from book to film is Stern's early and conspicuously ironic use of the Talmudic verse in the book—"He who saves the life of one man, saves the world entire" (54)—which, as Gillian Rose has argued convincingly, is given an all too literal meaning as a point of closure, a defining moment, in the film.[9] These crucial differences between book and film will be stressed throughout as key illustrations of the texture and concerns underlying Spielberg's *Schindler's List*.

The film closely follows the book, above all in recreating the tension between imaginative or colorful storytelling and authentic monochromatic documentation. That Spielberg wished his movie to have documentary authority can be seen from the prepublicity for *Schindler's List*, which emphasized the extent to which it was filmed, where possible, in the current sites of the Shoah. Because Kraków was left virtually undamaged during the war, Spielberg was able to forego his Hollywood studios and instead have as his backdrop the actual landscape of suffering. *Schindler's List*, to be sure, does attempt to incorporate European cinematography, not least because nearly all of its cast of actors, and much of its crew, are non-American. In a further bid at authenticity, many of the actors are the sons and daughters of Holocaust survivors or local Poles whose parents witnessed, to some degree, the events of the film.

That the film self-consciously imitates contemporary documentaries can be seen from the outstanding use of hand-held cameras with wide-angle lenses—often darting among a heaving mass of victimized Jews—which maintains the film's naturalistic illusion. Janusz Kaminski's skilled cinematography goes so far as to simulate the Podgorze ghetto in Kraków, the slave labor camp in Plaszów, and, astonishingly, even Auschwitz-Birkenau death camp. Such reproduction has been described negatively as a "Holocaust theme park": "The transport trains will roll, the ghetto will be populated and depopulated, even the chimneys of Auschwitz-Birkenau will belch forth anew."[10] But the didactic and popular recreation of the Shoah is a vital element in evaluating the film. The attempt of a mass-audience movie to illustrate the full panorama of genocide in all its bureaucratic horror obviously takes the film beyond the narrower character-based focus of Keneally's novel.

Nonetheless, the deliberate blurring of the borders between cinema and history in *Schindler's List* does generate a good deal of unease. On the one hand, the film frames itself in terms of a brief opening and concluding contemporary scene (in color), which qualifies its claim to documentary authenticity. This can be seen also in the deliberate embellishment of the young girl in a red dress (taken from the book) to dramatic effect. As with Keneally, the film self-consciously provides itself with a few moments of artifice to detract from its more ubiquitous rhetorical designs. *Schindler's List* is, after all, not merely a film within a film, but it is also based on a version of a true story within a novel. After the initial admiration of Spielberg's ambitious, often breathtaking naturalism, one also becomes aware of the overriding theatricality of *Schindler's List*. My argument, in short, is that the film is unable to sustain its well-meaning didactic pretensions and that, by the end, the uncertain certainties of its documentary naturalism are displaced onto a Manichaean aesthetic.

More than in any other popular film, Spielberg has struggled to turn into authentic images that which was thought to be unrepresentable. We see, re-created, the kind of dwarfish cubby holes that families—and especially children—were forced to use in the ghettos and camps to prevent them from being rounded up for the cattle trucks. We see them scurrying into preprepared hiding places in false walls and floors, pianos, cupboards, even latrines and sewers. The detail is staggering, but it is also reminiscent of more light-weight versions of similar episodes in *E.T.* or *Jurassic Park*. Since completing *Schindler's List*, Spielberg has spoken a great deal about the kind of adolescent anti-Semitic bullying that he suffered until his late teenage years.[11] As his films are obsessed with people (often children) leaving comfortable homes only to encounter strange, incomprehensible forces, it is possible to read Spielberg's biography back into his more accomplished popular movies such as *Duel* or *Jaws*. Such is the split in *Schindler's List* between Spielberg's autobiographical drive—which results in his recreating his own preoccupations in a multitude of forms—and his restrained impersonal account.

The unresolved tension between the film's flawed sense of its own limitations and its all too evident powers of lavish historical reconstruction takes many forms. Spielberg, interestingly, for a seemingly neutral rendering, is not unselfconscious about his debt to other films and filmmakers. The switch from the opening scene to the film proper transforms contemporary Sabbath candles into the smoke of a 1940s railway engine. This key image, moving from God-given redemption to mankind's degeneration, is clearly reminiscent of David Lean. Like Lean, Spielberg has been rightly viewed as creating a "sense of people caught in a cataclysm beyond their ken or control" as well as being fond of "processions winding into the distance [and] men on horseback."[12]

Other critics have thought of the after-image of the Cossacks in Eisenstein's *Strike* when viewing the SS liquidators clattering up the courtyard steps of the Podgorze ghetto in *Schindler's List*. Much of the movie also evokes the Polish filmmaker, Andrzej Wajda, whom Spielberg consulted and who has come closest, in *Kanal* and *Korczak*, to an equivalent and no less painstaking reconstruction of Nazi-occupied Poland. Above all, the photographs of Roman Vishniac and the popular iconography of the Holocaust—such as the well-known snapshot of the boy with the cap in the Warsaw ghetto with his hands in the air—are incorporated into *Schindler's List*. Coupled with his extremely adept use of the lighting techniques, crisp editing and sinuous camera movements of *film noir*, Spielberg's supposedly authentic documentary realism can be seen to be as mutually referential and artificial as his more self-conscious gestures to other filmmakers.[13]

As with *film noir* and the popular iconography of the Holocaust, much has been made of Spielberg's cinematic allusions to Claude Lanzmann's *Shoah*. This is not surprising since *Schindler's List* is framed with two pointed references to *Shoah*. The opening, ghost-like disappearance of the 1930s Jewish family who leave a set of empty chairs—which shrewdly become the absence addressed by the rest of the film—implicitly echoes the figure of that other "righteous gentile," Jan Karski, in *Shoah*. As Karski attempts to recall his eye-witness account of the scale of the atrocities in Europe, he breaks down and leaves an empty chair, which Lanzmann lingers over. The gulf between the unbridgeable loss of the past, and what we see on the screen, a notable preoccupation of *Shoah*, is also reflected in the last few frames of *Schindler's List* when the actual *Schindlerjuden* are placed next to their cinematic counterparts. Other aesthetic techniques, taken wholesale from *Shoah*, include the repeated references to the everyday machinery of genocide—typewriters, lists, tables, chairs, endless queues—which are eventually filled with dread, not unlike the constant shots of railway lines in *Shoah*.[14]

The most obvious reference to Lanzmann is, undoubtedly, the child actor in *Schindler's List* who slices his hand across his throat as the cattle trucks pass him by. This is filmed in quick succession (once in slow motion) from within the cattle trucks. In *Shoah*, an elderly Polish peasant told Lanzmann how, as a boy, he used to similarly indicate to the hordes in the cattle trucks, as they passed through his village, that they were heading to their death. Spielberg's conspicuous incorporation of the words of the elderly Pole is clearly a self-conscious and popular rejoinder to those who, like Lanzmann, emphasize the absolute impossibility of finding appropriate images to represent the past. While Spielberg attempts to give virtually every aspect of the apparatus of genocide a filmic equivalent for a mass audience, Lanzmann eschews the representation of history in a facile series of cinematic tropes. Such is the irresolvable exchange between the two films.

What is ironic about Lanzmann's dismissal of *Schindler's List*—for leaving our imagination in abeyance as we passively consume artificial images—is that *Shoah* is a surprisingly stable form of reference in the film. That is, the debate around the limits of representation, which locks *Schindler's List* and *Shoah* together in dialogue, does not touch on the wider and more acute question of what Gillian Rose has provocatively called the "fascism of representation." Levi, we remember, speaks of the "newcomers to the Lagers" who "expected to find a terrible but decipherable word" which was sharply divided into good and evil. Such Manichaeanism eventually monopolizes *Schindler's List*—and the representation of Jewish survivors—and fatally undermines its uncertain documentary realism. It is in these terms that, I believe, the "representation of fascism" in the film can be, as Rose maintains, indistinguishable from the "fascism of representation."[15] This contention is specifically illustrated with regard to one of the more telling and troubling sequences of *Schindler's List*—the episodes set in Auschwitz-Birkenau.

In a pivotal episode in the film (but not in the book), the three hundred women and children, supposedly destined for Schindler's Brinnlitz haven, find themselves mistakenly diverted to Auschwitz-Birkenau. They are taken to a delousing bathhouse and made to take a shower. Like the women on the screen, we are not sure if they are being locked into a real shower or not. Spielberg lingers a good deal over this scene as the women's cumulative screams are juxtaposed with the violins playing morbidly in the background. The audience is horrified less by the actual event than by the thought that absolutely nothing is going to be left unshown in this film. Such is the fragility of *Schindler's List* that it is hard to tell whether this is a moment of welcome self-consciousness or the restraint of an overweening appetite. In the end, mere water flows from the showerheads, and the women's screams are replaced by laughter. At this point, the film is finally forced to recognize the limits of what can and cannot be achieved on the screen. What is more, after this sequence, the uncertain certainty of its documentary realism begins to unravel disastrously and is displaced onto the film's underlying Manichaeanism.

In addition to noting the women's experience in Auschwitz-Birkenau, the book, it should be remembered, initially retold a similar experience undergone by their male counterparts in Gross-Rosen forced labor camp. The male experience makes the most telling and dramatic impact in the book. Given the timeless redemptive fantasies associated with Jewish women, it is significant that Spielberg should make the salvific waters of the delousing huts into a wholly feminine episode. The audience views the queues of the unknown masses waiting for the gas chambers in Auschwitz-Birkenau through the eyes of these women as they leave the showers. We also view Dr. Mengele through their eyes, and most of the apparatus of the camp "selection" processes is also mediated through them. At this point, the film's seductive realism breaks down and its uncertain certainties are sought elsewhere. No longer a neutral documentary, with flawless didactic pretensions, the audience's identification with the *Schindlerjuden* (here as the feminine sign of salvation) is, from now on, the narrative's overriding interest. The towering presence of Schindler, saving their children from the furnace in Auschwitz-Birkenau, similarly begins the process of transfiguring him into an unambiguous Christ-figure. One value, that of self-preservation, is aestheticized and replaces the uncertainty which surrounds the film's increasingly unrealizable naturalism.

Gillian Rose is correct to argue that the message of "water not gas" culminates in the film's unironic and sentimental point of closure: "He who saves one life, saves the world entire." As Zygmunt Bauman has also noted, this Talmudic saying, taken literally, is the ideological basis for an amoral survivalism that eventually permeates *Schindler's List*.[16] If the cinematic *Schindlerjuden* are left unchanged by their experience, left fully human in other words, then survival at any price becomes the primary ethic of the movie. What is more, the dehumanization and enforced complicity of the victims of genocide is left unrepresented. As Lawrence Langer has shown, with reference to the Fortunoff Video Archive at Yale University, survival should not be evaluated in terms of our conventional "bracing pieties," which invariably sentimentalize a supposedly "resourceful human spirit." In his volume, a victim recollects dragging huge numbers of corpses into mass graves and is asked by his interviewer: "when did you feel it was over?" His answer, "I didn't feel over *anything*," summarizes the inconsolable nature of the "ruins of memory" for Langer.[17] The depiction of an untroubled self-preservation can also be compared with Wajda's *Korczak*, an equally true story in which it is impossible for Korczak to go on living in a world where children are systematically murdered. Korczak, too, towers over "his" children in the Warsaw ghetto, but instead of choosing survival, he travels with them to Treblinka. The self-consciously mythologized ending of the movie offers a radically differing way of seeing the world as it once again makes human those who had been previously dehumanized.

That *Schindler's List* is initially troubled by a crude survivalism that leaves the humanity of the *Schindlerjuden* fully intact can be discerned in a number of key scenes. Once Stern is pulled from the cattle trucks by Schindler—prefiguring the later rescue of the *Schindlerfrauen*—Spielberg quickly cuts to a scene which is meant to establish the enormity of the death camps. Immediately after Stern is saved, a camera pans into a room adjoining the station platform where Jews are sorting out the piles of suitcases, glasses, and clothing of those dispatched to the gas ovens. This room simulates the present-day huge display bins at the museum of Auschwitz-Birkenau, where the "scattered artifacts" of those murdered represent, metonymically, their previous lives. The irretrievable gulf between such dismembered fragments and the lives that went before is similarly reproduced in *Schindler's List*.[18]

While Stern remains relatively unaffected by his ordeal, we are led by the camera to the disbelieving face of a Jewish worker who, as the scene ends, is given a large pile of teeth with gold fillings to sort out. None of this latter episode is in Keneally's account, which discloses that it was not Stern but Bankier and a dozen others who were rescued by Schindler. The book also ends on a suitably complicit note: "Now, the cattle transports told them, we are all beasts together" (137). In the film, the vacuous juxtaposition of life and death, survival and industrial genocide, culminates eventually in the happy scene in Brinnlitz (taken partially from the book), when one of the *Schindlerjuden*'s gold teeth is used to make the ring with the inscription, "He who saves one life, saves the world entire." It is as if the appalling pile of gold teeth seen earlier belongs to a different world.

What is perhaps most noteworthy about the inclusion of the disembodied remnants of the dead, at a relatively early stage in the film, is the degree to which they are meant to qualify an untroubling survivalism which eventually sets the tone of the film. Many of the ghetto scenes in *Schindler's List* are, after all, concerned with Stern extracting individuals from the various selection procedures. Families, elderly and young couples, rabbis, professors, adolescents, all become familiar faces who are resourcefully directed by Stern into Schindler's factory, the Deutsche Emailwaren Fabrik. This process of removing the *Schindlerjuden* from the queues of the condemned is repeated in scenes at Plaszów and, of course, Auschwitz-Birkenau. In the end, an unambiguous survivalism becomes a seductive and finally overwhelming point of identification which counters the horrific scenes of arbitrary and mass murder in the film.

To confound the "grammar of heroism"[19] offered by Stern's triumphs, there are a number of times in the film when the dehumanization of the victims—as opposed to their conspicuous survival—comes to the fore. During the liquidation of the ghetto, a mother and daughter attempt to hide with others, below a clothes chest at the end of a bed, and are told that there is no room for the mother. When the children frantically attempt to hide from a "selection" in Plaszów, one boy plunges into a latrine full of excrement and is told by the other children already there, "this is our place" (282). This latter instance is taken directly from the book, but Spielberg leaves out many more concrete examples of the dehumanization of the *Schindlerjuden* recounted by Keneally. We are told in the book, for instance, that the only hanging and criminal use of the furnace in Brinnlitz was when some of the *Schindlerjuden* killed a particularly brutal guard at the end of the war. When the final list was drawn up to transfer the *Schindlerjuden* to Brinnlitz, Marcel Goldberg, a clerk in Schindler's office, was extravagantly bribed so as to include many relatives and friends of those already on the list. Goldberg, the "Lord of the Lists" (320), had to rewrite Schindler's list alone from memory at Gross-Rosen. This decidedly equivocal act (where those with money could replace those on the list without) enabled Schindler's men to travel on to Brinnlitz. The fact that these stories of brutality and corruption were not included toward the end of the film—as they were in the book—says a great deal about the nature of the film. Instead of such ambiguities, the moral rectitude and humanity of the *Schindlerjuden* is insured, in the film, merely by dint of their survival.

The fact that Stern takes the part of Goldberg fatally idealizes his actions so that Stern can only either provide Schindler with an absolutely scrupulous moral framework for him to recognize eventually. To be sure, Schindler begins as a tabula rasa on which both the potential for good and for evil can be inscribed. He is, in other words, initially suspended between Stern's unequivocal virtue and Goeth's complete viciousness. That Goeth is left pointedly unseen in his relatively powerless state—after being imprisoned and sacked as the commandant of Plaszów for his black market activities—reinforces the film's Manichaean narrative. With Stern personifying the goodness of the *Schindlerjuden*, evil becomes melodramatically and harmlessly embodied in Goeth. Such aestheticized certainties mean that the film inevitably shifts from the victims to the perpetrators of genocide and, above all, ceases to implicate the audience in its story. If heroic self-preservation is the highest value in *Schindler's List*, then this particularly dubious virtue—in light of the dehumanization of the victims of the Holocaust—positions the audience as passive consumers of an already known ethic.[20]

As James Young has shown, the American memorialization of the Holocaust is radically different from its more skeptical European counterparts. This is largely because an American nationalist perspective inevitably wants to call attention to the great distance between itself and the Shoah.[21] For this reason, as Young demonstrates, the Holocaust has been increasingly Americanized in its many local museums and monuments, and Spielberg's *Schindler's List* is undoubtedly an important aspect of this process. The reworking of Keneally's text for an American audience can be seen particularly in the figure of Goeth, who is not quite as central in the book as he is in the film.

The focus on Goeth arbitrarily sniping at those below from his balcony inevitably evokes the very American fear of random acts of violence or killing for fun. This, in turn, has distinct resonances with other Hollywood movies such as Peter Bogdanovich's *Targets*.[22] The cinematic techniques and motifs of Francis Ford Coppola also contribute to the Americanization of *Schindler's List*. In Goeth's wine cellar sequence with Helen Hirsch, Spielberg speedily juxtaposes complementary episodes of Schindler kissing a Jewish woman and a couple getting married in his factory, which distinctly echoes similar intercutting techniques in the *Godfather* movies. When Jewish bodies are being ex-humed from their mass graves and burned in a heap at Plaszów, the focus on the deranged SS officer also echoes Coppola's *Apocalypse Now*. The rather kitschy SS officers playing either "Mozart or Bach," as the camera pans across the recently liquidated ghetto, similarly evoke this movie. These overt refer-ences to a distinctly Manichaean American cinematic tradition sit somewhat uneasily alongside those more skeptical European filmmakers (especially with regard to the Shoah) who are, as we have seen, also partially incorporated into *Schindler's List*.

If Goeth is, to some extent, reminiscent of B movie Nazis or of *Grand Guigonol*, as many have argued, then he is also a kind of post-Vietnam degen-erate who would not have been out of place in *Apocalypse Now*.[23] Goeth is Kurtz-like precisely because he is portrayed above all as a civilized beast who pre-sumably could have acted like Schindler. This identification is made possible largely because Spielberg closely follows Keneally in thinking of Goeth as Schindler's "dark brother" (185). Goeth and Schindler are both convivial womanizers, drunkards, and war-profiteers, ride horses and, in their different ways, have the lives of Jews in their hands. They are also meant to have a simi-lar physique, which is emphasized in the film by camera angles which, am-biguously, could refer to either of them. The film, like the book, attempts to bring Schindler and Goeth together in a range of ways just as it eventually unites Schindler with Stern.

When Schindler first meets the Jewish black marketeers in the local cathe-dral, he comments on their silk shirts. Schindler then teams up with the one black marketeer who promises to get him as many shirts as he wants. This scene is reiterated when Goeth, on first meeting Schindler, also comments on his silk shirt and asks him where he obtained it. Goeth, significantly, ends up wearing Schindler's shirt in the wine cellar scene with Helen Hirsch, which itself resonates with an earlier episode when a Christ-like Schindler tells Helen that he "knows her suffering" (an addition to Keneally's account.) The scenes with Goeth and Schindler dressed similarly, accompanied by Helen Hirsch in the wine cellar—one tormenting her, one comforting her—encapsu-late the increasingly crude Manichaeanism of *Schindler's List*.

However, the film does occasionally try to make Goeth into a more com-plex figure by showing him to be both an interpreter of Schindler (just as Schindler often interprets Goeth) and, at times, a cruel parody of him. During a selection at Plaszów, Goeth saves a woman because she looks healthy enough to work. His invented speech to his SS troops—"today is history"—similarly repeats Schindler's many set piece speeches in the film. The "Amon the Good" sequence, also fabricated by Spielberg, similarly portrays him as a grotesque, parodic Schindler. Such welcome points of ambiguity represent a blurring of a too easy identification with good and evil in the film. One should remember, in this regard, that before Goeth torments Helen Hirsch in the wine cellar, there is a peculiarly artificial exploration of his racist personality (not taken from the book) which invokes Shakespeare—"Hath not a Jew eyes"—in a bid to discover where Helen is "human" or not. But such humanizing moments quickly collapse into B movie clichés. The more the depths of Goeth's derangement become apparent, the more Schindler is transformed into his benign counterpart. By the end of the film, Schindler, in response to Goeth, is unequivocally deified (even to the extent of giving a final crypto-sermon on the mount in Brinnlitz). Stern's welcome skepticism and suspicion of Schindler also evaporates, leaving Schindler absolutely redeemed and the movie's audience passively consuming its "bracing pieties."

By the end, *Schindler's List* veers dizzily between crass sentimentality, in a tearful scene with Stern, and a more anxious, self-conscious restraint. At its worst, the *Schindlerjuden* descend from on high to the Promised Land as if they were the cast of the *Sound of Music*. But this unforgivably cheerful penultimate scene (taken ham-fistedly from Wajda's *Korczak*) is contrasted in the final frames of the film with the poised encounter with the actual *Schindlerjuden* and a reference back to the gravestone entrance of Plaszów. At this moment, the impossibility of fully ending any account of the Holocaust is skillfully made apparent. A film that can encompass such a massive range of possibilities, even in a few minutes, is clearly a frustrating accomplishment. Incorporating a welcome tradition of European skeptical modernism, as well as B movie Manichaeanism, *Schindler's List* maneuvers restlessly between clichéd pieties and a more neutral documentary realism. It is, however, finally unable to contain the uncertain certainties of its didactic pretensions and descends headlong into an irredeemable sentimentalism.

Notes

1. I am grateful to David Herman for usefully commenting on an earlier version of this article, "The Holocaust in the Picture-House," *Times Literary Supplement* 4742 (January 18, 1994), pp. 18–19.

2. Primo Levi, *Moments of Reprieve* (London: Michael Joseph, 1986), pp. 10–11.

3. "The Humane Uncertainty of Primo Levi," in Bryan Cheyette and Laura Marcus, eds., *Modernity, Culture and "the Jew"* (forthcoming).

4. Primo Levi, *The Drowned and the Saved* (London: Michael Joseph, 1988), p. 23 and chap. 2, passim.

5. Zygmunt Bauman, *Modernity and the Holocaust* (Oxford: Polity Press, 1989), p. 122 and chap. 5, passim.

6. Levi, *The Drowned and the Saved*, p. 11 and chap. 1, passim, and "Revisiting the Camps," in James Young, ed., *The Art of Memory: Holocaust Memorials in History* (New York: Prestel Verlag, 1994), p. 185.

7. Thomas Keneally, *Schindler's Ark* (London: Hodder and Stoughton, 1982) p. 9. References to this edition will be included in the body of the text.

8. Dina Rabinovitch, "Schindler's Wife," *The Guardian* (February 5, 1994), pp. 14–17.

9. Gillian Rose, "Beginnings of the Day: Fascism and Representation," in Cheyette and Marcus, eds., *Modernity, Culture and "the Jew."* It is significant that the Talmudic verse is a key aspect of the film's publicity. I am grateful to Gillian Rose for helping me radically rethink my initial response to *Schindler's List*, "The Holocaust in the Picture-House," published in the *Times Literary Supplement*.

10. Simon Louvish, "Spielberg's Apocalypse," *Sight and Sound* 4, no. 3 (March 1994), p. 12. For a similar critique, see also David Mamet, "Why Schindler Is Emotional Pornography," *The Guardian* (April 30, 1994), p. 30.

11. Steven Spielberg, "Why I Had to Make This Film," *The Guardian* (December 16, 1993), pp. 2–3.

12. David Cesarani, "Oskar's Den," *New Moon* (February 1994), p. 18.

13. Louvish, "Spielberg's Apocalypse," pp. 14–15. See also John Gross, "Hollywood and the Holocaust," *New York Review of Books* (February 3, 1994), p. 14.

14. Louvish, "Spielberg's Apocalypse," pp. 14–15, and Cesarani, "Oskar's Den," p. 20.

15. Rose, "Beginnings of the Day: Fascism and Representation."

16. Max Farrar, "Zygmunt and Janina Bauman on *Schindler's List*," *Red Pepper* 2 (July 1994), pp. 38–39 and in conversation.

17. Lawrence Langer, *Holocaust Testimonies: The Ruins of Memory* (New Haven: Yale University Press, 1992), p. 190.

18. James Young, *The Texture of Memory: Holocaust Memorials and Meaning* New Haven: Yale University Press, 1993), pp. 132–33 and chap. 5, passim for this account of Auschwitz-Birkenau.

19. This phrase is taken from Langer, *Holocaust Testimonies*.

20. As well as Claude Lanzmann's well-known critique, the above paragraph is reiterated, in different forms, in the articles cited by Mamet, Rose, Bauman and Louvish. See also "Jacobson's List," *The Independent* (February 2, 1994), p. 19.

21. Young, *The Texture of Memory*, p. 284 and chaps. 11 and 12, passim.

22. Farrar, "Zygmunt and Janina Bauman on *Schindler's List*," pp. 39.

23. Cesarani, "Oskar's Den," p. 21. See also articles by Mamet and Jacobson.

Contributors

Omer Bartov is Associate Professor of History at Rutgers University. He is the author of *The Eastern Front, 1941–45: German Troops and the Barbarization of Warfare*, *Hitler's Army: Soldiers, Nazis and War in the Third Reich*, and *Murder in Our Midst: The Holocaust, Industrial Killing, and Representation*.

Haim Bresheeth is a filmmaker and writer, Chair of the Film and Video Department at the London Institute, London. He is coeditor, with Nira Yuval-Davis, of *Palestine: A Profile of an Occupation* and *The Gulf War and the New World Order*. He is the author, with Stuart Hood, of *Holocaust for Beginners*. His most recent film is *A State of Danger*, a documentary on the Intifada for the BBC.

Bryan Cheyette is Lecturer in English Literature, Queen Mary and Westfield College, University of London. He is the author of *Constructions of "the Jew" in English Literature and Society: Racial Representations, 1875–1945* and editor of *Between "Race" and Culture: Representations of "the Jew" in English and American Literature and Jewish Writing in Britain and Ireland*. He has published widely on modern and contemporary literature and theory and is currently completing *Diasporas of the Mind: British-Jewish Writing and the Nightmare of History*.

Judith E. Doneson is Visiting Professor of Jewish History at Washington University, St. Louis, and was a fellow at the Center for Jewish Studies at the University of Pennsylvania. She is the author of *The Holocaust in American Film*, and her articles on the Holocaust and stereotypes of Jews in film have appeared in *Holocaust and Genocide Studies*, *Studies in Contemporary Jewry*, and other publications.

Miriam Bratu Hansen is Ferdinand Schevill Distinguished Service Professor in the Humanities at the University of Chicago, where she also directs the Film Studies Center. She has published widely on German and American cinema and is coeditor of *New German Critique* and *Public Culture*. She recently published *Babel and Babylon: Spectatorship in American Silent Film*, and she is currently completing a book on the Frankfurt School's debates on film and mass culture, focusing on Siegfried Kracauer.

Geoffrey H. Hartman is Sterling Professor of English and Comparative Literature at Yale University and Revson Project Director of the Fortunoff Video Archive for Holocaust Testimonies. He is the author of numerous books, among them *Minor Prophecies: The Literary Essay in the Culture Wars* and *The Longest Shadow: In the Aftermath of the Holocaust*. He is the editor of *Bitburg in Moral and Political Perspective*, *Midrash and Literature* (with Sanford Budick), and *Holocaust Remembrance: The Shapes of Memory*.

Sara R. Horowitz is Director of Jewish Studies and Associate Professor of English Literature in the Honors Program at the University of Delaware. She is the author of *Voicing the Void: Muteness and Memory in Holocaust Fiction* and is currently completing a book on gender, genocide, and Jewish memory. She is founding coeditor of *KEREM: A Journal of Creative Explorations in Judaism*, and she served as fiction advisory editor for *Jewish American Women Writers: A Bio-Bibliographical and Critical Sourcebook*.

Natasha Lehrer is a postgraduate student in the Hebrew Department of the School of Oriental and African Studies, University of London. She completed her undergraduate degree at Jesus College, Oxford. She was affiliated for the academic year 1993–94 with L'INALCO, University of Paris (Sorbonne), where she undertook research into the use of the Holocaust as a metaphor in the French press. She is a regular contributor to the *Jewish Quarterly*, *Jerusalem Report*, and the art magazine *Frieze*.

Yosefa Loshitzky is Senior Lecturer in the Department of Communication and Journalism at Hebrew University. She is the author of *The Radical Faces of Godard and Bertolucci*, and she is currently completing a book on Israeli identity. She has also written extensively on film, media, and culture for a variety of journals.

Jeffrey Shandler holds a Ph.D. in Yiddish Studies from Columbia University. In 1995 he was an Annenberg Scholar at the Annenberg School for Communication, University of Pennsylvania. He is currently writing a book about the presentation of the Holocaust on American television.

Liliane Weissberg is Professor of German and Chair of the Program in Comparative Literature and Literary Theory at the University of Pennsylvania. She is the author of *Geistersprache: philosophischer und literarischer Diskurs im späten achtzehnten Jahrhundert* and *Edgar Allan Poe*, and she has edited several books, including *Weiblichkeit und Maskerade* and the forthcoming critical edition of Hannah Arendt's *Rahel Varnhagen*. She is currently completing a study on German-Jewish acculturation in the early nineteenth century.

Barbie Zelizer is a Guggenheim Fellow and Associate Professor of Communication and Rhetoric at Temple University. She is the author of *Covering the Body: The Kennedy Assassination, the Media, and the Shaping of Collective Memory, Snapshots of Memory: The Image, The Word, and the Holocaust*, and *Taking Journalism Seriously: News and the Academy*.

Index